ON CRITICAL THEORY

ON CRITICAL THEORY

JOHN O'NEILL, editor

A Continuum Book

THE SEABURY PRESS/NEW YORK

This is Gregory's Book

1976

The Seabury Press, Inc.
815 Second Avenue
New York, New York 10017

Printed in the United States of America

Library of Congress Cataloging in Publication Data

Main entry under title: On critical theory.

(A Continuum book)
Includes bibliographical references.
1.Criticism (Philosophy)—Addresses, essays,
lectures. 2.Theory (Philosophy)—Addresses,
essays, lectures. 3.Social science research—
Addresses, essays, lectures. 4.Horkheimer, Max,
1895–1973—Addresses, essays, lectures. 5.Adorno,
Theodor W., 1903–1969—Addresses, essays, lectures.
6.Frankfurt am Main. Institut für Sozialforschung
—Addresses, essays, lectures. I.O'Neill, John, 1933–
B809.3.05   149'.9   76–21229   ISBN 0–8164–9297–2

CONTENTS

CRITIQUE AND REMEMBRANCE

JOHN O'NEILL

Men of good will want to draw conclusions for political action from the critical theory. Yet there is no fixed method for doing this; the only universal presumption is that one must have insight into one's own responsibility.

—*Max Horkheimer*

It is well for us to keep in mind Horkheimer's comment upon how it is we today are to respond to critical theory. In its own context, Horkheimer's remark pertained to his hesitation in publishing essays in a later and much changed political context than that which originally inspired them. Within this hesitation there resides the very life of truth as it is conceived by critical theorists. That is to say, human truth is beholden to the circumstances of its envisioning and it is as much to be judged by the weaknesses and failures in its circumstances as what is secure and unfaltering in them. Thus the time which has elapsed since the Frankfurt School of critical theorists began their work and were thrown into the historical turmoil of Fascism, World War II, and the Cold War has left many things changed. Death alone has taken its toll upon the Frankfurt School and if thought were wholly time's child then surely critical theory would be largely a thing of the past. Yet today more than before we are witness to a rebirth of critical theory. How are we to understand this and to foster it? In the first place, nothing separates us from the last fifty years of the world's suffering. Because we are now confronted with new forms of the bureaucracy of suffering and exploitation, no less than with new

1

forms of contentment and pleasure, what is required of critical theory is not at all that it separate itself from its own legacy. This would only be a temptation, as indeed it is a risk in the more recent work of Habermas, if critical theorists wished to make an alliance with those modes of scientific knowledge that are identified with the organizational power of the institutions of domination. In these institutions tomorrow's knowledge is better than today's, and human time is turned outwards towards what it can demand of the future without any care for what it has made of the past.

In separating themselves from traditional theory, critical theorists mean to reject what is common to the positivist sciences whether espoused as bourgeois or communist practice. In simple terms, critical theory remembers what it owes to the very bourgeois culture that it opposes. By the same token, it wants nothing of party Marxism that is forgetful of its own dead and cheerfully wedded to the future of socialist man. "The better, the right kind of society is a goal which has a sense of guilt about it."[1] This is not merely an expression of the cultural pessimism with which we may associate the writings of Horkheimer, Adorno, Benjamin, and Marcuse. Or rather, it is so only if we have not critically examined our philosophy of history or human time. The theory of the development of socialist society is merely a version of evolutionary theory unless Marxists think through the nature of human solidarity as that which grounds the revolution in a redemptive event that is owed to all men both before and after the revolutionary struggle. Therefore the revolution can never be the simple property of the party shouting historical materialism through futuristic slogans. "For all the optimism he [the critical theorist] has about changing situations, for all that he treasures the happiness which comes from solidarity among men and work for a changed society, he has a pessimistic streak as well. Past injustice will never be made up; the suffering of past generations receives no compensation."[2]

Socialism has its own dead to bury. It cannot be otherwise in a world where truth and justice have no privileged entry but have to be fought over like other things that men seek. But surely socialism is old enough by now not to arrogate to itself all the chances of the world's rejuvenation. To become critical theorists we must take a responsible stand towards the apocalyptic separation of the past from the future. When socialism was young it seemed as though nothing could be saved from the past that would be worthy of the future of man. Today, curiously enough, we regard the future, at least ecologically, as something to be averted by the remnants of sanity and good use that we find in the past and the present. We cannot assume that freedom will open up in the division of human time struck by a revolution that is itself subject to the painful making of human institutions. We ought not to forget that the separation of theory and practice is a wound of socialist experience and an instrument of the party, not just a matter of capitalist "false consciousness." We shall abuse critical theory if we read it only to sublimate Marxist theory still further, disclaiming the one-dimensionality of industrial society and ignoring that Soviet Marxism is also surrendered to the same logic of domination.

I believe that by stressing the fundamental notion of our historical memory of guilt and unredeemed suffering we recover the deepest grounds of the ethical materialism that motivates critical theory. Moreover, I think this is necessary inasmuch as Habermas's recent attempts to put the ideals of communicative competence above the values of suffering labor risk foreshortening the historical memory and utopian thought that is the mark of socialism. In *Knowledge and Human Interests* Habermas argued that Marx was unable to account for the genesis of critical science and its role in the self-constitution of the human species since Marx's version of historical materialism was tied to the category of productive labor or instrumental action. By contrast, Freud paid less attention to the cognitive orientation to labor and its natural environment. Instead, Freud focussed upon men's internal environment, so to speak, upon the internal compulsions of distorted and self-limiting communication.[3] According to Habermas, an adequate theory of the emancipatory interest of self-reflection can only be built upon a general theory of communicative competence. In this respect Habermas's linguistic turn depends upon the analogy between the dialogic reconstruction of the structure of a life history as the model for the critical interpretation of symbolic structures in general. What I want to stress in the genesis of critical theory is the role of historical remembrance and utopian will rather than Habermas's emphasis upon the normative function of rational discourse. The point of the difference in emphasis relates to the question of political mobilization which is crucial to the unresolved unity of theory and practice.

I believe that Marcuse's interpretation of the role of historical
memory, which also derives from Freud, is better related to Marx
than Habermas because Marcuse preserves the power of suffering and
its redemption to mobilize social criticism and political action.

> This ability to forget—itself the result of a long and terrible education
> by experience—is an indispensable requirement of mental and physical
> hygiene without which civilized life would be unbearable; but it is also
> the mental faculty which sustains submissiveness and renunciation. To
> forget is also to forgive what should not be forgiven if justice and
> freedom are to prevail. Such forgiveness reproduces the conditions
> which reproduce injustice and enslavement: to forget past suffering is to
> forgive the forces that caused it—without defeating these forces. The
> wounds that heal in time are also the wounds that contain the poison.
> Against this surrender to time, the restoration of remembrance to its
> rights, as a vehicle of liberation, is one of the noblest tasks of thought.
> In this function, remembrance *(Erinnerung)* appears at the conclusion
> of Hegel's *Phenomenology of the Spirit;* in this function, it appears in
> Freud's theory. Like the ability to forget, the ability to remember is a
> product of civilization—perhaps its oldest and most fundamental psy-
> chological achievement. Nietzsche saw in the training of memory the
> beginning of civilized morality—especially the memory of obligations,
> contracts, dues. This context reveals the one-sidedness of memory-train-
> ing in civilization: the faculty was chiefly directed toward remembering
> duties rather than pleasures; memory was linked with bad conscience,
> guilt, and sin. Unhappiness and the threat of punishment, not happiness
> and the promise of freedom, linger in memory.[4]

The timelessness of historically repressive societies merely represents the official sublimation of pain, disease, and death. Forgetfulness
closes history whereas remembrance keeps open both the past and the
utopian future of man. Remembrance is the womb of freedom and
justice and must be cultivated long before men are able to name their
slavery within the discourse of rational freedom and consensus. Remembrance is therefore cultivated as much in collective ritual, art and
music as in rational discussion. Remembrance is the bodily infrastructure of political knowledge and action. It holds injustice to account
and sustains the utopian hope that underlies the will to freedom and
equality. Remembrance is musical, it generates literature, art, song,
and poetry as well as the scientific culture of revolution.[5] Remembrance is at the heart of what I have called wild sociology or wild

politics.[6] I have in mind by this the necessary recognition of the claims of that anonymous labor in the history of man's senses and intellect which have left us a world with any vision of human solidarity. Habermas's attempt to ground the emancipatory interest in the universal pragmatics of rational discourse in my view abandons Marx's utopian unity of human sensuous activity as well as the potential unity of art and politics. The result of this separation of the cognitive and sensory interests in emancipation is to undermine the utopian motives of Marxism without which we cannot adequately formulate either the tasks of scientific analysis or the practical labor of political education and mobilization in colonial as well as advanced capitalist countries.

In an early essay on the concept of essence Marcuse made clear the importance of the role of remembrance and utopia in the unity of Marxist scientific analysis and ethics. He argued that it is not possible to separate the history of philosophy from the history of man's aspiration for happiness and freedom. The medieval and Platonic conceptions of essence, or of the unity and universality of being, were not purely epistemological but included critical and ethical elements. The premodern conceptions of being were concerned with the tension between essence and existence, in which *eidos* was a dynamic constituent of things moving toward their "true being" and "good," and subject to the moral critique of their unrealized potential or bad facticity. In modern philosophy, however, the concept of essence is reduced to a problem of logic and epistemology. The authentic potentiality of being was now sought in the exercise of subjective thought pursuing absolutely certain knowledge in a nature subject to mathematical calculation and the domination of applied science. Henceforth the method of philosophy was equated with the transcendental organization of experience and nature in the "concept of the unconditioned." The transcendental reduction in its various stages from Descartes and Kant to Husserl represents, in Marcuse's judgment, a progressive abandonment of the critical task of philosophy. In critical materialism the tension between essence and appearance becomes a historical theory of the development of man through specific forms of social and economic organization. The critical Hegelian-Marxist conception of essence does not refer to an immutable ontological difference, but to a historical relationship between men which is the motive for knowledge and for the transformation of society. The method of materialist knowledge is to relate particulars to wholes masked in inessential relations that determine immediate practice but can be seen historically to be disproportions *(Missverhältnis)* of the true development of man.

> In truth, an *a priori* element is at work here, but one confirming the historicity of the concept of essence. It leads back into history rather than out of it. The immemorially acquired image or essence was formed in mankind's historical experience, which is preserved in the present form of reality, so that it can be "remembered" and "refined" to the status of essence. All historical struggles for a better organization of the impoverished conditions of existence, as well as all of suffering mankind's religious and ethical ideal conceptions of a more just order of things, are preserved in the dialectical concept of the essence of man, where they have become elements of the historical practice linked to dialectical theory.[7]

It is important to understand the critical materialist theory of essence if we are to have any adequate grasp of Marx's economic analysis. For Marx did more than flirt with the Hegelian method in *Capital.* The determination of man's essence has traditionally governed idealist philosophy through historical contingencies external to its own formal interests. However, once reality is conceived as the totality of the relations of production—material, social, political, and ideological—then the interests of *domination* and *recognition* provide a structural organization in which form and content, essence and appearance, are separate only within particular historical patterns of community and class interests.

The result of this materialist conception is that critical theory functions at two levels: at one level concepts deal with the relations between reified phenomena, and at another level they deal with the real or essential relations between reified phenomena whose subjective constitution has been revealed as an historically specific praxis. Marxian economics therefore employs a first set of concepts such as profits, wages, entrepreneur, and labor, in order to present the real but "phenomenal" forms of the processes of production and reproduction. At the next level, the processes of production and reproduction are regarded as an antagonistic unity aimed at the realization of capital which then requires concepts such as surplus value to bring out the essential relations of class exploitation and to reveal the true content of the formal analytic categories employed at the first level. The two levels of analysis, however, are dialectically related through the utopian intentionality of the first level which is to "produce" man. The historical alienation of this first-level utopian structure can only be grasped through a second-level analysis in which the materialist dialectic furnishes a critical theory of economic reification.[8]

> The dialectical concepts [of Marxist political economy] transcend the given social reality in the direction of another historical structure which is present as a tendency in the given reality. The positive concept of essence, culminating in the concept of the essence of man, which sustains all critical and polemical distinctions between essence and appearance as their guiding principle and model, is rooted in this potential structure. In terms of the positive concept of essence, all categories that describe the given form of existence as historically mutable become "ironic": they contain their own negation. In economic theory this irony finds its expression in the relationship of the two sets of concepts. If, for instance, it is said that concepts such as wages, the value of labor, and entrepreneurial profit are only categories of manifestations behind which are hidden the "essential relations" of the second set of concepts, it is also true that these essential relations represent the truth of the manifestations only insofar as the concepts which comprehend them already contain—their own negation and transcendence—the image of a social organization without surplus value. All materialist concepts contain an accusation and an imperative.[9]

Marcuse embeds the concept of the essence of being and the subjective praxis of modern knowledge in the Hegelian unity of reason and freedom demanded by the critical concept of the essence of man. The concept of man is therefore as much an ethical as a rational one; it is critical as well as descriptive and in this respect its historical and political telos is effectively utopian. This critical utopian conception of the essence of man is opposed to the idealization of freedom and reason outside the real world in which the palace of ideas sits next to the hovels of the poor and hungry. Nor is it grounded in a simple materialism, although it rests on economic foundations insofar as these are transcendentally oriented to the "production" of a human world. It rests on science and technology. But its utopian nature asks questions about science that are beyond the pale of idealist and positivist reason. Its concern with the future *as a human future* lies beyond the predictive controls of science in general and, needless to say, of economics in particular.

I have appealed to Marcuse's critical analysis of the concept of essence because what I have called its *utopian* feature emphasizes an element in the teleology of critical reason which otherwise appears to be purely cognitive. By stressing the utopian nature of knowledge and critical rationality, we may be reminded that the crisis of reason is not just a matter of philosophical ennui or failure of nerve. It is a crisis in the utopian nerve of social-scientific knowledge, which is the form philosophical reason assumes in order to mediate human praxis. Moreover, it is only through its utopian dimensions that the Marxist concept of the essence of man can remain adequate to its intentional universality and to the present need to hold in theory what in the future will be an everyday reality.[10]

The *ethical* unity of Marxist knowledge remains, however, a programmatic ideal unless it is brought to the level of *pedagogic practice*. Here we encounter the problem of the role of Marxist knowledge in the relation between the party and the proletariat. In simple terms, communicative competence is likely to remain the one-sided talent of party theorists and organizers obliged to work with a silent and obstinate proletariat with little experience of the world of ideas, debate, and free consensus. The danger is that people may be herded together in the interests of their political leaders who have community on their lips or in their plans but not in their hearts.[11] This is a likely outcome whenever socialist leaders and party organizers adopt a rationalistic version of man's capacity for speech.

The oppressed are the instruments of a culture of silence in which the political control of language and education excludes them from critical reflection and its revolutionary practice.[12] The poor generally do not speak for themselves and are likely to be as dependent upon their liberators as they were previously upon their oppressors. Indeed, this is the probable outcome of the revolution unless, as Marx anticipated in his Third Thesis on Feuerbach, the revolution lays upon itself the task of *educating its own educators*. Here again I believe the notion of remembrance is crucial to the pedagogic practice of critical socialism. We need to remember that socialism is long suffering—that it works only with men and not upon men. But the labor of oppressed men teaches them to fear critical speech for they have identified with their oppressor's hostility to anything that challenges the dominant order. This will be the case even in fairly literate urban situations as well as among illiterate peasants. In our society common sense is at a disadvantage in the confrontation with planners and professionals whose technical language appropriates the presumption of rationality.

> Wild sociology will encourage radicalism. Yet it will be hard on its own radicalism, suspecting further evils from its own activity should it presume upon its relation to the lay community. It may well be that the daily practice of sociology encourages arrogance on the part of its members, undermining the very resources of humanism with a numb professionalism or the shrill cry of ideology. If this is not to happen wild sociology must make a place for itself, and to accomplish this it must engage hope and utopia. Hope is the time it takes to make the place in which men think and talk and work together. Thus wild sociology is essentially engaged in the education of the oppressed.[13]

The politics of communicative competence cannot be settled in the reciprocal presuppositions of an ideal speech situation. For unless the pedagogic practices between the oppressed and their leaders educate the leaders themselves to equality they stand only to alter the style of popular servitude. Therefore the pragmatics of communicative competence belong to a larger critical theory of socialist education which is broader than either the cognitive theory of proletarian consciousness or a linguistic approach to the critique of ideology. Socialist education cannot succeed except where men *love* the world and the society of men. The pedagogy of the oppressed therefore cannot be one-sided or manipulative nor can it be fostered by men who lack *humility* and are arrogant and domineering. Socialist humilty in turn has no place where a few men set themselves up and are unwilling to bend in the service of the people because they lack *faith* in the partnership of the oppressed. However, critical socialist pedagogy is more than a prescriptive ethic. As outlined by Paulo Freire, whose work I regard as a practical extension of Habermas's ideal of emancipatory communicative competence, the pedagogy of the oppressed involves an applied method of entry and organization of local communities whose critical tasks are opened up through the generative themes— slum, development, water, infant mortality—of daily life in the colonial world.[14] It would be an important and relatively easy intellectual task—as easy as in practice it is dangerous—to extend Freire's methods of "conscientization" to the education of the internal proletariat of industrial and urbanized societies where the challenge does not derive from absolute illiteracy but from the relative illiteracy that results from the increasing technical and professional practice of social change and reform.[15] In particular, the task of a critical theory of communicative competence under these conditions would require the development of adequate ethnographies and dramaturgies of lay and professional "accounting" procedures as competing epistemic and organizational strategies of communal order, conflict and change. It is along these lines that I believe critical theorists must work if those systematically excluded from having a voice in the legitimation processes of our society[16] are to realize their potential for citizenship.

Critical theory cannot remain an academic preserve. It must be broad enough to share the historical burdens of labor anywhere in the world. It therefore cannot weaken its grasp of political economy. At the same time, however, critical theorists must commit themselves to the ordinary work of a social science that will deliver competent ethnographies of the practical exigencies of daily living in the modern world. The accumulation of such knowledge requires that critical theorists develop a broad pedagogy that would restore the political relation between science and common sense knowledge and values. At this level critical theory must begin work wherever the opportunity affords itself, in quite local circumstances and over simple matters in schools, hospitals, supermarkets, the arts and social services as much as in the factories. Only after a long period of such work ought we to climb once more the ascending heights of theory.

NOTES

1. Max Horkheimer, *Critical Theory, Selected Essays,* trans. Matthew J. O'Connell and others (New York: Herder and Herder, 1972), p. ix.

2. Ibid., p. 26. Cf. Christian Lenhardt, "Anamnestic Solidarity: The Proletariat and its *Manes,*" in *Telos,* no. 25, Fall 1975, pp. 133–154.

3. Jürgen Habermas, *Knowledge and Human Interests,* trans. Jeremy J. Shapiro (Boston: Beacon Press, 1971), pp. 282–283. I have replied to Habermas in "On Theory and Criticism in Marx," in John O'Neill, *Sociology as a Skin Trade, Essays Towards a Reflexive Sociology* (New York: Harper & Row/London: Heinemann, 1972), pp. 237–263. In the early stages of the preparation of the present volume, we published a Review Symposium on Habermas, in *Philosophy of the Social Sciences,* vol. 2, no. 3, 1972.

4. Herbert Marcuse, *Eros and Civilization, A Philosophical Inquiry into Freud* (New York: Vintage Books, 1962), p. 212.

5. John O'Neill, "Gay Technology and the Body Politic," in *The Body as a Medium of Expression,* eds. Jonathan Benthall and Ted Polhemus (London: Allen Lane, 1975), pp. 291–302.

6. John O'Neill, *Making Sense Together, An Introduction to Wild Sociology* (New York: Harper & Row/London: Heinemann, 1974). It would be an interesting task to relate the notion of "remembrance" to Arendt's discussion of the place of "forgiveness" and "the promise" in political life. Cf. Hannah Arendt, *The Human Condition* (Chicago: University of Chicago Press, 1958), part V, chapters 33 and 34.

7. Herbert Marcuse, *Negations, Essays in Critical Theory* (Boston: Beacon Press, 1968), ch. II, "The Concept of Essence," p. 75.

8. For an analysis of the double structure of Marxist political economy, see John O'Neill, "For Marx Against Althusser," in *The Human Context*, Vol. VI, No. 2, Summer 1974, pp. 385–398, and "Marxism and Mythology" in *Sociology as a Skin Trade*, pp. 137–154.

9. Marcuse, *Negations*, p. 86. Cf. Norman Geras, "Marx and the Critique of Political Economy," in *Ideology in Social Science, Readings in Critical Social Theory*, ed. Robin Blackburn (New York: Doubleday Anchor, 1972), pp. 284–305.

10. "In the history of revolution, deep faith in man and deep faith in the world have long gone hand in hand, unmoved by mechanistics and opposition to purpose. But militant optimism, as the subjective side of real progress, also implies searching for the where-to and what-for on the objective side—of forwardmoving being without which there is no progressive consciousness. And the *humanum* is so *inclusive* in the *real possibility* of the *content of its goal, that it allows all movements and forms of human culture location in the togetherness of different epochs. The humanum is so strong that it does not collapse in face of a wholly mechanistically conceived cyclic time.*" [Ernst Bloch, *A Philosophy of the Future*, trans. John Cumming (New York: Herder and Herder, 1970), p. 140. Bloch's emphasis.]

11. Frantz Fanon, *The Wretched of the Earth*, trans. Constance Farrington, with a Preface by Jean-Paul Sartre (Harmondsworth: Penguin Books), pp. 152 and 157.

12. Paulo Freire, *Pedagogy of the Oppressed*, trans. Myra Bergman Ramos (New York: Herder and Herder, 1972); and *Education for Critical Consciousness* (New York: Seabury Press, 1974).

13. O'Neill, *Making Sense Together*, p. 80.

14. John O'Neill, "Le langage et la décolonisation: Fanon et Freire," in *Sociologie et Societés*, vol. 2, Novembre, 1974, pp. 53–65.

15. For an attempt to understand street politics as part of the demystification of expert politics, see John O'Neill, "Political Delinquency and the Iron Mountain Boys" and "Violence, Language and the Body Politic," in *Sociology as a Skin Trade*, pp. 41–56, 57–80.

16. Claus Mueller, *The Politics of Communication, A Study in the Political Sociology of Language, Socialization and Legitimation* (New York: Oxford University Press, 1973).

ON HAPPINESS AND THE DAMAGED LIFE

BEN AGGER

Critical theory chances to be either a museum-piece in the hands of its modern inheritors or a living medium of political self-expression. My argument is that critical theory can only be renewed—as Marx would have hoped—by refusing to concentrate on its philosophical inheritance and instead by writing the theory in a direct and un-mediated way. The old saw that to be a Marxist is to surpass Marx is just as true for critical theory: Adorno, Horkheimer, and Marcuse blazed the trail for a theory of late capitalism, yet now they can only be suitably remembered by new formulations of theory responsive to the altered nature of the socio-cultural world.

The central motif in this task of reinvigoration is that of language. Critical theory employs a vocabulary of hope and defeat. Marx's great contribution was his notion of theory as a stimulant to political action, if not as action's mere reflection. The rhetoric of critical theory emerges from the theorist's sense of the possibility of social change and itself contributes to fostering or deflecting emancipatory activity.

In this sense, Adorno's nearly unmitigated pessimism contrasts with Marcuse's guarded and sophisticated optimism about cracking the one-dimensional totality. Although *Eros and Civilization* states definitely that only the "surplus" of ego-constitutive repression can be purposefully eliminated, Marcuse remains hopeful about the prospect of lessening this surplus. Similarly, O'Neill's "wild sociology" defends the commonplaces of everyday life as the inalienable basis of any community, from which all radicalism must inevitably proceed. For Adorno, there was an *equivalency* between basic and surplus repres-

12

sion, and thus few opportunities for social change.

The language of critical theory is its own meta-language. Objective description of things contains a vision of an *Aufgehoben,* a transcended-reconstructed world. The dialectic is captured in the capacity of objective knowledge for political enlightenment. Critique in Marx meant the imagination and analysis of a world without exploitation, a human world. This must be embodied in the forms of critical expression such as social thought, art, music, and philosophy. A dialectical language both describes the dissonant world and bespeaks the possibility of redemption.

> The new sensibility and the new consciousness which are to project and guide such reconstruction demand a new *language* to define and communicate the new "values" (language in the wider sense which includes words, images, gestures, tones). It has been said that the degree to which a revolution is developing *qualitatively* different social conditions and relationships may perhaps be indicated by the development of a different language: the rupture with the continuum of domination must also be a rupture with the vocabulary of domination.[1]

Adorno employed a negative language and favoured negative culture. Marcuse was less negative because he glimpsed the point at which evil could be redeemed. Concretely, Adorno believed that the demise of a politically organized working class sealed the fate of Marxism, whereas Marcuse and O'Neill have responded to the libidinal rebellion of American youth as a potentially revolutionary phenomenon. However, O'Neill goes even beyond Marcuse's ingrained prejudice for high-culture in siding with Norman O. Brown against Marcuse in terms of what he calls "the Left version of the generation gap."[2] Whereas Marcuse flirts with turned-on youth, uncertain of their revolutionary potential, O'Neill celebrates them. Adorno saw negative theory captured in the mind-boggling rows of twelve-tone music where Marcuse and O'Neill hear the crash and flight of rock music as a new promise of freedom, providing a vision of the preverbal harmony of socialist life: the *carnal* grounds of socialism.

For too long, Marxism has been under the sway of a taboo prohibiting the depiction of the image of socialism. In Adorno's later work, there is barely a hint of the promised land. Critical theory, transplanted from Germany to North America, has become a crabbed style of philosophical analysis, replete with a scholastic structure of authority. My thesis is that this taboo must be lifted and Adorno's dismal reluctance to sing about socialism opposed. Marxism under the influence of its great founder has always assumed that history consisted in radical interruptions; Marx's eschatology revealed a temporal gap between the alienating present and *future* socialism. The taboo on graven images was erected because it was thought that the socialist future was too far off to admit of sensible description in the here and now. Yet in my opinion the "moment" of abstract negation—out of which Adorno's theory is built—must be superseded, and the temporal model of a long road to a redeemed future scrapped.

Marcuse explicitly rejects the model of critical theory as abstract negation; since his work on Freud he has concerned himself with depicting the *body politic* of the new society, its politics, sexuality, art, and philosophy. Freud enabled him to translate Marx's rationalism into naturalistic terms, into the body-language of a new version of critical theory. At the same time, Marcuse also rejected the notion of the long road to socialism and suggested instead that "revolutionary" forces could be perceived as emerging in the present society. Adorno's impatience with jazz and rock as culture-forms is rejected by Marcuse and O'Neill who search for oppositional impulses *anywhere,* even in *apparently* non-proletarian and non-political forms.

> This potential for transfiguration is not at all obvious amidst the vulgarity and garbage of Woodstock or the May revolution. But this is the way of wild sociology into the world; it can enter only through self-mockery, nihilistic flirtations and the very self-violence which it seeks to avoid. Its way is profane because its resources are nothing else than the world and its people struggling for improvement. It is easy to be cynical about the organizational and promotional features of "rock-ins" and "maybe's", to dissolve them in a phrase, to empty their *logos* into the waste-bin of fashion. Indeed, the spontaneity, festivity and refusals which constitute these events make it inevitable that the participants will "blow it," will be unable to sustain their enthusiasm and disintegrate as at Altamont, in Paris and elsewhere. The critics will observe failure and speak wisely of what is to be done within the limits of an untransfigured world which lives without fancy and avoids enthusiasm in favour of the pigeonholes of politics, history and sociology.[3]

Modern critical theory in Marcuse and O'Neill has therefore abandoned the traditional model of the politically organized working class. Opposition can come from any quarter; the nature of modern opposition consists in rejecting the division of labour and in the actual creation of a new political body. Dialectical thought today rejects the thesis of a long road and indeed all crisis-theory rooted in the classical Marxian terms of a proletarian revolution. Instead, critical theory must—as Marx taught time and again—sensitize itself to *all* on-going oppositional movements in attempting to channel them in palpably political directions. Critical theory cannot afford to remain in the 1920s and 1930s when—perhaps—the old working class model did apply.

My thesis about O'Neill's and Marcuse's sensitivity to non-traditional forms of opposition, in contrast to Adorno, turns on their approach to certain cultural forms like language and music. They have tried to conceive how modes of expression like music and theory *themselves* constitute a new body politic and socialist relations. Theory is a praxis which concretizes and communicates the image of socialism. It contains within itself, as does music, a sense of the future which is emerging *from* the present. I want to read Marcuse, O'Neill, and Adorno as singing the world in different ways, as engaging in different styles of cultural opposition. The way of O'Neill and Marcuse is a direct attempt to create a socialist body politic through the medium of musical and theoretic harmony. Adorno's way is a form of abstract negation through dissonance.

Both body-politics and abstract negation must be moments of oppositional practice today. Marx's famous notion of the dialectic between theory and practice really bespeaks the practical potential of theory itself as a form of cultural politics. O'Neill's and Marcuse's "critical theory" is the cultural practice of a *new sensibility;* it is not a form of life separable from political practice. Adorno's "theory" is an abject resignation before a seemingly intractable world. Marcuse and Adorno cannot be compared according to the lifeless epistemological standard of bourgeois social science but only in terms of their varying styles of cultural opposition. My view is that Adorno is unjustified in resigning from the effort to build a socialist society in the actual here and now of everyday politics.

One-dimensional society swallows up deviance but leaves the traces of idealism in theory, art, and music through which opposition can find its voice. Inasmuch as the thought of freedom remains conscious, there is a chance to create a society grounded in active and reciprocal expression. Once the thought of freedom is buried in the unconscious, hope withers along with the subject of hope. I want to restore the self-consciousness of action and vision to critical theory in turning it towards its own potential for speech and conviction, thereby combatting its ossification as another differentiated form of academic thought.

O'Neill and Marcuse remain hopeful that theory can transcend itself as a new science and technology, whereas Adorno wrote of his own irreparably "damaged life." Adorno's view was that theory remains imprisoned on the level of thought, that truth does not inhere in a collectivity or class. Theory in this vein is but a tragic expression of will, a theme reminiscent of Nietzsche and Schopenhauer. In a way, Nietzsche's *The Birth of Tragedy* represents one of the options of language and style open to critical theory today. Nietzsche writes of the sublation of tragedy by "Socratism" and its destruction of music as a pure expression of the unencumbered will. Socratic optimism in its modern genre employs the techniques of opera, romantic classical music, and rock, while the tragic version of critical theory takes refuge in the dissonance of twelve-tone music.

Adorno is the theorist of atonality, while Marcuse is the opera buff wavering between romantic high-culture and the youth-culture of rock and acid. Their difference is the split between tragedy and epiphany, the one humbly owning up to its essential impotence, the other committing the sin of pride and challenging the world to change. Critical theory has two broad cultural styles, the one tragic or Nietzschean, the other more optimistic or Hegelian-Marxian.

The "negative totality" of modern capitalism has produced one-dimensionality and reduced criticism to imitation and private language. Marcuse believes in the possibility of a concrete harmony between subject and object, while Adorno rejected all identity-theory found in Hegel and Marx. The alternative to the Hegelian optimism of Marcuse is a Nietzschean perspective of tragedy and eternal recurrence for which things either remain the same or get worse. *Dialectic of Enlightenment* by Horkheimer and Adorno is an echo of *The Birth of Tragedy*. Nietzsche believed that Aeschylus had been eternally wronged by Euripides and Socrates, whereas Horkheimer and Adorno thought that western civilization began to die with Odysseus' rationalism.

Marcuse has not been overly reluctant to hypostatize a worker-student-Third World coalition as the new collective subject. This has been largely an argumentative device, the alliteration of critical theory, in that Marcuse, like Marx and Lenin, never failed to reduce praxis to individuating acts. Hegel's phenomenology of mind underwrote Marx and Marcuse by offering them an image of the political nature of reflection and cognition. Marcuse's debt to Hegel is revealed in the second preface to *Reason and Revolution* where he writes that Hegel has restored the "power of negative thinking" in a time when the "second dimension" of transcendent critique has been assimilated to the positive affirmation of the given. But Hegel was not a tragic thinker in the same sense as Nietzsche. Hegel was a dialectical theorist who tried to comprehend how history was animated by its thought of itself, its essentially progressive reflexivity.

Critical theory mediates between the thought of freedom and the actuality of a free world. Mortal Marxism embodies in the struggling but hopeful subject the mediations which can let theory become a practice. The Nietzschean conception of the mortally self-limited subject differs radically from the Hegelian-Marxian idea of the potentially universal subject of world history. For Adorno, everything we do in the way of subjectively mediating present and future will end in disappointing failure; rebellion only strengthens the system. For Marcuse and O'Neill, we cannot avoid the attempt to translate emancipatory ideals into the concrete particulars of place, time and emotion.

> To think sociologically is to dwell upon a question we have answered long ago: How it is that men belong to one another despite all differences? This is the task of a *wild sociology,* namely, to dwell upon the platitudes of convention, prejudice, place, and love; to make of them a history of the world's labor and to root sociology in the care of the circumstance and particulars that shape the divine predicaments of ordinary men. The work of sociology, then, is to confront the passionless world of science with the epiphany of family, of habit, and of human folly, outside of which there is no remedy. This is not to deny scientific sociology. It is simply to treat it as a possibility that has yet to convince the world.[4]

Critical theory either translates the universal of Freedom into sensible dimensions of experience and language or it acts as a fatalistic expression of the heteronomous will. I think it can be argued that Adorno hoped that music itself could express a theory too abstruse for words. Nietzsche heard the sound of tragedy in the choral music of Aeschylus. Tragedy and a certain mortal finity were expressed through the song. Adorno considered Schoenberg to be a prophet of tragedy—a tragedy essentially beyond the reach of the discursive voice. The negative dialectic must be base enough to bespeak an evil world.

Marcuse speaks about human tragedy without ascending to Aeschylean heights in forgetting the potential of the positive. He searches for a language with which to express the Good contained within the shape of the present. Art and theory prepare us for the time when social relations will not scar the human face. Yet criticism will also preserve the distance between vital lived experience and the reconstructed experience of language. That is to say, each society needs critics and artists to idealize a higher order of freedom than that which has been actually attained. Whereas Adorno felt that the jargon of authenticity rendered language impossible, O'Neill and Marcuse want to reserve the most revealing languages for the time when a socialist order is itself in need of pretheoretical invigoration.

> Wild sociology will encourage radicalism. Yet it will be hard on its own radicalism, suspecting further evils from its own activity should it presume upon its relation to the lay community. It may well be that the daily practice of sociology encourages arrogance upon the part of its members, undermining the very resources of humanism with a numb professionalism or the shrill cry of ideology. If this is not to happen wild sociology must make a place for itself, and to accomplish this it must engage hope and utopia. Hope is the time it takes to make the place in which men think and talk and work together. Thus wild sociology is essentially engaged in the education of the oppressed.[5]

Praxis thus is anything we can do to remain critically alive, sensitive to pervasive dissonance *and* transcendent harmony. As its own metalanguage, critical theory is a praxis. It talks about the world as it assesses the social potential for freedom. My point is that for Adorno, O'Neill, and Marcuse theory is not always discursively set out but can assume prelinguistic forms. O'Neill draws from Vico's argument that poetry is the originary substratum of language and that critical theory must return to poetry in resurrecting the natural rationality of human expression. Vico implies that humanity can be redeemed *because* we are the original authors of our own humanity; we can hear the *sound* of our own humanity in non-discursive forms of expression like poetry and music.

Language fractures in the modern world because our speech is no longer
the reflection of anything that is ordered either inside or outside of us.
Every historical order ultimately collapses the literary, artistic, and
philosophical languages that for a time allowed an age to speak of itself
and to gather its particular goods and evils. It is an axiom of Vico's wild
sociology that if history is at all saved it is saved by language. For it is
in the history of our language that we recover our humanity. It is in
language that we discover the gradual making of the institutions that
have made us human.[6]

Music like poetry is a *form* of critical theory in that it stimulates
and solicits resignation or rebellion. Adorno felt that twelve-tone
music captured the negative dialectic of an insufferable society,
whereas O'Neill's patience with rock and drug culture emerges from
his contention that there is something elementally *political* in the
ecstasy of turned-on youth. In a sense, Marcuse is located somewhere
between Adorno's gloom and O'Neill's song of the inalienable commonplaces of humanity, less willing than O'Neill to relinquish the
Greek ideal of Reason in favour of the mundane rationality of the
body and voice.

Ultimately, critical theory develops an aesthetics of the good life.
Marx resisted writing such an aesthetics, although he gave ample
hints in the Paris manuscripts about the *sense* of socialism. Today,
this aesthetics must depict the form and feel of socialism, not merely
discursively, but through the *body* and *voice* of the new man, his art,
music, architecture, sexuality. Marcuse was the only Frankfurt theorist to take the development of this aesthetics seriously, relying heavily on Freud for the sexual underpinning of a new body politic.
O'Neill's concept of the "body politic" also renders this aesthetics as
a possible sociological artifact, an aesthetics produced by all the forms
of human expression. O'Neill's vision of a wild sociology is a version
of critical theory which sings of commonplace pain and hope and thus
constitutes itself *as* a form of music. The bittersweet harmony of
Beethoven or Dylan is joined with the pretheoretical affirmation of
common humanity which wild sociology provides. The organon of
Marcuse's "new science" and of O'Neill's "wild sociology" is the *body
politic.*[7]

In this sense, critical theory must *build* a body politic which has
three dimensions. Theory sings, paints, writes, makes love. In so
doing, it evaluates modern society against concrete criteria of socialist
possibility. Marx's ideal of dis-alienation is rendered phenomenologi-

cal in the translation of socialism into an actual political body. The taboo on graven images is explicitly rescinded, for the taboo robs us of an organizational device with which to redirect youthful opposition into political channels. Superficially, the Rolling Stones are not revolutionary for they are a product of late bourgeois society and the modern culture industry. Yet the libidinal responsiveness of the young to the sights and sounds of their music is a *potentially* political phenomenon, an essential component of the aesthetics of socialism.

The concept of praxis thus has a more allusive and negative formulation in Adorno; Marcuse and O'Neill locate the realm of praxis in the "infrastructure" of the psyche and body. The tragic form of theory has its roots in the philosophy of Nietzsche. I want to focus on the function of art in Adorno's view, a perspective which is not dissimilar to Nietzsche's own theory of music expressed in *The Birth of Tragedy*. Adorno says of music:

> Its truth appears guaranteed more by its denial of any meaning in organized society, of which it will have no part—accomplished by its own organized vacuity—than by any capability of positive meaning within itself. Under the present circumstances it is restricted to definitive negation.[8]

Negation of what? Of social forms of domination? Certainly not. "Aesthetic authenticity is a socially necessary illusion: no work of art can thrive in a society founded upon power, without insisting upon its own power."[9] Art negates only as it promises a different, better world and thereby breaks through the one-dimensional totality by the example of its own abrasive contingency. Yet Adorno unlike Marcuse does not sanction Brecht's concept of the estrangement-effect, an art which shocks and educates. Atonal music was not to contain anything but the experience of pain; it was not a pedagogy of the oppressed. Marcuse's fondness for romanticism contrasts with Adorno's utter lack of sentimentality, issuing from his tragic concept of the negative subject. Marcuse's subject, rooted in Schiller's "play-impulse," suffers greatly at the hands of the world yet can express his suffering in the hope of romantic redemption.

Aesthetic dissonance refuses to be sentimentally hopeful by giving in to harmony. Art mimetically mirrors the insane world. Rigour characterizes Schoenberg's music whereas sentimentality hiding only affirmative neo-objectivism taints the music of Stravinsky. Rigour can show us the evils of the world, but only subliminally through the preconceptual and precoherent effects of sound.

As Adorno and Horkheimer wrote in *Dialectic of Enlightenment,* "the triumph of advertising in the culture industry is that consumers feel compelled to buy and use its products even though they see through them."[10] Dissonant music serves as revolutionary advertising since it never falls on deaf ears. It insinuates its way into consciousness and tries to gain a foothold in the buried critical spirit of the subject. The clash of symbols reminds us however remotely of the din of the bourgeois city. Twelve-tone rows recall for us the seriality of our lives.

Music for Adorno is a social form because it is an element in a comprehensive social whole, almost a reflex of a noisy society. Music is not simply sold as use-value but gains its allure from its bourgeois purposive-purposelessness. Art is thought to have *no* use-value. The art-object delights because it represents the affluence of a culture which can afford to employ artists to do nothing in particular.

Theory itself for Adorno does not consist in a form of life exuding the positive character and need of its subject. Like dissonant music, it is socially useful noise. Its language cannot fail to be the language of the dominant society, extended to its limit of rationality. Adorno once believed that the social whole contained its own principle of contradiction to be revealed by a theory which comprehends the untruth of the whole. Theory is the critique of an ideology which does not penetrate its own veneer of half-truths and glosses. Theory opposes the premature harmony of liberal capitalism by denouncing the tragedy of liberalism, its ultimately cheerful seriality. Both Adorno and Nietzsche situated the originary mythologization of enlightenment in Socrates who first hoped rationally to eliminate tragedy. *Dialectic of Enlightenment* resonated the sentiment that Marxism had failed by breaking insufficiently with the ethos of the domination of nature and society. *Negative Dialectics* charts the self-consciousness of enlightened dominion which has produced a thoughtless world. Adorno has rephrased Hegel's cunning of reason as the cunning of unreason: the inexorable "progress" of enlightenment which can be depicted only in an enlightened, disenchanted music. Adorno ultimately abandoned Marx's hope that contradictions within society could be resolved and harmony created.

Like Marx, Adorno was concerned to reveal by reproducing the contradictions of the negative totality through ideology-critique.

Schoenberg's music became the ultimate critique of ideology in its abrasive reproduction of social dissonance. "The penetrating eye of consciousness" is an art which bespeaks the world as it has come to be and apparently serves us as the critique of political economy served Marx. Hegelian rationality reveals the essential *telos* of things by peering behind their commonsense appearances. Adorno believed that a discursive philosophy would fail in this effort; that only art and music could truly disclose the negative inauthenticity of the bourgeois world.

"Modern music sees absolute oblivion as its goal. It is the surviving message of despair from the shipwrecked."[11] Theory is the bottle in which the shipwrecked deposit their plea for help. But no bottle is ever found except when it survives long after the shipwrecked have perished. Negative or radical music evokes only the negative. It provides a mood for the "penetrating eye of consciousness" and enables it to comprehend the depravity of things. The whole is the untruth and critical theory fails to change the world.

The subject is so deformed by his presence in a brutalizing, privatizing world that he can *never* resurrect himself with the aid of discursive theory, precoherent art, or concerted activity. The sin of Socratism which tried to comprehend all mysteries has plagued every subsequent generation. The sin of pride scars the subject by forcing him outside himself in the externalizations of technology. Realism overwhelms the subject with the things themselves. Adorno contrasts the music of Schoenberg to that of Stravinsky which expresses the ideal of an unradical neo-objectivism.

> Stravinsky does justice to reality. The primacy of specialty over intention, the cult of the clever feat, the joy in agile manipulations such as those of the percussion in *L'Histoire du Soldat*—all these play off the means against the end. The means in the most literal sense—namely, the instrument—is hypostatized: it takes precedence over the music. The composition expresses only one fundamental concern: to find the sounds which will best suit its particular nature and result in the most overwhelming effect.[12]

Adorno felt that critical theory could restore the value of intention by asserting the primacy of music over against techniques to express sound. Radical music cuts to the heart of instrumentality by following out the logic of musical instrumentality to its ultimate conclusion. The "ideal of authenticity" for which Stravinsky's music strives is similar to the authenticity pursued by Heidegger's philosophy. Both forms of expression are jargons inasmuch as each sublates the objective subject by hypostatizing the abstract importance of technique and of care. Heidegger's *Dasein* is as inhuman as the subject of Stravinsky's composition—if indeed music has any conception of the subject, as Adorno would probably have claimed for it.

The annihilation of the ego is the residue of late bourgeois society which has collapsed the realms of ideology and reality. One-dimensional society contains no sensible criterion of unfulfilled actuality because reality contains every illusion and promise made by the ideology of limitless liberalism. Adorno's particular genius was to have recognized the phenomenology of one-dimensionality in its most insidious and abstracted socio-cultural forms.

Culture is the jutting tip of the iceberg of bourgeois society. But culture "progressively" penetrates downwards to affect the base by transforming the sensibilities and expectations of workers and their received ideology of the work-ethic and erotic renunciation. A phenomenology of advanced capitalism reveals the ground of the forms we invoke when we speak about a "one-dimensional" society.

Yet theory in Adorno's terms does not enlighten in the hortatory way in which Marx-the-rationalist conceived of theory doing. Theory merely acts as a bell-weather of domination by reflecting the deformations of subjectivity. The more insane is the object of critical theory, namely, late bourgeois society, the more allusive critical theory must be. The more that culture is disenchanted, the more theory will have to be mythological. Just here, dialectical theory in Marx's sense becomes frozen. Allusive theory responds reflexively to the deformations of culture. The dialectic of the real and the possible has been defused by the social totality and its metamorphosis into a universe which can liberally encompass deviance. Adorno understood that theory had become undialectical because the world had been totalized in its total evil to a degree which denied the critical immanence and transcendent quality of *thought*. Marx's conception of a critical theory which could reveal the *telos* of deformed things has been transformed in times when the negative totality of society has lost its principle of dynamic contradiction. Thus the falling rate of profit projected by Marx has not materialized in a final crisis as capitalism has "temporarily" curbed the disruptive principle of its own self-negation.

Adorno characterizes the damaged subject as a casualty of "social progress." The "fallen nature of man" is the existential reality to be treated and hopefully resurrected by theorists. Music and theory can only express the tragedy of a world which through liberal enlightenment has lost sight of tragedy. There can be no guarantees that the music or theory composed by damaged, neurotic subjects can be anything but damaged expressions. Dissonant music bespeaks the dissonance of community and man. Likewise, allusive and gloomy theory stands witness to the seemingly eternal fall of enlightenment into myth.

The Nietzschean root of Adorno's thought is revealed in Adorno's affinity for Nietzsche's *amor fati,* the love of fate. Eternal recurrence of tragedy occasions a love of fate which can be broken through only by total redemption, fallen from the stars, a product of the unpredictable cunning of insanity. The Baconian root of modernity is the manipulative scientism which purges doubt and uncertainty from human experience. What Nietzsche disparagingly called "Socratism" in *The Birth of Tragedy* was Socrates' belief in the purposive reduction of uncertainty through technical rationality *(epistemé).*

Music in its non-tragic form sings the positive love of the earth and the eternal recurrence of existential mortality. We succeed only because we comprehend that success will not render the person transparent. Redemption is our atonement for the sin of pride. Critical theory sings the world because it is disenchanted with Marxist and bourgeois system-builders. In the profound despair of Adorno there is a kernel of mortal love for all men and for nature. The kernel will burst out of its shell only if we banish the Socratic and Baconian notions of the reduction of uncertainty through the objectifying control of society and nature. Adorno's critical theory sings the falleness of the world only because it cannot truthfully engage in the superficial and insidiously affirmative dialogue of enlightenment.

Marcuse always believed that the "power of negative thinking" contained within it a rational kernel of positive hope. In fact, the theory of liberation offered by Marcuse treats the subject as a relatively undamaged agent of revolutionary praxis. The Hegelian power of reason, its determinate negation of the apparent world, informs Marcuse's hopeful conception of the objectively natural subject. Nowhere does Marcuse allude to the permanently fallen hopelessness of critical praxis. Even his notorious *One-Dimensional Man* holds out the possibility of redemption. "It is only for the sake of those without hope that hope is given to us."

Marcuse's "new sensibility," like O'Neill's "wild sociology," is an amalgam of bodily and mental senses, of libidinal and symbolic rationality. The bourgeois idealist concept of reason ignores the rationality of the body by concentrating solely on an abstract intellectual rationality, thus denying Freud's profound naturalism and his conception of the *objective subject.* [13]

> Beyond the limits (and beyond the power) of repressive reason now appears the prospect for a new relationship between sensibility and reason, namely, the harmony between sensibility and a radical consciousness: rational faculties capable of projecting and defining the objective (material) conditions of freedom, its real limits and chances. But instead of being shaped and permeated by the rationality of domination, the sensibility would be guided by the imagination, mediating between the rational faculties and the sensuous needs. The great conception which animates Kant's critical philosophy shatters the philosophical framework in which he kept it. The imagination, unifying sensibility and reason, becomes "productive" as it becomes practical: a guiding force in the reconstruction of reality—reconstruction with the help of a *gaya scienza,* a science and technology released from their service to destruction and exploitation, and thus free for the liberating exigencies of the imagination. The rational transformation of the world could then lead to a reality formed by the aesthetic sensibility of man. Such a world could (in a literal sense!) embody, incorporate, the human faculties and desires to such an extent that they appear as part of the objective determinism of nature—coincidence of causality through nature and causality through freedom. [14]

In *An Essay on Liberation* Marcuse suggests that any future revolution will have to emerge through a new infrastructure of undistorted human needs and instincts. *Counterrevolution and Revolt* elaborates this in terms of Marcuse's critique of the American New Left which has regrettably eschewed the critical function of rationality. He also discusses the political aesthetic of a future society and a new non-antagonistic alliance between man and nature. New science can reconstruct the exchange between humanity and nature. The object-world is but a proving-ground for liberated subjectivity which has an ineluctably objective component in the body and instincts. Marxian scientism has contributed to the decomposition of Marx's original notion of the sensuous nature of man. The person has been falsely and narrowly treated as a socio-economic cipher devoid of libidinal, emotional faculties. Mechanical Marxism ultimately has no conception of the objective naturalness of the subject, a conception derived by Marcuse from the great works of psychoanalysis.

> Behind these familiar traits of a socialism yet to come is the idea of socialism itself as a qualitatively different *totality.* The socialist universe is also a moral and aesthetic universe: dialectical materialism contains idealism as an element of theory and practice. The prevalent material needs and satisfactions are shaped—and controlled—by the requirements of exploitation. Socialism must augment the quantity of goods and services in order to abolish all poverty, but at the same time, socialist production must change the quality of existence—change the needs and satisfactions themselves. Moral, psychological, aesthetic, intellectual faculties, which today, if developed at all, are relegated to a realm of culture separate from and above the material existence, would then become factors in the material production itself.[15]

The historical nature of the subject itself stands at the ideological crossroads between the critical theorists. What is the nature of the subject? Can we even speak about the subject, except by very indirect analogy in our music or our science? Adorno supposed that the subject was an effete residual of bourgeois philosophy which perished in the Nazi death-camps. Marcuse and O'Neill by contrast argue that the kernel of positive opposition lies in the "libidinal rationality" beginning to emerge from the embodied subject. They have tried to harness the prepolitical reaction of subjectivity against surplus repression in building a new body politic.

Whereas Adorno read Freud as the prescient prophet of the completely eradicated subject, Marcuse employs the allegedly "gloomy" Freud to postulate a buried libidinal substratum capable of healthy creativity and socialist relations. The initial revolt of 1960s youth against an oppressive superego was not dismissed by Marcuse or O'Neill as merely another version of Oedipal reaction, but as indicating that the instinctual substratum was beginning to emerge. Marcuse's Freudianism enabled him to harness the natural subject as the new agent of body politics.

Marcuse and O'Neill want to restore the experience of the embodied subject to Marxism. Ideology-critique opposes the scientization of Marx in arguing that the fate and potential of the subject is important for oppositional activity. Although Hegel spiritualized the subject in terms of a world-historical Spirit, Marx re-objectivized and re-naturalized the concept of the subject through his labour-theory. Marx saw that contemplation was itself a kind of production, akin to work and possessing the same permanent objective residue. *The German Ideology* relentlessly criticizes the spiritualization of the subject in German philosophy and argues that the so-called objective spirit is a product of nineteenth-century ideology.

Restoring the bodily and libidinal health of the subject is for Marcuse and O'Neill tantamount to resuscitating the power of critical rationality. Adorno never believed that Hegel's concept of thought as negation was an adequate form of political activity; but negative thought was better than no thought at all. Marcuse believes that negative reason can actually be a form of praxis: the Great Refusal of what is. Hegel's concept of negation was revised by Marcuse to become a self-sufficient form of critical praxis: negation pregnant with the hidden positive. Marcuse's notion of the political character of sensibility turned the moment of thought into a directly political moment. Surplus repression was the libidinal counterpart of the extraction of surplus value.

Adorno's conception of the frozen quality of the social totality denied even the critical power of thought. The subject was so damaged —with no libidinal prepolitical potential—that his thought and speech were but determinations of the society's material and ideological forms. Total domination could *not* occasion total opposition unless opposition mirrored the form of domination.

Adorno's dialectic was defused and bent away from the social totality. Dialectic no longer reveals the unfulfilled purpose of things, but instead simply mirrors a "negative dialectic" of society which successfully reconciles all social contradictions. Dissonant music apes the prematurely de-structured dialectic which becomes sedimented in eternally contradictory social institutions. For example, increasing private leisure-time occasions a more thorough-going domination of the subject by corporate prerogatives. Indeed, leisure itself is captured by the culture industry as needs are turned into commodities. Critique has no field for its expression in that it would fall upon deaf ears. Everything can be made to seem affirmative, even Marxism.

The aesthetic theories of O'Neill, Marcuse, and Adorno all respond to the premature reconciliation of contradictions in late bourgeois society. O'Neill's turn towards a political aesthetic responds to the deformation of the subject and yet remains sensitive to nascent opposition on the level of body politics. Marcuse's hope of re-sensitizing the subject lies in an active conception of libidinal rationality and preservation of the transcendent function of art. Adorno argued that the dialectical method was stagnant, archaic; the only possible form of negation remained on the mimetic level of dissonant thought. Praxis, the self-externalization of the labouring subject, always fails to achieve its purpose, namely, the liberation of other men. Thought alone could conceivably remain undamaged by the pernicious totality.

In *Negative Dialectics,* Adorno argues that the conception of the subject itself is a remnant of bourgeois idealism. The subject could not be thought without thinking the object which dominated it. To subjectivize social theory was falsely to represent the actual powers of the nearly impotent, voiceless person. Theory was circumscribed by its own inability to theorize about a separate entity called the human being. In reality, the subject was almost perfectly synonymous with the objects to which it was politically subordinated. Thus, the subject is a trivial and forgotten moment in a dialectical method which charts the progress of the object's preponderance.

It is clear that Adorno does not completely banish a concept of the subject from his musicology, for music needs an audience. The culture-critique of Adorno deals with culture as an objectified domain of spirit which has somehow gone wrong. *Minima Moralia* is characteristically embellished with the sub-title "Reflections of a Damaged Life." In *Philosophy of Modern Music* Adorno says that the avant-garde's rejection of Schoenberg's music which hides behind the apology of incomprehension masks their real hatred of the abrasive atonality of the music. Each sentence in Adorno's work likewise resonates a harshly dissonant quality through which he tries to capture the frozen quality of the dialectic.

Marcuse's theorizing makes thought practical by embedding thinking in the totality of the sensuous person. In O'Neill, "sensibility" is a combination of good sense and of good senses, intellectual and libidinal rationality. The ego itself is a dialectic between unfulfilled hopes and concrete possibilities. Thought thinks of the future and grapples with the "chance of the alternatives" which springs from the present circumstance. There can be no dialectical movement without the complicity of the self-conscious subject, a subject not as damaged as Adorno supposed. Whereas for Adorno culture was merely a domain for the system's ugly self-reflection, culture for O'Neill and Marcuse is a potential launching-pad for oppositional projects.

Negative theory for Marcuse works to create the aesthetic of socialist forms; it contains the positive within the negative. In O'Neill the Great Refusal breaks into song. In Adorno, the Refusal peters out in a vague imitation of social insanity by the crazy composer. There is a tendency both on the part of Adorno and his modern inheritors to reject youth culture as a superficial spin-off of the affirmative culture industry. Marcuse by contrast recognizes the *ambivalent* nature of the 1960s youth phenomenon. Events like Woodstock are obviously corporate rip-offs, yet they *also* represent a real attempt to create a new order of political togetherness, the beginning of a new class consciousness. Woodstock was an ambivalent phenomenon because American youth lacked the political structures—like an organized Left—within which to situate their erotic-aesthetic rejection of inner-worldly asceticism. Marcuse and O'Neill, unlike Adorno, see the positive within the negative, the real concretization of socialist experience within an otherwise disorganized, pre-ideological youth movement.

Rock music and drugs are sources of prepolitical ecstasy which in their ecstatic moments free the person from the spacetime of serial bourgeois life. Atonal music merely mocks seriality. Marcuse and O'Neill both attempt to force the moment of prepolitical ecstasy into the mold of a new body politic. The ecstasy of habitual, free and easy togetherness experienced at rock concerts can be recollected as an authentic mode of socialist co-existence. Ultimately, the ecstatic forms of youth culture constitute aspects of the everyday life of a socialist body politic. The naive, pre-ideological honesty of gentle folk can thus be preserved as a vital archetype of the post-ideological socialist personality. Marx's icon of the Paris Commune as the epitome of communism is replaced today by the icon of the "be-in."

It is insufficient merely to reject these moments of cathartic subjectivity as fodder for the culture industry. Social change is effected between the moments of subjective abandon and objective sobriety; Marx roughly distinguished cultural from economic modes in accepting this motif. Yet nowhere did he rule out the *objective potential* of initially subjective rebellion. The "counter" culture is not actually against culture; it is against cultural forms which are serially divorced from political forms. The archetypal hippie, for all his apparent prepolitical innocence, actually rejected the bourgeois segregation of culture from economics and politics, and in this was engaged in a quintessentially political form of opposition. The "counter" culture opposed the categorial boundaries *between* bourgeois culture and politics. Indeed, Marcuse's new science and O'Neill's wild sociology are forms of cultural opposition against this very fragmentation of the modern lifeworld. Wild sociology attempts to reunite fractured humanity in rejecting the vulgar Marxist dichotomy between "superstructure" and "base." It is a dialectical sociology because it digs beneath the apparently unpolitical surface of phenomena like Woodstock and the Rolling Stones and turns them towards the political light of day: towards the new dawn of a truly socialist world.

Adorno accepted a very deterministic model of the relation between economics and culture. Marcuse imputed less determinative force to the structure of capital and more to a relatively autonomous cultural sphere. I would argue that Marcuse's model is closer to that of Marx in that Marx also tried to discover prepolitical modes of opposition before they entered the schema of class-conflict. Today it is imperative to move *further* away from Adorno's model of a frozen, totally managed world in reassessing certain non-proletarian cultural forms for their contribution to the creation of a new body politic. It is also imperative that we reject Marx's model of the politically organized working class and the theory of crisis which supports it. In Marx's *spirit,* but not slavishly imitating him, we must become sensitive to untraditional modes of political opposition.

> For Marxian theory, the location (or rather contraction) of the opposition in certain middle-class strata and in the ghetto population appears as an intolerable deviation—as does the emphasis on biological and aesthetic needs: regression to bourgeois or, even worse, aristocratic, ideologies. But, in the advanced monopoly-capitalist countries, the displacement of the opposition (from the organized industrial working classes to militant minorities) is caused by the internal development of the society; and the theoretical "deviation" only reflects this development. What appears as a surface phenomenon is indicative of basic tendencies which suggest not only different prospects of change but also a depth and extent of change far beyond the expectations of traditional socialist theory.[16]

We have contrasted Adorno, Marcuse, and O'Neill better to comprehend the alternative of critical theory as music and critical theory as the activist sin of pride, as praxis itself. Adorno thought that everything we do in the way of praxis is wrong, or at best insufficient; theory contemplates freedom which can only be expressed atonally:

there is no collective subject anymore. The primacy of the object forces the subject into a meek and abstract compliance with the interdictions of the object. In late bourgeois society, Schoenberg sings the truth, although it is a dismal, negative truth. The dialectical blockage of dynamic forces issues in the death of opposition. We can only sing the tragedy of a world which has forgotten tragedy.

Adorno thinks that science has no song but that of mathematics. Nietzschean tragedy has been banished from memory by the instrumental success of scientism. Culture has been made an industry by those who attempt to harmonize the fundamentally tragic universe; culture is a painless ideology, another great myth.

Marcuse is less Nietzschean than Hegelian in that he does not accept the inherent tragedy of human existence. In fact, his conception of the mortal subject is based on Freud's essentially constructive matrix of instincts: natural man. His own theorizing presupposes Marx's optimism about eliminating domination. Critical theory can perhaps even serve as an expressive medium for the recreation of sensibility. The Great Refusal is a form of praxis, but dissonant music is not. Music is merely negative theory, resigned to its heteronomous quality. Marcuse's theory transcends itself in becoming a form of embodied sensibility, a political structure of needs and feelings. A dialectical theory must herald the *negation* of contradiction, couched in historically comprehensible terms and forms, which is to say that it must be a theory of *hope*.

Adorno's negative theory does not negate dissonance because it cannot rise above the terms of discourse of a dissonant world. O'Neill transcends pain through an optimism rooted in the *natural* or *wild objectivity* of the instinctual body. Without this source of naturalism critical theory will fail to rise above tragedy. Critical theory has become scholastic because its second generation could not come to terms with psychoanalysis and its theory of the objective character of subjectivity. Marcuse's *Eros and Civilization* failed to convince enough Marxists that the objectivity of subjectivity was a wellspring of hope, not despair. Therefore, in failing to assimilate Freud, critical theory runs the risk of neglecting vital cultural forms of opposition which kick surplus repression in the teeth.

Freud provides what Marx neglected: a transmission-belt between economic structure and cultural forms, the objective subject. Ultimately, Marx did not understand *why* the collapse of capita¹ *could* emerge in a new order of society; he did not theorize the political sensibility which stands between the moments of structure and consciousness. Capitalism survived because workers could not translate the pain of hard labour and their fundamental insecurity as wage-labourers into a sensible language which pointed towards a new order. Marx himself did not tell them what the future could be like; he did not tell them what socialism would *feel* like.

Critical theory today must do so, even if it uses a crude, sensory language like that of freaked-out youth. The one-dimensional totality denies the experiences of imagination and union, experiences which are essential to the non-linear spacetime of rock and drugs. It is in this sense that the language of a critical theory which transcends its own scholasticism must portray the raw feeling of ecstasy through media which somehow escape the levelling influence of the culture industry.

We are not faced with a discrete choice between culture-forms like symphony, opera, jazz, or rock. Atonal music recollects the painful disassociation of meaning under alienating society; rock recollects the libidinal rationality of good times, the promise of living ecstatically beyond instrumental rationality. If critical theory is a discourse, it must talk even when ordinary language has been exhausted. Between Adorno, O'Neill, and Marcuse there lies the distance between disappointment and the cautious reawakening of hope, a distance vital for a practice with eyes wide open to a history which occasionally delights as well as disappoints.

Critical theory itself is a culture-form, a product of history and place. In singing the world, this theory chooses either to deny or affirm the possibility of a resurrected humanity arising from *this* earth. Atonal music evokes the scream of tortured Jews, appropriate to its time. Rock sings of sexual rationality and the transcendence of functional differentiation. Between Auschwitz and Haight-Ashbury critical theory has changed its tune, first Adorno, then Marcuse. As I said initially, critical theory must surpass *itself* in remaining within the dialectic of the real and the possible. New science recovers grounds for positive rebellion in the carnal body, the body politic. "Critical theory" is not a school but rather the way we choose to oppose inhumanity in different songs of joy.

NOTES

1. Herbert Marcuse, *An Essay on Liberation* (Boston: Beacon Press, 1969), pp. 39–40.

2. John O'Neill, *Sociology as a Skin Trade* (New York: Harper & Row/London: Heinemann, 1972), p. 53.

3. John O'Neill, "Gay Technology and the Body Politic," in *The Body as a Medium of Expression,* eds. Jonathan Benthall and Ted Polhemus (London: Allen Lane, 1975), p. 299.

4. John O'Neill, *Making Sense Together* (New York: Harper & Row/London: Heinemann, 1974), p. 10.

5. Ibid., p. 80.

6. Ibid., p. 34.

7. See John O'Neill, "Gay Technology and the Body Politic," pp. 291–302.

8. Theodor W. Adorno, *Philosophy of Modern Music* (New York: Seabury Press, 1973), p. 20.

9. Ibid., p. 216

10. Max Horkheimer and Theodor W. Adorno, *Dialectic of Enlightenment* (New York: Herder and Herder, 1972), p. 167.

11. Adorno, *Philosophy of Modern Music,* p. 133.

12. Ibid., p. 172.

13. See Russell Jacoby, *Social Amnesia* (Boston: Beacon Press, 1975).

14. Herbert Marcuse, *An Essay on Liberation* (Boston: Beacon Press, 1969), pp. 37–38.

15. Herbert Marcuse, *Counterrevolution and Revolt* (Boston: Beacon Press, 1972), p. 3.

16. Marcuse, *An Essay on Liberation,* pp. 58–59.

THE WANDERINGS OF ENLIGHTENMENT

CHRISTIAN LENHARDT

The arrival in North America and England of some of the major works of the Frankfurt School had long been hoped for by a few insiders who knew the original texts or had heard about them. Now that these writings are finally appearing in fairly rapid succession, I for one find myself in the awkward position of suspecting that their coming is not only overdue but also too late. At least some of them will only be of antiquarian interest to the English-speaking public. It will be quite impossible to share the intellectual excitement caused by the *Dialectic of Enlightenment* in Germany during the 1950s. The impression that something important arrives too late is reinforced by the spectacle of disintegration which the Frankfurt School presented during the last decade. Some people say it never existed, insofar as it did not generate an orthodoxy save perhaps in matters of style and literary mannerism. While Max Horkheimer and Theodor W. Adorno kept emphasizing to the very end that their philosophical outlook was the same, thereby fostering the stereotype of a "school," Jürgen Habermas went off on a philosophical journey of his own which has had few points of contact with that of his mentors. In short, four or five years ago, at a time when it began to be exported, German critical theory had undergone a process of diversification, if not dissolution, which is bound to affect its reception abroad. Moreover, much from the pen of Adorno that once had a deep impact on the post-war German Left was subsequently shrugged off as defeatist verbiage and esoteric elitism by the activist student movement in its return to Marxist-Leninist orthodoxy. I have no doubt that a similar fate will befall Adorno's writings in England and America: The aura that once surrounded them and German critical theory, in general, will not be transported abroad.

The conceptual focus of my commentary is the idea of fear; its textual basis is the excursus on the *Odyssey* in the *Dialectic of Enlightenment* which Adorno wrote with Max Horkheimer.[1] It is clearly inspired, if the term is not out of place, by the time in which it was written, but many of its more speculative theses depict the archaic context from which much that is contemporary has sprung. As a result, the new appears in the light of the ever-the-same, whereas the old makes greater sense as its "modernity" is revealed. Written in America before 1944, the *Dialectic of Enlightenment* stands out as a kind of synopsis of the diverse fields of enquiry and philosophical concerns of the Frankfurt School. It sketches the outlines of the Frankfurt critique of positivism; it provides more than just a glimpse of Adorno's aesthetic theory; it exemplifies the kind of qualitative analysis of mass culture typical of critical theory; it deals with the interpretation of racial prejudice; and it tries to take stock of the so-called rationalization of capitalism. In short, it assembles all or most of the themes which have been of concern to the Frankfurt School in one way or another. It also throws light upon the *lacunae* in Horkheimer's and Adorno's thought, *lacunae* which have never subsequently been filled and which have been a constant source of frustration and disenchantment to sympathizers and disciples. If the *Dialectic of Enlightenment* is among other things a book about the then contemporary scene, about the objective spirit of American capitalism, why does it pay so much attention to Metro-Goldwyn-Mayer and none to General Motors? Why does it analyze the politics of the motion picture industry and not the politics of the New Deal? Why does it mention Mickey Rooney and not Franklin Roosevelt? Somehow, the blind spots in the *Dialectic of Enlightenment* are as typical of Horkheimer and Adorno as its explicit themes. In sum, the book is a microcosm of the manifold theoretical interests of its authors and, in a wider sense, programmatically delineates a position which was to become a kind of trademark of critical theory, Frankfurt style.[2]

As the subtitle of the German edition announces, the conception of the book is fragmentary. This is a bit of an understatement. For although the particular seems to gain the upper hand as the text unfolds, at least the first three sections have a thematic unity and systematic quality which the subtitle "Philosophical Fragments" only serves to conceal. Appropriately, it was deleted from the American edition. The book is much less fragmentary than it seems, its unity consisting in the continuity of the theme. This theme is encapsuled in the dialectical formula that "myth is enlightenment and enlightenment degenerates into mythology" (6/XIV). What may strike the reader, especially the English-speaking reader, as a lack of ordered progression of discourse is not the authors' incompetence and inability to think clearly, but derives from the erratic logic of the history of reason itself. That history has been one of fragmentary progress, hence the only adequate medium of literary exposition must needs be fragmentary as well. One cannot describe a discontinuous historical totality in a systematic framework of formal classifications and rubrics. It is this material element which accounts for a certain lack of methodicalness that is such a conspicuous—and deliberate—feature of all critical theory.[3]

The *Dialectic of Enlightenment* is not about the period in the history of philosophy which goes by the name of Enlightenment. The central figures of the Enlightenment are hardly touched upon at all. Instead the book is about enlightenment, without the definite article and with a small "e." It is about enlightenment in general. In philosophical parlance, enlightenment is the emancipation of man from the despotism of myth. Horkheimer and Adorno take exception to this traditional definition which led to the errors of rationalism and progressivism. Far from being straightforward emancipatory, enlightenment has had a dialectical career, carrying within itself the seeds of regression. Horkheimer and Adorno speak of the *aporia* of enlightenment, for it is at once emancipation from myth and the destruction of areas of freedom already won. What is new about this argument is that it views enlightenment as constitutive of problems which modern rationalism has tended to chalk up to archaic countertendencies extraneous to enlightenment itself. As the authors put it, "the causes of enlightenment's relapse into mythology are not so much to be found in those nationalistic, pagan and other mythologies which have been expressly trumped up for the purpose of regression, as in the fact that fear of the truth spellbinds enlightenment itself" (3/XIII).

This argument sets the dialectical critique of enlightenment ideology off from other intellectual approaches which likewise try to come to terms with the self-destruction of civilization. Unlike so many conservative defenders of culture, Horkheimer and Adorno do not make a plea for the preservation and affirmation of so-called eternal cultural values in the face of the continuous onslaught of instrumentalism, commodity production, and everything else that reeks of mundaneness. "What is needed today is not the preservation of the past, but the fulfilment of past hopes" (5/XV). In effect, the abstract humanism of writers like Huxley, T.S. Eliot, and Ortega y Gasset can be diagnosed as an integral part of the regression of enlightenment. In any event, the affinity their critique of modern civilization seems to have with a dialectical theory of culture is spurious.[4]

Much as it would like to do so, a dialectical theory of civilization cannot skirt the tricky question of historical origins. In order for its analysis of contemporary mass culture to gain meaning, it must be grounded in knowledge, no matter how hypothetical, of undifferentiated primitive being. Admittedly, this is treacherous terrain. Marx and Engels clung to their prehistorical vision of primitive communism with a mixture of dogmatism and selective perception, eagerly citing Lewis Morgan but ignoring contrary evidence. More circumspect than Marx, Adorno and Horkheimer discard the idea of primitive communism but not the speculation about archaic origins itself. As Adorno puts it in one of his later works,

> To ask whether antagonistic social relationships are simply an extension of the history of nature which is governed by the principle of *homo homini lupus* or whether they are *thesei,* that is, artificial, is no idle speculation. Nor is it idle to ask if, assuming they are artificial, their coming into existence was occasioned by the need for survival of the species or by arbitrary acts of seizing power. If we suppose the latter to be the case, the origin of social antagonisms would be contingent. As a result, the whole construction of a world spirit would fall apart. The historical universal, the logic of history, which is caught up in the necessity of the historical trend, would then be based on contingency, on something external to the logic of things. History would not have had to be what it was.[5]

What is being radically questioned here is the idea of historical totality. This is the sense of Adorno's dictum that "the whole is the untruth," which signals the Copernican turn critical theory has effected in dialectical thought, Hegelian and Marxist alike. History has no *telos* or design. But it is not contingent either. There are distinct strands of continuity within it. That is why the idea of historical totality need not be dismissed entirely.

We must construe and at the same time deny the existence of universal history. In the face of the past catastrophes and future ones, it would be cynical to assert that a comprehensive world plan manifests itself in history, moving it forward toward perfection. But we must not therefore deny the unity which has fused the discontinuous and chaotically fissioned moments and phases of history. This is the unity of domination of nature progressing to domination over man and ultimately over inner nature. Universal history does not lead from savagery to humanity; it does indeed lead from the slingshot to the megabomb.[6]

History is the unity of necessity and contingency. Considered together in their dialectical union, these two forces have produced catastrophic results on end. "If I were to give a definition of the world spirit . . . it would have to be that world spirit is a permanent catastrophe."[7]

In fact, an irrational act of will to power and domination in primal history was the *first* catastrophic event.[8] Likewise, all subsequent catastrophes were acts of repression. The two terms seem to tend toward synonymity. In ordinary usage, catastrophes are by definition unpredictable; but we do appoint investigating commissions to sift the debris after the fact so as to get at the causes. Conversely, Adorno's catastrophic caricature of world spirit makes prediction possible (in a sense) but not explanation. Domination is not only a permanent experiential catastrophe for those subject to it; it is also a catastrophe for consciousness: a blank spot. We do not know how to account for it except by hypostatizing it, whereby it becomes an historical universal, an aspect of the human condition. For a dialectical philosophy of history this is not good enough. Universals, which are merely *in* themselves, cannot speak *for* themselves. They are mute, meaningless. Thus, even if we know nothing about the origin of domination we must hold fast to the concept of origination itself, lack of evidence notwithstanding. As soon as we abandon the idea of historical genesis, we serve notice that the study of politics and conflict is the legitimate concern of the scientists, which it is not. Adorno's desperate language game—desperate because it brings him into dangerously close contact with apocalyptic and Gnostic premises—reflects the awkward dilemma of having to choose between the idiom of *Genesis* and that of universal science. The makeshift notion of catastrophe is introduced to save the day for a dialectical interpretation of social domination and to shield the last glimmer of hope against the danger of being snuffed out by the positivistic chatter about human nature. For, ironically, if domination has been a catastrophe, it need not have occurred because it is a contingent particular. By the same logic, future catastrophes could be avoided; domination could be negated.

In the *Dialectic of Enlightenment*, the precatastrophic, prehistorical stage has the earmarks of Rousseau's state of nature rather than of Marx's aboriginal communism. At least the authors do not explicitly mention primitive socialization. Their savage acts in a setting characterized by the omnipresence of nature, to which he adapts through mimesis, making himself like her. He has no ego, no consciousness of himself, no identity apart from nature. There is no science which opens a window upon this world of undifferentiated unity. But the differentiation of an individual consciousness, enlightenment for short, is a long historical process which culminates in the idealistic philosophies of the 18th and 19th centuries. Therefore, by tracing the steps of this enlightenment backward we witness the gradual effacement of the individual. Mimetic integration of man in nature then becomes the conceptual limit for self-reflexive enlightenment.

What Adorno and Horkheimer attempt to do in their excursus on the *Odyssey* is to assess the costs of enlightenment. The average reader of the epic has no trouble recognizing that here is a work about the advancement of human intelligence and the repression of the dark forces of myth. It is Odysseus alone, the schemer and inventor of subtle tricks, who returns home, overcoming all obstacles put in his path by divine malefactors, while his superstitious companions perish. The ancients took no exception to the fact that the many were sacrificed to the rescue of the one. They did, however, take a jaundiced view of Odysseus' blasphemy, suggesting that he should not have got away with it. His status as hero was thus tarnished from the start. In the eyes of the literate Greeks of the fifth and fourth centuries B.C., Odysseus symbolized an emancipation of consciousness which was bought at the price of insubordination, hybris, and other moral traits that are of dubious value. The victory of reason as a loss of universal moral harmony—this was the dialectics of costs and benefits the ancient Greek readers of Homer tended to perceive in the poem. By contrast, Adorno and Horkheimer essentially view the *Odyssey* as an allegory about the rise of the bourgeois. While the transformation of the relationship between man and the gods may be a significant evolutionary process in the epic, the adventures of Odysseus unmistakably reveal the sociocultural dialectical link between the growth of self-consciousness and the repressiveness of man's behaviour toward his own kind. "The history of reason, liberality and bourgeois values *(Bürgerlichkeit)* goes back much further than is assumed by historians who date the notion of the bourgeois from the end of medieval feudalism" (51/45). The late-romantic German scholars of antiquity realized as much, and so did the fascist interpreters of Homer, for they branded his work as one dealing with merchants and seafarers, which led them to dismiss it as overly rational and enlightened. This dismissal, however, is too facile because it would have us believe that myth and reason are clearly separable. The key assumption of the *Dialectic of Enlightenment* is that they are not. While this is a general proposition, it holds true *a fortiori* of the story told in the *Odyssey.* "No literary work testifies more eloquently to the interconnectedness of enlightenment and myth than Homer's which is the fundamental text of European civilization" (52/45–6).

Odysseus and his party of Greek warriors constitute a society of unequals. In the end, he survives and they die. This is of great importance for an understanding of modern social inequality. We are told that inequality today is epiphenomenal, enlightened, not a matter of death and survival, therefore we can afford not to worry so much about it, especially since a level of general comfort is the basis on which inequality has, as it were, been superimposed. Homer may serve to disabuse us of this complacent view. The corpses that line the path of Odysseus' homecoming are stark reminders of the logic of inequality, which literally goes over dead bodies when it has to. Perhaps the future will see a remythologization of inequality of Homeric proportions, once natural resources become scarce enough to push inequality to its inherent existential limit of meting out death to supernumerary mouths.

How does Odysseus, the castaway on the island of the Phaeacians, earn the supreme privilege of saving his naked life? The answer is that he earns it only in part. Tradition does the rest. Surely his subjective reason must have inspired his companions' awe, an attitude which they normally reserved for the Olympian Gods, minor deities, and spirits. But there is also his inherited social position as a landowner accustomed to commanding the deference of propertyless vassals: He rules the ship because he used to rule an estate and will rule it again. In Odysseus, the man of reason, and the king, two strands of a theory of legitimacy converge. His domination is grounded on achievement

and ascription, enlightenment and myth. The paradigmatic significance of Odysseus as commander of a gang of veterans of the Trojan
War is that he instils a belief in the power-legitimating nature of
human reason. Had he been merely a feudal lord, his role as the ship's
commander would not have withstood the ordeal of the voyage. But
since he is more than a bearer of traditional entitlements he can
change the nature of his appeal to obedience. Under the pressure of
circumstances, Odysseus abdicates as king in order to take the helm
as a bureaucrat exerting political domination in the name of reason.
By doing so he defeats a myth (not knowing that he creates another
one in its place). But note the extreme conditions under which his act
of enlightenment was achieved: his crew was literally in the claws of
an everpresent death. If they did not heed the commands of the wily
Odysseus their fate was sealed: they would die. They died anyway. But
while they were alive, to obey and to acknowledge the supremacy and
shrewd rationality of a leader seemed to them to hold out the only
promise of salvation. They could either abandon themselves to the
mythical forces right away or else put up a fight against them by
becoming serfs of the domineering Odysseus.

The social situation of modern man is strikingly dissimilar and yet
reminiscent of this first attempt to survive by establishing a repressive
order based on reason. No one actually believes today that he will lose
his life if he refuses to confer political privilege upon those in the
know. There may be widespread fear that if this sort of obedience is
withheld, modern society will regress to a more primitive stage. But
probably this fear, if it is indeed empirical,[9] is a far cry from the
psychic terror of prehistoric vagrants trying to make their way
through unpredictable dangers lurking in a world populated by demons and hostile gods. They knew what it was to be afraid. We don't
anymore. Our normal everyday lives are free of this sort of psychic
terror. It too vanished, like myth itself, with the growth of enlightenment. Or so we think. Horkheimer and Adorno know better. Just as
myth survives today in the interstices of rational society, so panic is
an omnipresent possibility. We must all be prepared day after day that
a rap on the door signals our impending imprisonment by fascist
police. In this respect the *Dialectic of Enlightenment* is a highly
personal work, as I noted before, for it is informed by subjective
experience. Not just fascism, but the experience of the worst excesses
committed by fascism against individual lives, forms the backdrop of

the book. And it may well be that the major obstacle to understanding the argument of the *Dialectic of Enlightenment* is our distance from the experience of panic, the concept or consciousness of which becomes the counterpoint of reason in the historical process of enlightenment.

The predominance of the notion of fear, variously addressed in the text as *Furcht, Schrecken,* or *Grauen,* is obvious. The first chapter begins with the statement: "Since its inception enlightenment in the most comprehensive sense of progressive thought has aimed at freeing man from fear and installing him as master" (9/3). Fear is the mainspring of rational thought and action. Not only do the henchmen of Odysseus subordinate themselves to him out of fear and therefore act rationally; according to Adorno and Horkheimer the same reflex reverberates in such late products of enlightenment as modern positivism. "He [man] believes he is free of fear when nothing is left that is unknown. This has determined the trajectory of all demythologization and enlightenment. . . . Enlightenment is mythical fear that has become radical. Its latest product, the pure immanence of positivism, is nothing but a universal taboo, as it were. Nothing at all is to be left outside of it because the mere thought of an outside is the actual source of fear" (22/16). Another passage in which the idea of psychic terror is introduced in a kind of *a priori* and perhaps unintelligible way reads as follows: "Fatality, which in times immemorial vitiated the inexplicable fact of death, has its direct counterpart in our own lives which are now being exhaustively explained to us. The noontide fear which made man suddenly conscious of nature's divine character (Allheit), has found its counterpart in the panic which nowadays threatens to break out at every moment. Man expects that this closed, exitless world will be set on fire by a divine agent which he is himself but over which he has no control" (35/29).

Fear is a psychological category. Unlike related concepts, such as interest and reason, the concept of fear cannot be dislodged from the analysis of the empirical ego and shifted over to some kind of intelligible character or transcendental self or even historical *nous.* Nor is this what Adorno and Horkheimer have in mind here. They do speak of fear as experienced individually and prereflectively. Given this necessarily psychological status of the notion of fear, one might ask whether the *Dialectic of Enlightenment* hypostatizes the accidental, or whether this psychological premise is necessary. I will return to this problem.

The *Ideologiekritik* of the Homeric poem not only uncovers the fact that enlightenment sets in motion a dialectic of master and slave. It also points up the dialectic of bourgeois individuation. Enlightenment is the formation of a subject or human self which survives the onslaught of ever-present mythical dangers. This is achieved as the amorphous I gains upright carriage through self-discipline and defiance of nature and of its own passions. Again, Horkheimer and Adorno take issue with all too linear interpretations of this process by pointing out the mediations between developed ego-identity and the evanescent I of mythical man.

Odysseus, the individual *in statu nascendi,* is constantly beset by temptations which threaten to divert him from the "track of his logic" (53/46). These temptations are necessary assaults by the forces of superstition upon the inchoate self. Without them the formation of the subject would abort. What is more, Odysseus abandons himself to them, or pretends to do so like an "uneducable learner" (53/46).

The book gives a concise micrological analysis of the precariousness of the Odyssean subjectification. Time and again Odysseus runs into situations where regression is not imposed upon him, as in the incident with Circe, but becomes a wilful, though temporary, adaptation, such as when Odysseus, trying to escape the vengeance of Polyphemus, declares his name is Nobody. Adorno and Horkheimer take this to be paradigmatic of the vagueness of Odysseus' individuality, which must occasionally efface itself in order to survive. But no sooner has Odysseus escaped from the grip of the giant than he reveals to him his real name, thus deliberately and unnecessarily endangering his life because Polyphemus, still within striking distance, showers the fleeing boat with rocks. Horkheimer and Adorno interpret this scene as a model of the kind of compulsive reassertion of subjectivity which characterizes many of the adventures of Odysseus. It is "as if . . . he thought that the mythical world was still strong enough to make him a nobody if he just calls himself that, unless he restored his identity right away by means of the magical word" (75/76–8), i.e., by shouting his real name.

Here, in a nutshell, is what future ages were to pervert into the capitalist apology of profit in terms of risk-taking. Only those who give precedence to restless curiosity and enterprise over serene enjoyment can attain the status of political citizens because they are assembling a fortune. In the *Odyssey,* the idealistic side of this process comes out most clearly; Odysseus is not directly interested in property or the accumulation of goods. But his behaviour is not unlike that of the entrepreneur in the classical tradition of political economy. He takes risks, the proceeds of which are intangible. "Like the heroes of all real novels, Odysseus throws himself away in order to attain his self" (54–5/47–8).

It has often been remarked how ambivalent the bourgeois attitude toward pleasure is. On the one hand, when an entrepreneur saves in order to invest money in new means of production, he is said to forego the pleasure of immediate consumption. This is rationalized, on the other hand, by adding that the renunciation is really no more than a postponement of gratification: bourgeois economic man saves in order to enjoy more in the end. How little this sort of explanation really explains has always been apparent to critics of bourgeois economic theory. They either denounced it as a fraud (Marx) or supplemented it with the idea of religious motivation (Weber).

Risk-taking and the renunciation of pleasure are also the ideological elements of Odysseus' encounter with the sirens. The principle of risk-taking prevented Odysseus from closing his ears along with those of his crew. Had he done so, his passage would have been safe and uneventful. Only by exposing himself to the danger was he in a position to steel his nascent self. But the risk he took was a calculated one. The ropes which chained him to the mast made sure that he would not be able to indulge himself in mortal pleasures. This is the counterpart to bourgeois risk-taking: renunciation. Odysseus listens to the alluring sounds, but the more attractive they become the tighter become the fetters he has placed upon himself, "just as later the bourgeois foregoes happiness the more tenaciously the more he realizes that his increasing power has put it within his reach" (40/34).

The scene has additional allegorical qualities which the book spells out masterfully. Odysseus, in chains, bodily feels the tension between his desire for emancipation from nature and the urge to regress to prerational pleasure. He reconciles the antagonism by sublimating the alluring stimulus. Art, subjectively the cultivation of a capacity for *interesseloses Wohlgefallen,* is his method of mediating the claims of enlightenment and myth. Likewise, the adventure shows the class character of art. The contemplation of art and the performance of manual labour begin to draw apart and have stayed apart ever since. Art becomes the prerogative of an enlightened class of rulers. "The curse of the irresistible progress is irresistible regression" (42/36).

Perhaps the clearest illustration of what Horkheimer and Adorno do when they engage in literary criticism *qua* critique of ideology is the analysis of the phenomenon of sacrifice in the *Odyssey*. Much like James Frazer, whose work they seem not to have been familiar with, the authors attempt a materialistic-rationalistic interpretation of sacrifice. In this view, the phenomenon of magic is not, as many of its students have claimed, an outgrowth of mythical, prerational perceptions, but is sustained and transformed by the dialectic of reason and superstition. For Frazer, sacrificial magic had a proto-scientific dimension[10] which was lost with the rise of theistic religions only to surface again with the demise of Christianity and with the modern secularization of thought, beginning with Bacon and Descartes. In contrast to the *Golden Bough* the *Dialectic of Enlightenment* emphasizes not so much the implicit scientific *intention* in sacrificial rituals, which Frazer believed were designed to help control a contingent object world, as the bourgeois aspects of sacrifice in animistic and polytheistic cultures.

Here we come to the unequivocally seamy side of the prehistoric portrait of the bourgeois. So far we have chiefly heard something about self-denial, repression and sublimation of instincts, individuation—all of which evoke an ambivalent attitude in us. We cannot denounce them as fake without denouncing ourselves. Short of outright glorification, we tend to look upon the secretion of an impregnable ego from a life-world of superstition, gullibility, and conformity to tradition as an important achievement, even though we also discern in this process the genesis of a privileged class to which we belong (but which we may pursue with hatred). Individuation is at once real progress and illusory ideology. But when we turn to the phenomenon of sacrifice we face ideology in the form of deceit. This too is an element in the syndrome of bourgeois rationality—the sort of rationality which later hit upon the idea of swapping glass beads for gold and calling that an exchange of equivalents. "All human sacrifices, carried out according to a plan, deceive the divine power which they are supposed to aggrandize or appease, for they subordinate god to human purposes, thereby whittling down his power. . . ." (57/50). Odysseus is not the first to commit deceit by sacrificial acts. He is only the first to raise deceit to the level of consciousness, thus helping to destroy the illusoriness of myth, although belief in it, Adorno and Horkheimer speculate, may never have been so deep-seated and unconditional as we nowadays think. "Very old indeed must be the experience that symbolic communication with god through the medium of sacrifice is not for real" (58/50–1).

This idea makes sense when we consider that, according to the mythical mentality, the gods and the demons of primitive religion could be swayed and reconciled by sacrifices, not of divine scale, but of human scale. The gods did not demand sacrifices that were out of proportion to human abilities, but they demanded such sacrifices as were humanly possible. Perhaps this is one of the strongest reasons —one that Frazer overlooked—for arguing that primitive magic was rational. However powerful the gods were in their intercourse with human beings, they never went to the extreme of stating the terms of their contract with man in an unfulfillable form. Even the sacrifice of human beings, rare as it was, is a cost which can be borne by a community as a whole. The same goes *a fortiori* for nonhuman sacrifices.

Primitive gods were the first accountants even before Odysseus tried to trick them. In other words, the bourgeois traits of enlightenment are directly visible, not only in prehistorical mythical heroes using magic as a tool but in the supernatural projections of the primitives themselves as well. The gods and spirits of Homeric Greece behave as if they know the difference between necessary labour and surplus labour, and that the continuous flow of offerings depends on some kind of physical-economic reproduction of human labour power. One could almost say that they have accepted a contractual obligation vis-à-vis man not to annihilate him.[11]

Adorno and Horkheimer do not say this in so many words, but they imply much the same when they allude to the almost petty-bourgeois griping of the gods of the *Odyssey*, especially Zeus and Poseidon, who kept complaining about the fact that Odysseus was able to pile up more wealth from the exchange of gifts than he would have had in his possession if Poseidon and the other gods had allowed him to travel unmolested, taking home his full share of the Trojan loot.[12] In other words, Poseidon's wrath is caused by the result of a calculus in which he weighs exchange values like a bookkeeper. This is symptomatic of the attitude imputed to all the Homeric gods to whom sacrifices are due. They demand no more than a man can afford to give without perishing, and often considerably less than that. "While economic exchange may be viewed as a secularization of sacrifice, it is equally true that sacrifice is the magical prototype of rational exchange" (56/49).

Switching back to the human side of the sacrificial relationship, we notice that while the gods exact what they consider to be a just tribute, the prostrate believer begins to learn to calculate very shrewdly how he can get away with paying less. This is exactly what Odysseus does. He experiments with disobedience. Sometimes he haggles over the price, as if to operationalize a crude criterion of sufficiency. At other times, he pays with counterfeit money, such as when he heeds a mythical contract imposing a sacrifice on him, but fulfils it only according to the letter and not the spirit, which he knows only too well.

All this amounts to saying that the bourgeois principles of exploitation and marginalistic economic behaviour are already well entrenched in the mythical world into which Odysseus enters. He only magnifies the scope of these principles through deceit and enlightened bargaining, thus exposing the relativism inherent in the notion of equivalence. "The benevolence of the deities is expected to have something to do with the *specific magnitude* of hecatombs" (56/49), not with the offering of just any sacrifice whatever. The Odyssean cunning explores the variability of that magnitude. In doing so, Odysseus frees the price system of mythical sacrifices from its traditional pegs and controls. His deceit challenges and subjects to "market forces" the notion of fair price embodied in the mythical contract which underlies the materialism of sacrificial acts.

However, as we have seen before, the figure of Odysseus symbolizes also the transformation of sacrifices into self-sacrifice. "The history of civilization is the history of the introversion of sacrifice" (62/55). Thus, although Odysseus marshals cunning to minimize the ransom exacted by the gods, he subjects himself deliberately to the opposite logic by shouldering the burden of sacrifices he could well have avoided or forced others to pay in his place. This is the element of self-abnegation which seems to run counter to the linear progression of his subjective ability to cut costs and find loopholes in the contracts of religious tradition. In the latter ability we recognize bourgeois rationality, in the former we recognize bourgeois idealism, which was never quite the sort of monstrous lie to which vulgar materialists have degraded it. "This very self-denial [of man's nature] is at once the core of all civilized rationality and the breeding ground of a teeming mythi-

cal irrationality. It renders opaque and confused not only the *telos* of
the external conquest of nature but also the *telos* of man's own life"
(61/54). The mortification of human passions which Odysseus effects
within himself already points to the loss of meaning suffered by enlightenment in its late capitalist phase where means have arrogated
the place of ends. The story of Odysseus exposes enlightenment as
absurd. In his self-abnegation he "surrenders more than he gains"
(62/55). He wastes his life.

We cannot dispel the absurdity surrounding the life of the errant
seafarer unless we take into account the Utopian idea of history as a
totality. Only by doing so can we reap the fruits of his self-sacrifice
which was bound to be meaningless for *him*. For depending on what
we make of the narration, he may have "sacrificed himself for the
abolition of sacrifice" (63/56). The privations he endured by carrying
on his struggle against myth can be redeemed, since they created the
conditions for a society free of privation. Such conditions may exist
today, but the society itself does not. That is why, in the last instance,
the dialectic of the Odyssean enlightenment to this day has not
reached its reconciliation.

I now return briefly to the theme of fear in order to explore a few
lines of possible reflection. Admittedly, they are almost embarrass-
ingly simple and impressionistic. Fear has never been a philosophically respectable category. Especially the historico-philosophical systems of the nineteenth century knew nothing of fear. Nature in Hegel
and Marx was not a repository of dynamic life-threatening forces but
an empty nothing, subject to potential domination. Not the least
important motive for Kierkegaard's anti-Hegelian crusade may have
been this total neglect of fear in Hegel, although other more momen-
tous concerns occupy the foreground of his argument against Hegel.
Kierkegaard gave fear a new philosophical status, but he did so at the
price of dehistoricizing philosophical analysis—a price which is surely
too high. In this connection, the *Dialectic of Enlightenment* reads like
a synthesis between a dialectical science of history and certain Kier-
kegaardian motifs: If the historical mission of enlightenment is a
man's progressive deliverance from fear, this means that nature, the
seat of mythical threats, is not an indifferent otherness which has
progressively become "for us" through toil and the thetic-constitutive
powers of the subject. Instead, archaic nature was determinate, satu-
rated with spirit, and man existed "for it." This is the sense of man's

primordial subjection to nature, from which all human fear arose. The neutralized, clawless concept of nature in Hegel and Marx was no more than a product of modern secularization and demythologization, not nature as natural man saw it. Their historicism was a bit too ontological in this one respect: The nature of which they speak is an abstract universal susceptible to encroachment and transformation by man. It is implied that the further we go back historically, the more nature reveals its abstractness free of human mediations. This is patently untrue. The *Dialectic of Enlightenment* gives us a sense of the complexity of archaic nature and of its embeddedness in subjectivity. In comparison with the fear-engendering nature of archaic superstitions, the ontological purifications which pass for nature in philosophy are pale constructs of a modern will to power.

Horkheimer and Adorno are correct in claiming a central place for fear in their dialectical theory of civilization. Still, on a level of unreflective experience one is inclined to throw the whole idea out as anachronistic. Increasing numbers of people today agree with the position that enlightenment is bound up with regression. In effect, the phrase "myth of progress" is fast becoming a staple of the sort of daily world-historical criticism dispensed by newspaper editorials. To that extent, the *Dialectic of Enlightenment* seems to be vindicated by popular sentiment on a large scale. But would anyone agree with its assertion that fear of nature is an ever-present possibility in the midst of a technological civilization? Not very likely. We live in a world of material comfort which seems to shield us so effectively against nature that we forget it is there. What is there left to be afraid of in nature? In short, whatever costs and mythical regressions the history of enlightenment may have entailed, one thing seems to have been definitely accomplished, and that is the "dephobization" of human life. What does this mean concretely? (I stress concretely because I do not know yet what it means philosophically.) Has the continuity between us and prehistorical stages been interrupted?

In encountering monsters and gods, especially the chthonic god Poseidon, Odysseus experiences fear which Homer describes in vivid language, for instance in the Scylla-and-Charybdis scene. Typically, fear is evoked in the *Odyssey* by the appearance of mythical agents who threaten to draw the hero into the oblivion of the sea. There is no escaping the sea and its elemental destructiveness for one who, like Odysseus, must reach the distant island of Ithaca: The voyage by ship is the only way. We have seen before that Odysseus may on occasion seek trouble.[13] We have also seen what the function of his deliberate flirtation with, and exposure to, danger is, namely, the formation of identity. However, Odysseus never goes so far as to prolong unnecessarily his panic at sea. He prefers to meet threats to his evanescent identity as a person on land. There he can more easily hold his own, whereas, at sea, he is at the mercy of his archenemy Poseidon.

That fear is not a constant of human psychology or, deeper yet, the human condition, is suggested by the description of the Phaeacians. Homer casts them as a tranquil and peace-loving people when Odysseus arrives in their land. They used to engage in violent feuds with the Cyclopes, but have long stopped this practice. They are civilized and expect no harm from any source whatsoever, although they continue to sacrifice to the gods—just in case. They fear no human or divine disturbance of their serene life. Why is this? Homer makes it appear that a mixture of divine benevolence (the Phaeacians consider themselves "dear to the gods," as Nausicaa says) and subjective ability is involved here. It is interesting to note that among the skills in which the Phaeacians excel Homer singles out shipbuilding and navigation as the most conspicuous.[14] In other words, there is a way to conquer fear, the fear of the elements: It is to acquire the knowledge of a good pilot. Though sharing this know-how, Odysseus did not have nearly enough of it and thus remained anxiety-ridden as long as he did not have solid ground underfoot.

To be free of fear is to be a good helmsman, or the slave of a good helmsman, for, as we have seen, servitude is an aboriginal form of enlightenment precisely because it quells fear. Here the motorized masses of North America seem to be the heirs of Odysseus rather than of his underlings. Their method of conquering fear is distinctly bourgeois, if not feudal, *herrenhaft*. In general, the often-noted disappearance in the West of the proletariat as a class may have less to do with the general embourgeoisement attendant upon a rising standard of life, than with the influence of *specific* commodities which strengthen the workers' identification with the dominant classes, commodities such as cars which make everybody's daily homecoming a matter of freedom from fear provided he is a seasoned pilot. I do risk sounding trivial. The point is that no one has ever studied seriously the variable impact of different consumer durables on the erosion of class consciousness. This whole problem would seem to deserve careful analytical attention.

The millions of individualized *Odysseys* which occur daily thanks to automobile technology and production have generated their own dialectic. Out of their interplay comes that horrible spectre of violent death which the Homeric hero sought to banish by learning how to maneuver his vessel. Traffic deaths in France are approaching a figure of 20,000 annually, which is one inhabitant in every 2,500. Calculated over an average 50-year life-span of the active driver, the life-to-death ratio becomes one in 50. Add those maimed and disfigured by traffic accidents, and you get an even more gruesome statistical probability that "you" will be among those whose homecoming is marred by disaster. The statistics are appalling but not striking in themselves. What I do take to be highly revealing here is modern man's unflinching reaction to them: It seems that the lethal probability calculus which everyone can refine for himself—in terms of hours spent annually in the car or miles driven—has induced psychological panic only in the rarest cases. Somehow accident statistics and similar information fall on deaf ears. The question is therefore whether, with all the continuity linking enlightenment and myth, there is not an element which has dropped out of the historical dialectic. This element is fear of death. No theory can desubjectivize fear. Either it is felt or, if it is not, it is a bogus issue. The *Dialectic of Enlightenment* I think wrongly implies that fear and panic are the psychic accompaniments of everyday life in an age of computerized welfare.

The suggestion that present-day life is, as it were, free of the scourge of mythical fear may strike one as inaccurate. But is it really? It is true that modern society imposes unprecedented strains on the psyche of the individual. However, we know from psychoanalysis that anxiety and fear are two different things and also that anxiety is generated by objective factors in the situation of the child. This sort of emotional response may well have been on the rise with the development of bourgeois society in the last 300 years, although according to Freud the possibility for it was always present. But we are not dealing here with anxiety. Odysseus cannot be said to be a captive of neurotic fears. His fear is the result of reality-testing based on mythical constructs. We say he was wrong in fearing the wrath of Poseidon because Poseidon is a figment of the imagination. But we could not conclude on the basis of this that Odysseus was neurotic by modern standards of psychopathology, because his criteria for empirically testing what is real and what is imagined were public rather than deviantly private ones. To repeat, then, the dread which obsesses Odysseus when he hears from Circe what further troubles the passage to Ithaca has in store for him is real psychic terror stemming from a conventional assessment of divinely governed necessity.

I am claiming that dread of this sort afflicts us to a much smaller extent today. It seems to be vanishing as a species of emotional experience. This seems to have nothing to do with the development of a scientific outlook itself. For instance, there are still reasons why fear might be an ingredient of the emotional household of the "normal" person today. I have mentioned automobile traffic. In addition one need only think of the destructive potential of weapons surrounding us. It is said they serve to protect us, but there is no guarantee that they will. On the contrary, we know only too well that they protect us only at the price of threatening others with annihilation. Their protection is at best costly, at worst self-destructive. According to the official theories of deterrence, their protective potential hinges on a system of universalized fear. But where is this fear in practice? Quite obviously, if it exists, it is enormously diluted. Few people experience the threat of annihilation continuously and with the same immediacy Odysseus did when he hung on that tree over the raging Charybdis.

I am driven to the paradoxical conclusion that in the present order of things, where people speak of apocalyptic "scenarios" as if concrete possibilities of life were nothing but scripts for diverse variants of unreality, it may be very important indeed to cultivate the phobic psyche in the midst of modernity. Concretely, it may become a task of progressive political rhetoric to heighten the public sense of fear, in deliberate opposition to the suasion of technocrats and sundry other ideologues who try to disarm critical reflection by pretending that enlightenment has brought us release from the devastations of panic. By itself, freedom from fear is scarcely the sort of world-historical *telos* worth arriving at.

The *Odyssey* is not a microcosmic story of universal historical reason. It only brings out some of the connections between progress, suffering, domination, and fear which have characterized the overall historical trend of enlightenment. Not the least difficulty in "teleologizing" the *Odyssey* is its affirmative ending. Horkheimer and Adorno never were Marxist enough to afford the thought of homecoming and bliss for mankind as a whole. They held that while such an idea could be postulated and was in a sense logical, its very postulatory character contravened the Marxist demand for unity of theory and practice.

They issued no reassuring proclamations that Ithaca had been sighted.

Everything we do is wrong no matter how generously or radically it is conceived. And since all of us do something, even those who do nothing like Adorno himself, we all share responsibility for the continued existence of a society whose organizing principles are domination and fear. A key phrase Adorno invokes frequently as a synonym for society or being-in-society is "universal context of guilt." The term alludes to the impossibility of completing anything in the spirit in which it is conceived: we act in order to extricate ourselves from the ravages of enlightenment in its capitalistic and fascist phase, but we get tangled up in them even more deeply. We reinforce their power. Why does Adorno speak of guilt in this connection? Surely he is aware that people do not experience this guilt; quite the opposite, they are blind enough to launch their boats again and again, like Odysseus, registering failure after failure without remorse. How can there be guilt when there is no conceivable course of right conduct, no moral code for the autonomy-seeking subject? This is the point where Adorno unwittingly assumes the posture of a kind of world spirit, one who behaves, to be sure, more like a vengeant fury than a benefactor of mankind or an embodiment of its highest aspirations. For after having postulated that all traditional theories of virtue are invalidated by a colossal *aporia* in their midst—that we ought to, but cannot, do anything right—he goes on to use the moral language of guilt and responsibility. In doing so he takes the place of the great world-historical umpire rendering judgment *sub specie aeternitatis.* But there is no logic in his verdict. If no *one* can be singled out for special praise or condemnation, the judge's discretion becomes infinite because he can pronounce us *all* guilty or blameless. I believe Adorno in his black gown is rather harsh and lacking in compassion when he hands down his guilty verdict. And it makes no difference that he refuses to exempt himself. Thus he states in the prefatory dedication of the *Minima Moralia:* "I wrote the bulk of the book during the war years, under conditions not unfavorable to contemplation. At that time I had no adequate conception of the force which had driven me out of Germany. I was not ready yet to realize that I, too, was guilty because of the mere fact of talking about the individual *(Individuelles)* in the face of the unmentionable which was being perpetrated collectively."[15] While he subsequently realized this guilt, he remained unaware of another, greater one. What Adorno did not see was that, in the presence of negative totality and the ontological facticity of eternal defeat, the damnation by the spectator of his contemporaries is no more just than their absolution. To make a choice at all—and worse, to make a choice in favour of what looks like the rigoristic alternative —is the pretension of which Adorno is "guilty" in the very ordinary down-to-earth sense that some*one* is abusing his intellectual authority. Under the heading of "Crab Apples," Adorno offers one of his lighter aphorisms which states that "in England and America, whores look as though they were dispensing not only sin but along with it the punishment of damnation in hell."[16] I sometimes think Adorno himself may have done precisely that.

Let us stick to the this-worldly aspects of Adorno's gnosticism which are problematic enough. The difficulty Adorno runs into is that of totalizing and deconcretizing evil. Just as all individual or collective acts tend toward qualitative self-sameness by virtue of their inability of living up to the ideal of transformatory praxis, so all particular phenomena within the totality seem identical because all are equally evil. Equally evil? There is, as we saw, a historical differentiation of the negative, a tendency toward rigidification of the infernal. Hence the ever-the-same gains its identity by mediation and absorption of the new. To that extent the identity of evil is dialectical, historical. Looking at the spatio-temporal here and now, say, of twentieth-century Germany, is there a sense in which it can be said that everything is equidistant from the gravitational center of evil? Or, as other critics have put it, does Adorno fail to see the difference between Auschwitz and Frankfurt? The problem is that of the relativity of evil, of the difference between the bad, the worse, and the worst. Undoubtedly Adorno saw this difference. Like other émigrés of his generation, notably Jaspers and Hannah Arendt, he tried to find words for the horrifying uniqueness of the death camps and the shock of being alive in the aftermath of the genocide. He spoke of a new categorical imperative which Hitler had imposed on posterity: that there not be another Auschwitz. The mass liquidations, a deadly combination of anti-Semitism (myth) and modern paper-pushing efficiency (enlightenment), represented a new low of terror. If the species man is to have any collective future at all, that future is contingent on our accepting the imperative that this must not happen again. The apodicticity of the rule corresponds to the extraordinary nature of the phenomenon it seeks to ban. In accordance with his hierarchy of evils, Adorno dealt in a series of topical essays with social, especially socio-pedagogical strategies which might facilitate the inculcation of the new moral norm.[17] In fact, his entire preoccupation with social psychology during the late 1940s was motivated by a desire to instil that imperative, which was not at all self-evident to many people, even after 1945 and even in America. But his commitment to praxis, if one may call it that, was shortlived and went no further than trying to prevent the worst. Time and again, the Gnostic idea of a *civitas terrena* where all cows are black and all things indistinguishably evil gained the upper hand over the discriminating perception and critique of determinate socio-political landscapes. This levelling of the negative resulted from Adorno's stubborn refusal to let go of the transcendent concept of reconciliation, in view of which every existent was radically deficient. From the standpoint of the transcendent *(das ganz andere)*, Auschwitz and Frankfurt were indeed one and the same.

For Adorno, enlightened praxis, in the naive sense of telling people what they must do or think in order not to work against their own interest, had narrow limits. Critical theory had to foreswear praxis save perhaps in instances where historical trends were coupled with the large-scale incidence of psychic regression. The less than absolutely bad, therefore—the routine agenda of oligopolies, the daily reification of consciousness and the mutilation of nature—did not call forth in Adorno the same desperate response to legislate and to change as the phenomenon of the Nazi terror. A desperate response it was indeed, for it would lead, if not to certain failure, at least to indifferent results. Still, the imperative had to be enunciated and the avenues to its enforcement explored.

Conversely, the collectively legitimated mass murder was not an isolated anachronistic irruption of savagery into modern civilization, but the crystallization of its organizing principle which on a psychological level Adorno identified as frigidity. What we need most but seem to be running after in vain is a panacea for the malaise of frigidity, which is the malaise of man in his state of unfreedom. While the old therapy of liberal tolerance might contain genocide, it cannot stamp it out because genocide is part of a larger pathological complex. Since Odysseus, frigidity is the inevitable shadow of individuation: To be able to see one's companions devoured by the monster without experiencing guilt, and perhaps even physical pain, was the condition of subjectivization. Consequently, the reconciliation of mankind, of Odysseus and the men he sacrificed to his ego, would require some kind of radical healing of the deformations of subjectivity. Not knowing how this is to be achieved, Adorno is all the more convinced *that* it is the logical issue of the history of enlightenment. This "it" "cannot be known, but can only be pointed out as an indeterminate negation."[18]

NOTES

1. Published by Herder and Herder, New York, 1972. The German original, *Dialektik der Aufklärung*, went through two almost identical editions, the first published in Amsterdam in 1947, the second by Fischer Verlag, Frankfurt, 1969. Page references, in the text of this essay, are to the second German edition and, after the slash, to the English edition. E.g., 100/94. Translations are my own.

2. The authors of *Dialectic of Enlightenment* have insisted time and again that their book is the fruit of collective thought, that many sections and passages are the outgrowth of joint reflection. If this is true, then the work is all the more remarkable because never before has an important philosophical book been composed jointly to the extent asserted by Horkheimer and Adorno. My own guess is that the claim is only partially true. In many instances, a really knowledgeable reader would probably be able to tell who the author of particular passages and ideas is.

3. Adorno discussed this built-in barrier against an axiomatic and complete mode of philosophical discourse frequently in his work. See in particular "Der Essay als Form," in *Noten zur Literatur I* (Frankfurt, 1958), pp. 30–49, where he writes: "The demand for continuity of thought presupposes some degree of harmony in the object under discussion." (p. 34)

4. Compare also T. W. Adorno, "Kulturkritik und Gesellschaft," in *Prismen* (Frankfurt, 1955).

5. T. W. Adorno, *Negative Dialektik* (Frankfurt, 1966), p. 313. [*Negative Dialectics* (New York: Herder and Herder, 1973), p. 321.]

6. Ibid., p. 312.

7. Loc. cit.

8. This is repeatedly hinted at, although the idea is left vague and tentative. *Negative Dialektik* speaks of the "assumption of an irrational catastrophe at the beginning [of history]." (p. 315) In a different context the prehistorical institution of sacrifice is viewed as the "stigma of an historical catastrophe." *D.E.,* p. 58/51.

9. The ubiquitous tool of survey analysis has never so far investigated this rather important question of how strongly people feel that they must pay for their ignorance with the coin of political servitude and whether they would not rather pay with a different currency, or perhaps whether they would not rather sacrifice some of the intelligence which experts are putting at the disposal of society as a whole in order to assert their autonomy.

10. See I. C. Jarvie and J. Agassi, "The Problem of Rationality in Magic," in *British Journal of Anthropology,* vol. 18, 1967.

11. By contrast, the god of the Old Testament demands absolute belief, denying the existence of any contractual relationship with man whatever. The trials of Job are a

case in point. Cf. the discussion in Norman Jacobson, *Thomas Hobbes as Creator* (New York: General Learning Press, reprint, 1971).

12. Homer, *Odyssey,* 5.36–40.

13. See also the excellent but speculative analysis of George E. Dimock, Jr., "The Name of Odysseus," in Charles H. Taylor, Jr., *Essays on the Odyssey* (Bloomington: Indiana University Press, 1966) whose approach has much in common with *D.E.*

14. *Odyssey* 7.34–36, 2.227–229, 8.246–253, 8.557–563.

15. Adorno, *Minima Moralia* (Frankfurt, 1951), p. 11.

16. Ibid., p. 55.

17. Adorno, *Eingriffe* (Frankfurt, 1963).

18. Habermas, "Urgeschichte der Subjektivität und verwilderte Selbstbehauptung," in *Philosophisch-politische Profile* (Frankfurt, 1971), p. 195.

TIME, AESTHETICS, AND CRITICAL THEORY

IOAN DAVIES

The problem that we confront in contemporary sociology, or indeed any of the social sciences, is that the categories that we use to interpret reality have become an obstacle to viewing that reality. In fact the terms or conceptions employed by the social scientist have themselves become short-hand jargon in everyday life which make the social scientist the victim of his own codification. If we ask a worker questions about his work, the chances are that he will reply using words like "role," "class," "status," "alienation," or "solidarity," words which he believes will give his responses some validity in the ears of his questioner. George Orwell's castigation of the destruction of the English language through the use of imprecise political terms looks mild against the banality of social science discourse which makes of all language a quantified commodity.

But the sense of meaning will hardly be restored by a return to that linguistic analysis which characterized political philosophy in the years after 1945: to say that we can say nothing because we can never be sure of the exact meaning of words is perhaps the ultimate abdication of analysis.[1] The route from Wittgenstein need not be a cul-de-sac: the search for meaning in communication cannot start with words themselves but with the structural basis of our communication systems. My argument is that a critical theory of politics is necessarily a critical theory of mythology, of narrative and of the forms of communication we employ to construct our stories. But by "critical" we introduce the idea of a vantage-point from which we conduct our analysis. What that vantage-point is will be developed below. Sufficient at this point to indicate that *all* theory (whether it calls itself critical or not) has a vantage-point: that it *reveals* itself is the distinction of critical theory.

I

The study of mythology and communications tends to fall between developmental approaches and structuralist ones; in other words between accounts which try to tell us why things have changed and those which emphasize the continuities. Much developmental sociology or history is heir to the work of J.G. Frazer or Herbert Spencer and, through Durkheim, Weber, or Talcott Parsons, it plots the social structures and the *occasions* for the change. There is the sense of reading history as an occasion for understanding the present, or as Benjamin put it, "with establishing a causal connection between various moments in history. But no fact that is a cause is for that very reason historical. It became historical posthumously . . ."[2] The problem with developmental social theory is that it distorts the experiences of those who lived in order to make sense of our own experiences. We think we understand ourselves because *they* have been consigned to a museum catalogue. We live because they are dead, and somehow, therefore, our stories are superior to theirs, even to their stories about themselves.

The structuralist attempts to save us from this condescension by pointing out that our myths and stories are essentially the same as theirs. If only we understand the logical patterns of mythology we will understand all thought-processes. Or, as Edmund Leach puts it, "If we put the so-called primitive beliefs alongside the sophisticated ones and treat the lot with equal philosophical respect we shall see that they constitute a set of variations around a common structural theme."[3] Structural anthropologists such as Levi-Strauss, Leach, or Mary Douglas have spent time applying this form of analysis to such diverse topics as the early books of the Bible, religion in the Congo, and eating habits in Brazil and the South Seas. But if they show the commonality of myth they are less than adequate in showing the uniqueness of particular myths or even the variations of form within which myth may be found. The attempt by the developmentalists to understand change is ignored by the structuralists in their attempt to understand continuity and repeating patterns.

But perhaps both approaches are doomed to frustration or banality because the problem of vantage-point is not explicitly confronted. It is certainly true that anthropologists or sociologists often make a fetish out of their objectivity and even their militancy,[4] but this largely consists of making academic discipline the vantage-point. Critical theory has to make another definition to avoid being swallowed up in uncritical professionalism.

In developmental sociology, communications are closely related to changes in the social structure, although whether one predates the other is never clear. We understand the growth of literacy in conjunction with industrialization, the invention and diffusion of print, demographic trends, and so on. It is possible in this kind of communications analysis to deal serially with such issues as the rise of the novel,[5] the influence of mechanization on art and architecture,[6] the effect of print,[7] or the impact of radio on a non-industrial society.[8] It is even possible—in more absurd moments—to correlate "development" with the ideology of school textbooks.[9] One of the temptations of such analysis is to use as vantage-point either the notion that what things are becoming is necessarily better (which makes McClelland's or Lerner's work so absurd), or, alternatively, that they are getting worse. In both cases the judgements are made for quantitative reasons: more means worse or more means a lot more which must be better. If we set this against structuralist analysis we are clearly faced with a dilemma, for here we discover that difference means the same. The form is, in a sense, taken for granted: the message never varies because all men are intrinsically the same and respond to social changes in fundamentally similar ways. Vantage-point therefore is the enlightenment cynic whose sole object is to diffuse the magic of myth by emphasising common logical symmetries.

It is a short step from these two apparently discrete approaches to a solution which would seem to unite them in blessed matrimony: the content is dictated by the form. Developmental sociology is about changing forms, structural anthropology (which tends to confine itself to one form) is about similar messages bounded by different forms. Marshall McLuhan can thus emerge as the Aquinas of Communications theory: the changing forms emphasize a similar message because the thought patterns revealed in those forms have continuous elements. The messages are only revealed in their embodiment: the message of television is its encapsulated visibility just as the message of the Eucharist is transubstantiation.

Clearly this does not take us very far if we are concerned with developing a critical theory of communications. We have always known that there is a relationship between form, content and time: to say that they are one and the same invokes ritual but not analysis. In a fundamental sense it is to abdicate analysis in the face of an apparently overwhelming evidence of discrepant information. And yet McLuhan *does* provide us with one interesting observation: that the communications patterns developed in one social situation or in the context of one form may be reproduced *in content* in quite another form. The idea of the Global Village is perhaps banal, but it raises interesting questions about the reversability of form and content that can be developed in another context.

II

For this reason we spend our time, as individual actors, not in confronting the form within which the messages are transmitted, but in debating the content within the form. If our worlds are obscured by form, our discussions are based on the relationship of content to experience. We may, *à la* McLuhan, recognize that the media frames the language of the message we wish to transmit without conceding that the media is the message. There *is* little difficulty in tracing the growth of the novel as a form through the seventeenth, eighteenth, and nineteenth centuries without accepting that the novel would have to be, in perpetuity, a middle-class genre transmitting middle-class messages. Even if we accept that ways of seeing are influenced by the media in question, we do not have to conclude that formal perception *equals* content. To say that form is content is to reside in an area that takes *dress* or *face* as being reality. We might say that a naked body is a naked body is a naked body. This is patently untrue in human experience: a body in a morgue is not a body in bed or in a doctor's office or in a burlesque theatre. The context obviously affects the perception and the intention of the body. A naked body dancing is not necessarily the same thing in any context. As the structuralists show, a naked body (or any body) may be a subject of taboo in one culture and veneration in another. The subject of the problem at this level must be, therefore, to determine how the same object can be seen to serve different purposes in different contexts, and how new objects can serve the same purposes as those they replace. In this sense we confront the functionalist-developmentalist by saying that different objects do not necessarily mean different ends, and at the same time we challenge the structuralist who might claim that the symbolic structures are the same whatever the developmental systems.

I have chosen Walter Benjamin to illustrate both the problem and the indicative solutions because he seems, in different sections of his writing, to go in both directions and, in others, to suggest a way out.

III

Benjamin's major *oeuvre* was to be a study of Paris in the nineteenth century. His essays on this theme are collected in English in a posthumous book, *Charles Baudelaire,* and in *Illuminations.* On the face of it this study is an exercise in the history of social change. Benjamin himself seems to be tracing a *Marxisant* equivalent of Spengler's *Decline of the West.* His central figure is Baudelaire who "took the part of the asocial. He achieved his only sexual relationship with a whore."[10] The mythological figure of the *flaneur* seems to parallel Spengler's mythological *Man of Blood.* Benjamin's *flaneur* is a weak, endearing figure (akin to Spengler's Faust); Spengler's Caesar is a tough, decisive figure (akin to Benjamin's evocation of Brecht's *Arturo Ui*). Structurally the two authors seem to provide polarities of each other, and yet both seem to read alike. For example, Benjamin's conception of the turning point in culture (see his essay "The Storyteller" where the implication is that we cannot tell stories anymore) or Spengler's that "since Kant—indeed since Leibnitz—there has been no philosopher who commanded the problems of all the exact sciences,"[11] *seem* to be saying that, for the past 200 years, we have been unable to tell stories or read science. Both of these authors appear to be predicting doom for similar reasons: the end of civilization is due to a failure in cultural decisiveness. If only we could make sense of the connections, we would not be subject to the whim of the destroyers (technology, mechanization, or division of labour). For Benjamin the solution seems to be the *flaneur,* who preserves the sense of wholeness; for Spengler it is Caesar (or Plato) who can make the necessary connections.

But we may stop at the point we make these comparisons because clearly, they were saying different things and it does not require a critique of the absurdity of Popper to convince us that we have to stand back against the structural symmetries to understand the intrinsic messages.[12]

For example, if we take form as the context within which issues are raised, it is clear that the same form may be altered by the issues themselves. Benjamin introduces the problem of the social uses of architecture. In his essay, "Paris, Capital of the Nineteenth Century," we are given a synoptic treatment of forms being derived from social intent and subsequently being used for quite different purposes.

Haussmann's urbanistic ideal was one of views in perspective down long street-vistas. It corresponded to the tendency which was noticeable again and again during the nineteenth century, to ennoble technical exigencies with artistic aims. The institutions of the worldly and spiritual rule of the bourgeoisie, set in the frame of the boulevards, was to find their apotheosis before their completion. Boulevards were covered over with tarpaulins, and unveiled like monuments . . .

Haussmann attempted to shore up his dictatorship and to place Paris under an emergency régime. In 1864 he expressed his hatred for the rootless population of the great city in a speech in the Assembly. This population kept increasing as a result of his works. The increase of rents drove the proletariat into the outskirts. The Paris quarters thereby lost their characteristic physiognomy. The red belt appeared. Haussmann gave himself the name *artiste démolisseur*. He felt a vocation for his work and stressed the fact in his memoirs. Meanwhile, as far as the Parisians were concerned, he alienated their city from them. They no longer felt at home in it. They began to become conscious of the inhuman character of the great city. Maxime Du Camp's monumental work *Paris* owed its origin to this consciousness. The *Jérémiades d'un Haussmannisé* gave it the form of a biblical lament.

The real aim of Haussmann's works was the securing of the city against civil war. He wished to make the erection of barricades in Paris impossible for all time. With the same purpose, Louis-Philippe had already introduced wooden paving. Nonetheless, the barricades played a role in the February Revolution. Engels gave some thought to the technique of barricade fighting. Haussmann intended to put a stop to it in two ways. The breadth of the streets was to make the erection of barricades impossible, and new streets were to provide the shortest route between the barracks and the working-class areas. Contemporaries christened the undertaking "strategic beautification". . . The barricade was resurrected anew during the Commune. It was stronger and safer than ever. It extended across the great boulevards, often reached first-storey level and shielded the trenches situated behind it. As the *Communist Manifesto* ended the epoch of the professional conspirators, so the

Commune put an end to the phantasmagoria that held sway over the freedom of the proletariat.[13]

It seemed worth quoting this account at some length because of the demonstration that artistic and literary form has a social intent, but also because that intent is by no means fully realized, and indeed in certain circumstances may be overturned. Benjamin's thesis on form and content, therefore, differs substantially from that of Lukács where, notwithstanding the different media discussed by the two authors, the major distinction made is that the great work of art must express a *totality* of experience and conflict. Or as Lukács puts it in discussing Mann's *The Magic Mountain:*

> To see what is new in this novel we need merely to recall that in its initial stages the great novel of realism was oriented towards the "totality" of objects found in older ethics, in order to be able to portray the reality of society in its entirety, and at the same time in its sensuous and palpable unity.[14]

In spite of his attempts to show that form changes, Lukács is insistent on this totality (which clearly has to do with content) which in turn dictates certain forms. We have the uneasy feeling that the totalizing form in fact is more important than either formal or content changes. How else can we explain the remarkable statement that "Solzhenitsyn is heir not only to the best tendencies in early socialist realism, but also to the great literary tradition, above all that of Tolstoy and Dostoevsky"?[15] Because a novel is long, has many characters and deals with prisons camps does not mean that it is socialist! If Lukács had lived to read *The Gulag Archipelago* he might have concluded that mesmerization with the totalizing form is inherently reactionary. The problem with the Bolsheviks was not that they abolished radical content, though they did that too, but that they abolished innovating forms. By working within the Proletcult definition of form, Solzhenitsyn produced for us a series of Czarist novels. Benjamin's notes on Haussmann's architecture are warnings on the danger of not taking form seriously enough.

This digression is important if we are to understand the apparently developmental side of Benjamin. As with Lukács, Benjamin is concerned with preserving aesthetics from a purely diachronic approach. With Lukács the relationship between art, society, and time is treated as a metaphor of multilinear evolution. A critic writes:

In this metaphor art and other "receptive and reproductive forms of a higher order" are compared to some very unique "tributaries" of the "great river" of life, "tributaries" that originate, branch off from this "river" and feed back into it only to repeat the entire process again and again, endlessly. This is a carefully constructed metaphor, consistent with Lukács' materialistic philosophy, for the "tributary" of art does not originate from mystical realms but rather from objective reality, the needs of social life, reflecting these in accordance with the principles peculiar to aesthetics.[16]

Thus with Lukács time is both synchronic and diachronic. We are conscious of the "everflowing stream" but at the same time, with T.S. Eliot, there is the sense of aesthetic circularity, of loss and rediscovery:

> And what there is to conquer
> By strength and submission, has already been discovered
> Once or Twice, or several times, by men whom one
> > cannot hope
> To emulate—but there is no competition—
> There is only the fight to recover what has been lost
> And found and lost again: and now, under conditions
> That seem unpropitious.[17]

But if Eliot's sense of retrieval and circularity is quietistic and fatalistic ("But perhaps neither gain nor loss./ For us there is only the trying. The rest is not our business"), for Lukács the sense of circularity is also bound up with a sense of progress:

[The metaphor] is consistent also with Lukács' belief in art's positive role in improving the "quality of life" by contributing to the aesthetic-ethical growth of the "total man." The "tributary" of art does not bring new "waters" from unknown sources to enlarge the "river"; it returns the old "waters" in a purified, qualitatively improved form.[18]

With Lukács, then, the reading of history in relation to art and social change requires searching for those totalizing forms which reflect the wholeness of experience. Consequently Lukács says little about painting, sculpture, poetry, or short stories, where the vision is necessarily fragmentary. His subjects are epics, novels of social realism, and satires (such as *Gulliver's Travels* or *Oblimov*), which deal with life and philosophy on a grand scale.

Benjamin also seems to be concerned with the synchronic and diachronic, but his treatment of artistic matter is both more eclectic and more technical than Lukács'. More than this, his treatment of time and aesthetics is precisely the reverse of Lukács'. With Lukács we understand both the synchronic and diachronic by looking for the totalistic epic or novel; with Benjamin our reading of history requires a double perspective. Historically and socially our perspective is synchronic: *we read history because we have been here before.* Aesthetically our perspective is necessarily synchronic: *we will never be able to write the same things again.* What are our grounds for making such a distinction? It is worth examining in some detail the materials that are relevant to understanding the scope of Benjamin's Paris Project.

In the "Theses on the Philosophy of History," and the various versions of "What is Epic Theatre?" Time and History are treated as material, like any other, which can only be "useful" to those who live in the present. Consequently we cannot treat history as a series of causal sequences, whether we are socialists or capitalists, because such a causal analysis deprives us of our power to act, abdicating our powers to "eternity." "The historical materialist leaves it to others to be drained by the whore called 'Once upon a time' in historicism's bordello. He remains in control of his powers, man enough to blast open the continuum of history."[19] To do this he has to recognize that in history itself there is no progress.

> There is no document of civilization which is not at the same time a document of barbarism. And, just as such a document is not free of barbarism, barbarism taints also the manner in which it was transmitted from one owner to another. A historical materialist therefore dissociates himself from it as far as possible. He regards it as his task to brush history against the grain.[20]

How then can the historical materialist read history? First he has to recognize the deep implications of the opening lines of the Communist Manifesto:

> The history of all hitherto existing society is the history of class struggle. Freeman and slave, patrician and plebian, lord and serf, guild-master and journeyman, in a word, oppressor and oppressed, stood in constant opposition to one another . . .[21]

Benjamin adds bitterly, "Only that historian will have the gift of fanning the spark of hope in the past who is firmly convinced that *even the dead* will not be safe from the enemy if he wins. And this enemy has not ceased to be victorious."[22]

Once the historical materialist has recognized the parameters of historical circularity as well as its trajectory, his task is to arrest its flow. Writing on Brecht's Epic theatre, Benjamin provides a metaphor for the historical materialist's method:

> Epic theatre, then, does not reproduce conditions but, rather, *reveals* them. This uncovering of conditions is brought about through processes being interrupted. A very crude example: a family row. The mother is just about to pick up a pillow to hurl at the daughter, the father is opening a window to call a policeman. At this moment a stranger appears at the door. "Tableau," as they used to say around 1900.[23]

Thus the task of the historian is to understand continuities by intercepting them at critical moments. The sense of the whole is arrived at by interrupting the gestures of the participants. But the vantage point is always the present. Benjamin quotes a maxim of Brecht's: "Don't start from the good old things but the bad new ones."[24]

This sense of reading history deliberately from the present is bound up with two other significant variations from the work of Lukács. The first is the sense of the importance of minutiae, of matter and of technology, something which is central to all of Benjamin's analysis but almost totally absent from Lukács. As Ernst Bloch commented:

> Benjamin had what Lukács so enormously lacked, a unique eye precisely for significant detail, for the marginal . . . for the impinging and the unaccustomed, unschematic particularity which does not "fit in" and therefore deserves a quite special and incisive attention.[25]

This sense of the particular is important if we view the Paris Project. We interpret the gestures of the actors in mid-nineteenth-century France not simply to examine relationships between people, but between people and *things*. And for this purpose history itself is a thing, a material reality which is a reality only because it is revealed in the present as an object. But the importance of things enables us to come to terms with poetry, painting, architecture, fashion, machines, books, windows, rooms. If Marxism is a dialectical materialism, Benjamin is the materialist *par excellence*. The bourgeois politicians and merchants turned matter into a spiritual wave of progress. The historical materialist confronts matter as matter, and progress as the débris of matter:

> A Klee painting named "Angelus Novus" shows an angel looking as though he is about to move away from something he is fixedly contemplating. His eyes are staring, his mouth is open, his wings are spread. This is how one pictures the angel of history. His face is turned toward the past. Where we perceive a chain of events, he sees one single catastrophe which keeps piling wreckage upon wreckage and hurls it in front of his feet. The angel would like to stay, awaken the dead, and make whole what has been smashed. But a storm is blowing from Paradise; it has got caught in his wings with such violence that the angel can no longer close them. This storm irresistibly propels him into the future to which his back is turned, while the pile of debris before him grows skyward. This storm is what we call progress.[26]

But if matter is to be treated without the spiritual aura with which the bourgeoisie or the aristocracy tried to envelop it, how do we retrieve from matter the spirituality of the present? The second important feature of Benjamin's historical analysis is the social ground of spiritual hope. If Lukács' definition of hope is the totalizing form of the Tolstoian novel, with Benjamin it is the transcendence of a specific form of struggle. On Proust he writes:

> This disillusioned, merciless deglamorizer of the ego, of love, of morals —for this is how Proust liked to view himself—turns his whole limitless art into a veil for this one most vital mystery of his class: the economic aspect. He did not mean to do it a service. Here speaks Marcel Proust, the hardness of his work the intransigence of a man ahead of his class.[27]

Again on Kafka he wrote:

> This much Kafka was absolutely sure of: first, that someone must be a fool if he is to help; second, that only a fool's help is real help. The only uncertain thing is whether such help can still do a human being any good. It is more likely to help the angels . . . who could do without help. Thus, as Kafka puts it, there is an infinite amount of hope, but not for us. This statement really contains Kafka's hope . . .[28]

The hope that Benjamin speaks of is not contained in the material artifacts themselves, but with the moments salvaged out of the debris in which the relationships and visions were what mattered, and the present "is the 'time of the now' which is shot through with chips of Messianic time."[29] The relationship between the moments salvaged from the past and the future "gate through which the Messiah might enter" is indeed the man who is sufficiently in control to "blast open the continuum of history."

With this in mind it is worth returning to the concepts of form and content. With Lukács form and content are united in blessed harmony, and the symbiotic relationship establishes for us a necessary structure for engaging in a discourse with ourselves and others. For Benjamin form is a structure that I must confront in the same way that I confront a department store, a book, a tank, or indeed reified history. Thus although I can see continuities in history, and although I must arrest the gestures of the actors in order to understand, I also know that the material conditions that I confront today have changed. The world of the now includes fragments of the past as artifacts which I necessarily have to relate to because they litter the streets, the museums, the legislatures, or my apartment room. Knowing this I face a paradox. The time of the Now has social structural similarities with the time of Then, but aesthetically it is different because matter is different. My expression is therefore different.

In the Paris Project, Benjamin attempted to tease out a specific moment of Time by exploring the similarities with the past in order to understand the uniqueness of that Present. It is worth examining this exercise in some detail.

IV

The problem for Benjamin is not whether there are eternal verities or whether there is such a thing as "universal man," but how do men encounter and transform the social and material structures that they inherit. For Lukács the only artistic works worth discussing are those which are complete and all-encompassing. For Benjamin there is perhaps more interest in discussing the fragmentary, the scraps, and the incomplete:

> To do justice to the figure of Kafka in its purity and its peculiar beauty one must never lose sight of one thing: it is the purity and beauty of a failure. The circumstances of this failure are manifold. One is tempted to say: once he was certain of eventual failure, everything worked out for him *en route* as in a dream.[30]

Other critical theorists who have attempted to establish a vantagepoint for evaluating society have normally chosen an external parapet: Catholicism, the Promise of Revolution, or simply by providing a negative of existing social relations. Benjamin invites us to partake of a much more dangerous task: to view society from the perspective of those who failed or who threw up their hands in despair. It is in this context that we must view his treatment of Baudelaire and mid-nineteenth-century Paris.

If historical materialism allows us to read history from the perspective of the Now, as an exercise in seeing structural symmetries, we are still left with the problem of the *moments* of difference and similarities and also with our accounts of seriality. If we can return to historical accounts, interrupt the gestures and contemplate the meaning of the tableau, one thing we can be sure of: although we feel we understand the social structure, we also know that the structure we are understanding is not *their* structure, but ours, and that the language we use defines us in a way that they would never have used to define themselves because, and hence the paradox, *their* language in our structure inhibits our speech. Thus the importance of the Failure. He knows that certain things cannot be said anymore, not only the same way, but in any way because, as Marx reminded us,

> The tradition of all the dead generations weighs like an incubus on the brain of the living. And just when they seem engaged in revolutionising themselves and things, in creating something entirely new, precisely in such epochs of revolutionary crisis they anxiously conjure up the spirits of the past to their service and borrow from them names, battle slogans and costumes in order to present the new scene of world history in this time-honoured disguise and this borrowed language.[31]

The importance of the Failure is that he is aware that this experience is cumulative, but that the attempt is necessary, that

> each venture
> Is a new beginning, a raid on the inarticulate
> With shabby equipment always deteriorating
> In the general mess of imprecision of feeling.[32]

The essays on Kafka, Kraus, Proust, and on Translation are illustrations of this problem. The Paris Project and in particular the essays on Baudelaire are attempts to come to grips with the moment of failure.

The subject of this failure inhabits the same milieu that Lukács takes as the scene of artistic success, that is, the nineteenth-century city. But where Lukács takes the social realistic novel as the measure of comprehension, Benjamin takes the existential language. Lukács has a definition of the whole by which men might work out the interconnected parts; Benjamin deals with individuals and groups attempting to come to terms with the material world through the languages they inherit.

Of course the most significant cumulative effect on language in the nineteenth century has been technology, a technology which affects architecture, weapons, roads, lighting, painting, sight, transportation, music, theatre, and language itself. But perhaps, above all, what technology (and with it capitalism and urbanization) does to communication is to fragment it. In an essay on Leskov, Benjamin recounts the idea of the storyteller and remarks that "the art of storytelling is coming to an end. Less and less frequently do we encounter people with the ability to tell a tale properly."[33] The reasons are many but substantially because modern technology and war have broken our sense of the continuous, so that communication avoids conversation or listening to "the man who could let the wick of his life be consumed completely by the gentle flame of his story."[34]

The city is the arena in which technology and power coalesce. The poet, like the storyteller, uses a language and form which predates the industrial-commercial city. Unlike the storyteller, he has no tale to tell, but on the other hand he uses images and a tradition of poetry which emphasize both the continuity and break with that tradition. Precisely because the poet is an anachronism, he has more to say; he is the stranger who attempts to interrupt the gestures of the crowd, the architect, or the politician. That he fails is the theme of Benjamin's analysis.

The Baudelaire of Benjamin's essays is the man who attempts to establish a critical stance in relation to the new social classes and in particular the geographical embodiment of social class—the crowd. Benjamin contrasts Baudelaire with Victor Hugo who places himself in the crowd as *citoyen*. For Baudelaire the poet places himself as *hero,* but a hero who changes from the ancient romantic hero to the pimp-hero "whose deeds are reported by the *Gazette des Tribunaux.* "[35] For Baudelaire the dandy, the *flaneur* is successor to the days of heroism, but the age which Baudelaire calls the "modern" does not allow him the opportunity of the exploration. The symbols of traditional exploration and heroism have become either simply nostalgic or have been reversed to being motifs of decadence. Flowers, ships, the sea, romantic love, fantasy all become terrifying images of the "sunken city,"

> Je ne vois qu'en esprit tout ce camp de baraques,
> Ces tas de chapiteaux ébauchés et de fûts,
> Les herbes, les gros blocs verdis par l'eau des flaques,
> Et, brillant aux carreaux, le bric-à-brac confus.[36]

Baudelaire's hero inhabits a city where it is impossible to take the situation of hero seriously. "The modern hero is no hero; he acts heroes."[37] There is little doubt why Benjamin finds in Baudelaire such an important metaphor for understanding the relationship between Time, Aesthetics and Critical theory. If our argument on Benjamin's sense of synchronic and diachronic time is correct, Baudelaire himself is clearly a metaphor of the impasse: the author who feels that any period of time is his subject matter, who is acutely conscious of the repetitiveness of history as situation, but who is also aware of living in the present in terms of metaphors which do not make much sense. Baudelaire is the actor who interrupts his own gestures by recognizing that his mythical sense has itself been interrupted by that very modernity which he sought to command as Hero:

> Perdu dans ce vilain monde, *coudoyé par les foules,* je suis comme un homme lassé dont l'oeil ne voit en arrière, dans les annés profondes, que désabusement et amertume, et, devant lui, qu'un orage où rien de neuf n'est contenu, ni enseignement ni douleur.[38]

The man who sought to be the hero against the crowd is himself buffeted by the crowd, but he remains, as Benjamin remarks, no *flaneur.* If he adopted the style of the *flaneur,* as an approximation to the mythical hero, it was in order to establish a stance from which he could both understand and combat the tendency of the crowd to be dominated by commodity. The *flaneur* himself idealizes his independence from the masses by adopting the style of the aristocrat. Rapidly, however, he is appropriated by the market-mechanism. He becomes the trend-setter, the man of fashion, and even the anti-revolutionary leader of counter-insurgency warfare. His "independence" itself becomes a commodity which the bourgeoisie can adopt to control the crowd. The *flaneur* who began his career as the symbol of aristocratic detachment, ends up as the propagator of faddish modernism. Baudelaire can only view this development with cynicism and the sense of maintaining the *form* of Dandyism at all costs with no respect for the changes in the content of style against external formal changes. In his poem "L'Amour du Mensonge" (The Love of Deceit) he satirises form alone as a means of deception:

> Mais ne suffit-il pas que tu sois l'apparence,
> Pour réjouir un coeur qui fuit la vérité?
> Qu'importe ta bêtise ou ton indifférence!
> Masque ou décor, salut! J'adore ta beauté.[39]

That Baudelaire was able to see all this and yet fail to communicate to us any sense of alternatives is the theme of Benjamin's work: the man who maintains his critical stance but who feels impotent against the piles of debris that make the remembrance of times past not memories of spirituality or of social awakening but moments of un-consoled nostalgia. The memory of time is that of a time in which the nostalgia of remembrance is outweighed by the bitterness of the super-natural externality of metaphor. The supernatural is not the sense of transcendence, but the knowledge of the damned who wander inde-pendent of time. If we have festivals which attempt to reconstruct our sense of the nostalgic, prior experiences, in the end it is extemporal damnation that holds our attention. Church bells do not call us to recreate, they shock us into forgetting:

> Des cloches tout a coup sautent avec furie
> Et lancent vers le ciel un affreux hurlement,
> Ainsi que des esprits errants et sans patrie
> Qui se mettent a geindre opiniatrement.[40]

With Baudelaire the past becomes the extraterrestrial saga of dam-nation which points to our failure. For Benjamin it is that recognition of failure that provides the occasion for establishing the grounds for reconstructing our critical hope.

V

For the functionalist or the evolutionary social scientist, our hope rests in the knowledge that the artefacts of contemporary society provide structures which allow us to ignore the metaphysical uncer-tainties of transition by resting on the hope of an emerging social structural symmetry. The structuralist warns us against this utopian-ism by pointing to the symbolic continuities of our attempts at making sense: we will never be different because, being men, our language has always produced recurring patterns which help us to cope with our social situation in substantially similar ways. Our hope rests in our eternal sameness.

With both of these approaches we have little stance for critical awareness. Critique is subsumed by method. Action and thought are never interrelated. In the one instance action derives from social structure; in the other it is occluded by thought structure. The classic issues of enlightenment and post-enlightenment philosophy are not confronted but swept under the rug so that we are asked, not to examine the dust and the garbage, but to contemplate the rug. Critical theory invites us to look again at the garbage, but not only that: because the rug is now firmly placed above the garbage, we have to examine the rug as well.

The work of Walter Benjamin is of major importance for critical theory because it tempts us to pursue different routes. The motifs in Benjamin (as contrasted with Baudelaire) contain all the paraphernalia of our refuse and our attempts to order them. And our refuse is none other than the garbage-can of history: our dreams, words, artistic artefacts; our stories, monuments, histories; our lives, deaths and eschatologies. For Benjamin the order which I choose to impose on the artefacts is as important a theme of investigation as the artefacts themselves. There are no etceteras in Benjamin's margin.[41] There is no margin: the etceteras are in the centre.

In one sense this is no progress. The Surrealists and Dadaists said it all before. In an important sense they said nothing. Their nihilism provides a vantage-point from which we collect the etceteras in order to establish, simply, that they *are* etceteras. With Benjamin we collect them in order to point to another centre: the door through which the Messiah might enter. The vantage-point for viewing the present and the past is not the "good old things" nor merely the "bad new ones," but the "chips of Messianic time," not as "Jewish" time (for that would relate back to the "good old things"), but as the time of the Now in which any one might be the Messiah. Or as a Canadian poet has written:

A poet's colours
are green and black

the colours of life and death
And his Internationale begins:
    let's all fart in the ears
        of commissars and priests

And I'm here
    in this faded city only
        because I hope to find
            behind all these scurrying bones
                one unfearing authentic man.[42]

For Benjamin the point of critical theory is that every man should
be his own Messiah, or the "one unfearing authentic man." The man
who might come through the Messianic gate could be the man (who
is Everyman) who has seen through the art of the collector or the
rug-cleaner and has collected with him all the other rug cleaners who
know that the time of Tomorrow is the time of the Now without the
broomsticks or the vacuumcleaners. The time of Tomorrow is the
time without the homogeneous vacuum. It is the time of Man.

NOTES

1. A good example of this genre is T. D. Weldon, *The Vocabulary of Politics* (London: Penguin, 1953). See also Alan Blum, *Theorizing* (London: Heinemann, 1974).

2. Walter Benjamin, *Illuminations* (London: Jonathan Cape, 1970), p. 265. [New York: Schocken Books]

3. E. Leach, "Virgin Birth" in *Genesis as Myth and Other Essays* (London: Jonathan Cape, 1969), p. 86.

4. "If anthropologists are to justify their claim to be students of comparative religion, they need to be less polite. So far they have shown an extraordinary squeamishness about the analysis of Christianity and Judaism, religions in which they themselves or their close friends are deeply involved. Roth's Bulletin No. 5 on the North Queensland Aborigines was an ethnographic document of considerable interest; so is chapter 1 of the Gospel according to St. Matthew. Serious anthropologists should treat the two works on a par; both are records of theological doctrine." Ibid., pp. 109–110.

5. I. Watt, *The Rise of the Novel* (Harmondsworth: Penguin, 1963).

6. S. Giedion, *Mechanization Takes Command* (New York: Oxford University Press, 1948).

7. Marshall McLuhan, *The Guttenberg Gallaxy* (Toronto: University of Toronto Press, 1954).

8. D. Lerner, *The Passing of Traditional Society* (Glencoe, Ill.: Free Press, 1957).

9. D. McClelland, *The Achieving Society* (New York: Free Press, 1967).

10. W. Benjamin, *Charles Baudelaire: A Lyric Poet in the Era of High Capitalism* (London: New Left Books, 1973), p. 171.

11. Oswald Spengler, *The Decline of the West* (London: Allen and Unwin, 1954), p. 425.

12. In *The Open Society and Its Enemies* (London: Routledge and Kegan Paul, 1945),

Popper invites us to accept a version of McLuhanism in which we are asked to agree that although the actual messages in Plato, Hegel, and Marx are different, we must reject them because the form of their arguments is the same.

13. Benjamin, *Baudelaire*, pp. 174–5.

14. G. Lukács, *Solzhenitsyn* (London: Merlin Press, 1970), p. 36.

15. Ibid., p. 35.

16. Bela Kiralyfalvi, *The Aesthetics of Gyorgy Lukács* (Princeton: Princeton University Press, 1975), p. 142.

17. T. S. Eliot, *Four Quartets* (London: Faber and Faber, 1956), p. 31.

18. Kiralyfalvi, op. cit., p. 142.

19. Benjamin, *Illuminations*, p. 264.

20. Ibid., pp. 258–9.

21. K. Marx and F. Engels, "The Communist Manifesto," in E. Burns, ed. *A Handbook of Marxism* (London: Gollancz, 1935), pp. 22–3.

22. *Illuminations*, p. 257.

23. Benjamin, *Understanding Brecht* (London: New Left Books, 1973), pp. 4–5.

24. Ibid., p. 121.

25. Quoted in ibid., p. vii.

26. *Illuminations*, pp. 259–260.

27. Ibid., p. 212.

28. Ibid., pp. 147–8.

29. Ibid., p. 265.

30. Ibid., p. 148.

31. Burns (ed.), op. cit., pp. 116–7.

32. T. S. Eliot, op. cit., pp. 30–31.

33. *Illuminations*, p. 83.

34. Ibid., pp. 108–9.

35. Benjamin, *Baudelaire*, p. 80.

36. Baudelaire, "Les Cygne" in Angel Flores (ed.), *An Anthology of French Poetry* (New York: Doubleday, 1958), p. 305. Translation by Joseph Bennett, p. 32:
> I see only in mind all this camp of hutments,
> This heap of roughed-out capitals and shafts,
> The grasses, the large stone blocks greened by puddle-water,
> And, shining in the windows, the jumbled bric-a-brac.

37. Benjamin, *Baudelaire*, p. 97.

38. Quoted in Benjamin, *Baudelaire*, p. 153. "Lost in this mean world, jostled by the crowd, I am like a weary man whose eye, looking backwards, into the depth of the years, sees nothing but disillusion and bitterness, and before him nothing but a tempest which contains nothing new, neither instruction nor pain."

39. P. 311 in Flores, op. cit., trans. Dwight Durling, p. 39.
> Shall not the semblance alone suffice for me,
> To rejoice my heart, since Verity I forswore?
> What matters stupidity or indifference?
> Hail, mask, dear counterfeit! I bow, adore!

40. Benjamin, *Baudelaire*, p. 144.
> Suddenly bells leap forth with fury,
> Hurling a hideous howling to the sky
> Like wandering homeless spirits
> Who break into stubborn wailing.

41. Contrast with Harold Garfinkel, *Studies in Ethnomethodology* (Englewood Cliffs, N.J.: Prentice Hall, 1967), in which the Etcetera is an important issue. Garfinkel's

etcetera is clearly related to Parsons' or any economists' "all things being equal." With Benjamin no things are equal. That is the point of the enquiry.

42. Irving Layton, "Budapest," in *The Pole Vaulter* (Toronto: McClelland and Stewart, 1974), p. 25.

AESTHETIC EXPERIENCE AND SELF-REFLECTION AS EMANCIPATORY PROCESSES: TWO COMPLEMENTARY ASPECTS OF CRITICAL THEORY

SHIERRY M. WEBER

I. THE PROBLEM

The aesthetic and liberation

The political history of recent years indicates that the interest in freedom must encounter the aesthetic—the dimension of art, the imagination, and the experience of beauty. The political demands of the sixties included not only changes in institutional structure but also changes in the quality of daily life, culture, and the environment. The slogan "All power to the imagination" expressed one of the central ideas of the May '68 uprising in France.

The connection between the aesthetic and freedom has also been a major concern of the theory that has emancipation as its aim, critical theory. This is true not only of the writings of such members of the Frankfurt school as Theodor Adorno, Herbert Marcuse, and Walter Benjamin, but also of those of major figures of the period in which critical theory has its origins, that of German Idealism. Kant, Schiller, and Hegel all devoted works to the question of the relation between beauty and freedom.

What is the link between the aesthetic and critical theory? This question is most easily answered if we think of critical theory not so much as Marxism and its variations but rather as theory which is dialectical in method and has liberation as its content and aim. Conceived this way, critical theory would extend from German Idealism through Marx to the work of the twentieth-century Frankfurt school. The essence of liberation as conceived of in critical theory is the recovery of wholeness or the abolition of alienation. That wholeness may be defined as a non-alienated relationship between man and nature, man and others, subject and object, or the various aspects of a single person's existence. It is this concern with wholeness that makes the aesthetic a persistent part of critical theory's concerns. For critical theorists have always seen the aesthetic as embodying precisely such a non-alienated relationship between man and nature, subject and object, and reason and the senses. They have seen the aesthetic both as a model of such an emancipated relationship and as an indication that such a relationship can exist beyond the limits of the aesthetic dimension.

Self-reflection in critical theory

At the same time, critical theory (again taken in the broader sense) has been equally concerned with the connection between reason and freedom; more specifically, with the emancipatory power of reflective thought. Critical theorists have consistently pointed to the critical and dialectical activities of thought and have claimed that in liberating man from the domination of false conceptions they increase human freedom. This emancipatory process of thought may be called self-reflection, for in it reason, or the reasoning human subject, reflects not only on its objects but on its own relation to its objects, that is, on its own capacities and its own products. In the process the reasoning subject transforms both its conceptual and its normative frameworks and its objects insofar as they are constituted within those frameworks. Kant's critical philosophy, the Hegelian dialectic, Marx' critique of ideology, and the Frankfurt school's dialectical social theory are all self-reflective in this sense.

Like the aesthetic, the process of self-reflection entails a mediation of subject and object, and its claim to emancipatory power rests on that mediation. Yet although critical theorists have claimed emancipatory value for both the aesthetic and the process of self-reflection, and on the same basis, they have never systematically explored the relationship between them. It is true that the aesthetic has been viewed primarily as a *model* of a free relationship, while self-reflection has been conceived as an emancipatory *process*. But this distinction is not entirely accurate, nor does it suffice to define the relationship between the aesthetic and self-reflection. The issue lies deeper than that, as is evidenced by the fact that in the history of critical theory, self-reflection and the aesthetic tend to function as alternative foci of interest. The same thinker may focus on the aesthetic in one work and the nature of reason in another, and certain periods accord more attention to the aesthetic than others. A sketch of the history of critical theory will illustrate this variability of interest.

In the later eighteenth century, theory became concerned with the problem of liberation. Reason was seen as the goal of the historical process, and its realization was thought to include the realization of freedom. At the same time, the idea that reason would gradually be realized was recognized to be problematic, both because of the nature of reason and because of the problem of the agency of its realization. During the same period, the relation between the rational and the non-rational was at issue in the field of aesthetics, and the relationship between history, reason, and the aesthetic came to be a focus of much interest. When Marx in his historical materialism reformulated the problem of liberation in terms of social conflict and the social organization of the means of production, the role of reason and consciousness in attaining freedom became even more ambiguous, and the aesthetic came to be seen as a derivative phenomenon without a major role in the struggle for liberation. In the twentieth century, the Frankfurt school, while retaining the Marxian focus on the historical specificity of social oppression, devoted much attention to the problem of the subjective co-constituents of oppression and to the role of thought in liberation, and the aesthetic became a matter of central interest again. Most recently, in the work of Jürgen Habermas, interest in the subjective or interactional components of domination has led to a more systematic return to the original problems of the nature of reason and its role in history, without, as yet, a similar reconsideration of the nature of the aesthetic and its relation to reason.

The aesthetic and self-reflection
as dialectics of reciprocity

The above sketch should indicate that it is high time to consider the relationship between the aesthetic and the self-reflective structure of critical theory. It is time to begin to define what the aesthetic and self-reflection have in common, as well as how they are different and complementary in their emancipatory functions. In this paper I will present some initial suggestions as to the nature of their relationship. Briefly, I will propose the following:

1. Critical theorists have been working to develop a truly dialectical conception of the relationship between subject and object, nature and reason, individual and universal. As the deficiencies of both the idealist dialectic and the materialist dialectic have become evident, the endeavor has come to focus on the nature of the dialectical relationship itself. Both the aesthetic and self-reflection provide examples of dialectical relationships between those poles, and that is the basis of critical theory's interest in them. In both, I propose, the dialectical relationship is characterized by a reciprocal structure in which the two poles or moments are present as different levels, each of which is in turn subordinated to the other, so that reciprocity can be defined as coordinated subordination of levels. It is this structure that the aesthetic and self-reflection share (strictly speaking, this structure characterizes aesthetic experience, and it is the presupposition and effect of the process of self-reflection), and this structure that critical theorists have seen as providing a model for freedom.

2. The dialectical conceptions of the relationship between nature and reason or subject and object that are involved in the aesthetic and self-reflection as formulated in critical theory imply certain redefinitions of each of the poles. In particular, nature or the sensuous comes to be defined as the infinite particular which is the locus of individuality, and reason is redefined as self-reflective and complex in its functions. At the same time, this shared dialectical structure does not mean that the aesthetic and self-reflection can be reduced to one and the same process. For critical theorists, the aesthetic continues to represent the mediation of nature and reason in the particular, whereas the process of self-reflection is focused more on man conceived in his universal aspect as a rational member of a socio-historical species.

These theses will be explicated at greater length in the third part of this paper. In the second part I will present in more detail the history of critical theory's interest in the aesthetic and the development of the idea of self-reflection.

II. THE ARGUMENTS

In the first part of this paper I introduced the question of the relationship between the aesthetic and self-reflection as seen in critical theory, and I indicated my answers to that question. In order to substantiate those answers, I would now like to present in more detailed form some of the points in the history of critical theory which are most relevant to the problem under discussion. I have chosen twelve arguments, or theoretical positions, which, viewed as a whole, both constitute the problem and provide the material for the conclusions I have presented. Each of them bears on the central problem in at least one of the following ways: as a statement of the problem of emancipation, as an assertion about the emancipatory nature of the aesthetic or of self-reflection, or as an assertion about the nature of an emancipatory relationship between poles of an important dichotomy such as subject and object.

In attempting to deal with this highly abstract problem in a small amount of space, I have chosen for the most part to forgo documentation and argumentation. Thus what I present is of necessity a highly stylized version of each author's position. Nevertheless, I have tried to convey in each case what I consider to be the crux of the position, as well as my own view of what problems it leaves unresolved. I have also tried to provide some sense of the historical continuity of the arguments.

1. Late eighteenth-century philosophy of history (example: Kant's *Idea for a Universal History with Cosmopolitan Intent*)

Late eighteenth-century philosophy of history may be regarded as the starting point of our problem insofar as it poses the fundamental question of reason's role in history, that is, of reason's relation to its context. Thus philosophy of history is self-reflective theory; reason reflects on its own role in history. Furthermore, insofar as the philosophy of history tries to describe a course of history in which reason is brought to perfection or realized within the social world, it has a practical (moral) intent.

However, philosophers of history in that period do not adequately recognize the self-reflective and practical aspects of their undertaking. This deficiency leads to a crucial unresolved paradox in their enterprise, which may be stated as follows: philosophers of history conceive the course of history as an evolution from nature to reason, with reason as the ultimate goal. Reason is the goal of history both in the sense of ultimate value and in the sense of ultimate authority. However, since the presupposition of this conception of history is that nature precedes reason and that reason is to develop out of nature, reason cannot be conceived as the agent through which the goal is realized. Instead, in this respect nature is seen as the authority. Hence the course of evolution must consist of a transition from heteronomy (determination of man or reason by nature) to autonomy (reason's self-determination). Without a self-reflective concept of reason, however, this model cannot describe a transition from heteronomy to autonomy. Rather, it must posit an absolute origin of reason. Further, since man remains a natural as well as a rational creature, reason can be realized within the natural context only in the form of an authority over nature, and consequently in the form of the authority of (rational) man over (natural) man. Thus the complete autonomy of the individual is impossible. In short, the unresolved problem for late eighteenth-century philosophy of history is the mediation of, or transition between, nature and reason; failure to solve that problem leads to internal contradictions which manifest themselves in the form of hypotheses about ineradicable origins and authorities.

2. Kant: the nature of reason *(The Critique of Pure Reason)*

Kant's *Critique of Pure Reason* is an attempt to resolve the problem of the mediation of nature and reason, although in the context of epistemology rather than philosophy of history. Kant's attempt is important to us for several reasons. First, it explicitly acknowledges the self-reflective activity of reason. Self-reflection is the basis of the critical philosophy; reason reflects on its own contribution to the object of knowledge and on its own limitations. Second, Kant identifies synthesis as the crucial element in the production of knowledge. The understanding synthesizes perceptions with its *a priori* categorical framework to form concepts of objects. Thus Kant describes scientific knowledge as made possible by a synthesis of nature and the *a priori* contribution of the mind. Third, in thus describing scientific knowledge, Kant also makes possible a clear distinction between theoretical and practical (moral) knowledge, which is realized in acts of freedom.

However, Kant's solution to the problem of nature and reason raises further problems of mediation. In order to describe the *a priori* contribution of the mind to scientific knowledge, and delimit objective knowledge of the world of experience from practical knowledge, Kant must posit something other than and beyond the limits of the understanding, something which forms the material of the synthesis of knowledge and the agent of moral action in the world. He postulates the thing-in-itself, and he postulates a noumenal, free self. These hypotheses raise important questions: what is the ultimate relation between freedom (the noumenal self) and the basis of sensibility (the thing-in-itself), how is it possible for freedom to intervene in the objective world of experience constituted through the understanding, and what is the ultimate relation between the different aspects of reason and the knowledge they produce? In effect, Kant raises the question of other types of synthesis than the one involved in scientific knowledge. Furthermore, although Kant employs the self-reflective capacity of reason, he does not examine it, and thus does not confront the question of what type of knowledge his critical philosophy is and how it is possible. As with the philosophy of history, this failure to explore the dimension of self-reflection is correlated with thinking in terms of origins and *a prioris* rather than in terms of historical processes.

These problems which are shared by the philosophy of history and by Kant's critical philosophy, namely the problems of mediation, the nature of self-reflective reason, and the nature of the historical process, remain the central issues in critical theory, and the development of aesthetic theory and dialectics within critical theory may be seen as attempts to resolve them.

3. Kant: the aesthetic as mediator
(The Critique of Judgment)

For Kant an investigation of the nature of aesthetic experience provides the answer to one of these questions, namely, how freedom can be effective within the natural world. Kant sees the aesthetic as linking nature and the noumenal self that is the locus of freedom. His description of the aesthetic judgment (the judgment that something is beautiful) is crucial to his reasoning. In the aesthetic experience, he says, perception of objects is in harmony with the cognitive faculty, the understanding. At the same time, the aesthetic judgment. based on this experience is not a form of scientific knowledge; the aesthetic object cannot, like the scientific object, be classified in terms of concepts and laws of nature. The judgment that something is beautiful is based rather on the subject's perception of his own disinterested (and thus presumably universalizable) pleasure in the form of the beautiful object. This formulation is important in that it points to a notion of a free, non-subsumptive relationship between both subject and object and universal and particular. The aesthetic object is perceived as both unique and ideal; the aesthetic subject is both a sensuous experiencer and a disinterested self. Kant says that the idea of a universal sensibility (sensus communis) underlies the possibility of aesthetic judgment. This idea links the infinite particularity of the natural or sensuous world with the universality of reason (both the understanding and moral reason) and thus links the natural world with freedom.

This is critical theory's initial formulation of the mediating role of the aesthetic. In it the aesthetic is seen as linking both reason and freedom on the one hand, and reason and sensuous experience on the other. Kant's formulation, however, does not resolve the problems posed by the philosophy of history in that, since Kant still does not focus on the self-reflective process of reason, he cannot connect these mediating qualities of the aesthetic with the possibility of self-reflection as evidenced by his critical enterprise. Further, since his definition of the aesthetic remains formulated in epistemological terms, he does not confront the problem of mediation with the historical as opposed to the simply natural world.

4. Schiller: the aesthetic as mediator in history
(Letters on the Aesthetic Education of Mankind)

Schiller's *Aesthetic Education* may be seen as an attempt to remedy the latter problem of the *Critique of Judgment*. Schiller attempts to use Kant's formulation of the nature of aesthetic experience to show how nature and reason may be mediated within the process of history. Thus he attempts to show how the aesthetic may function not only as a model of a free, non-subsumptive relationship but also as an emancipatory process which will help to realize freedom in the natural world. Schiller's position is this: the French Revolution has shown that reason cannot simply impose itself on the historical, natural world. Domination of nature by reason is destructive to both. The aesthetic, however, can provide a peaceful transition, as it were, from nature to reason. Schiller bases this assertion both on Kant's definition of the aesthetic and on a reinterpretation of the course of history as it was conceived by late eighteenth-century philosophers of history. Schiller asserts that man's nature includes both a natural, or material component and a rational, or formal component. These two components are harmonized in aesthetic activity, which is typified by play. Thus it is in play that man is fully human. The elements are harmonized through the reciprocal non-subsumptive relationship that prevails in the aesthetic: nature and reason are each subordinated to the other, but in a context in which the constraint of nature and the constraint of reason are both suspended. Once introduced into nature in the aesthetic context, reason can develop without dominating nature. From this point of view, Schiller contends, the problem of history can be seen to lie not in an insufficient development of reason but rather in a structure of civilization in which nature and reason have unnecessarily constrained and distorted each other.

Schiller's attempt, like Kant's, is limited by his failure to consider the self-reflective nature of reason and thus of his own theory. This limits both his ability to formulate the connection between the aesthetic and philosophy and his ability to conceive the historical process. As a result, although he deliberately sets out to bridge the gap between a formal definition of the aesthetic as mediator and his conception of the aesthetic as an instrument of intervention in the historical process, he cannot do so. On the concrete level, his suggestions are limited to a naturally determined origin of the aesthetic on the one hand and the fantasy of an aesthetic state on the other.

5. Hegel: the dialectic as the historical movement of reason (*The Phenomenology of Mind, The Science of Logic, The Philosophy of History*)

Hegel's philosophical system may be regarded as an alternative to Schiller's conception of an aesthetic education: each uses ideas advanced in one of Kant's critiques to attempt to solve the problems posed by the philosophy of history. Schiller uses Kant's view of the aesthetic; Hegel uses Kant's conception of the critical activity of reason. Hegel is thus the first thinker to make the self-reflective, self-formative activity of reason the agency through which freedom is to be realized in history.

The essence of Hegel's notion of this self-reflective process (which he calls the dialectic) is this: Reason perceives contradictions in its subject matter, and the perceived contradictions are resolved through a change in categorical framework which in fact constitutes a new stage in reason's development. The development from Kant's critical philosophy to Hegel's own system is an example of this process: Kant put himself in a self-contradictory position, Hegel says, when he claimed that we could know only appearances, i.e., objects as constituted within our *a priori* framework for possible experience, and that the thing-in-itself is unknowable. For by positing the thing-in-itself reason had already known it in some sense, and by delineating the position of the subjective individual knower and his contribution to knowledge, reason had already constituted an objective knowledge. Thus the critical philosophy leads to Hegel's objective idealism. The end point of reason's process of reflection is the absolute idea, in which reason is no longer subject to any limitations since it already contains all contradictions within itself. This process of overcoming limitations is equivalent to the process of realizing freedom, Hegel says, and, accordingly, to the historical development of political forms.

The problem with Hegel's system is that it both is and is not based on a self-reflective notion of reason. On the one hand, Hegel claims to show how each position that reason takes evolves out of the contradictions of the prior stage; thus reason becomes historical. On the other hand, however, Hegel presupposes the absolute idea as the ultimate end of the process, and this leaves the relation between the individual human subject of knowledge and the subject of the absolute idea ambiguous. Thus Hegel's system, like earlier philosophies of history, contains a contradiction between a historical and reflective view of reason on the one hand, and one which implies an absolute, thus an origin and an external authority, on the other.

6. Hegel: the aesthetic as subordinate to the dialectic
(Lectures on Aesthetics)

Hegel's aesthetics are important to our problem in that they are an attempt to synthesize a view of art as mediation between nature and reason with a view of reason as self-reflective or dialectical and with a notion of historical development. According to Hegel, art is one of the objectifications of the *Weltgeist;* it is objectified spirit. Art is the appearance of the Idea in sensuous form, a mediation of the Idea with sensuous material. This very essence of art, however, is unstable, since the Idea by nature is continually transcending its involvement with the sensuous. Since the Idea is in the (historical) process of realizing itself as absolute Idea, art too is constantly evolving. The history of art may be seen as a gradual movement from a preponderance of nature in the images to a preponderance of spirit. At the midpoint of this development, in the classical (Greek) period, art realized *its* idea, the perfect adequation of the Idea with its sensuous form, in the Greek vision of the human body. At present, in the romantic (modern) period, art has in fact already transcended its idea. It has become more and more subjective, dominated by the Idea as the Idea becomes more self-substantial.

From the point of view of our problem, the paradox of Hegel's aesthetics is that in describing the relationship between art and self-reflective historical reason, Hegel necessarily comes to the conclusion that art is transcended as the Idea moves toward its fulfillment. Thus, correlatively, although art is seen as a mediator between reason and the sensuous, as in Kant and Schiller, it has no unique emancipatory value. Ultimately, reconciliation is accomplished through the process of self-reflection in which the absolute Idea develops itself.

Hegel's view of the aesthetic, of course, is subject to the same criticisms as his view of the dialectic; there is a contradiction between the claim to an imminent self-reflective development and the claim to an absolute culmination of the process. Nevertheless, Hegel's aesthetic is important in that it represents the first attempt in critical theory to formulate the relationship between the aesthetic as mediator and self-reflection as an emancipatory process.

7. Marx and Marxism: The dialectic and materialism[1]

Kant and the philosophy of history posed certain basic questions which Schiller and Hegel, both elaborating on Kant, attempted to resolve through the aesthetic and self-reflection respectively. For both of them the historical dimension remains a problem, which they attempt unsuccessfully to resolve by postulating an original priority of nature or an absolute reason.

It is precisely on this point that Marx makes a decisive contribution. He makes the historical dimension central to his thought in a way that will remain in force in the work of the twentieth-century critical theorists. For the problem at hand, one of the most important facets of Marx and Marxism is Marx' critique of Hegelian idealism and his attempt to construct a materialist dialectic. Marx rejects Hegel's absolute idea as the subject of history and conceives concrete human beings and groups of human beings as the agents of history. He still considers contradictions to be the motor of history, but sees them as arising out of the structure and social organization of the production process. Thus they are specific to specific socio-historical situations. Accordingly, Marx sees the realization of freedom in history (the original problem posed by the philosophy of history) not so much as a matter of developing reason but rather as a matter of changing a specific, historically developed organization of the production process. Thus he avoids the philosophical problem of absolute origins, as well as the problem of introducing reason into history. It is emancipation from domination rather than from nature that is the problem.

An important implication of Marx' attempt to formulate a materialist dialectic is that since the social interaction of man with nature through the labor process is seen as the determinant of contradictions and of ideas and consciousness, consciousness is necessarily limited by the particular stage of evolution of these social conditions. Therefore art as a product of consciousness is also historically determined. It no longer serves as a model for realized freedom. Rather, at best it reflects objective historical contradictions and at worst it propagates the ideological deformations of consciousness which reinforce social oppression.

There is a central contradiction or at least ambiguity in Marx' thought: For Marx, the historical determination or limitation of consciousness need not negate the emancipatory power of self-reflection.

Marx retains the claim to reason's emancipatory power in that he makes the proletariat's accession to true consciousness crucial to the revolutionary process. This accession is presumably aided by such critique of ideology as is to be found in his own work. On the other hand, Marx does not directly confront the nature of self-reflective reason as a philosophical or epistemological problem. Thus his theory remains ambiguous on the question of the relation between socio-economic determinants and consciousness.

8. The Frankfurt school[2]: dialectical thought as negation in one-dimensional society

The Frankfurt school's "critical theory of society" represents an attempt to deal more adequately than Marx did with problems of culture, ideology, and consciousness. In doing so, the Frankfurt school has recourse to some of the ideas of German Idealism while retaining the central premises of Marx' historical materialism. It considers the need for such a synthesis to be due to historical developments—the failure of the world revolution predicted by Marxism, the "triumph of unreason" in Nazi Germany, and the development of one-dimensional advanced industrial society. In one-dimensional society, as Marcuse calls it, the contradictions and conflicts which formed the content and the hope both of bourgeois philosophy and of Marxism seem to have been levelled, so that although no emancipation has taken place there is no longer a hold for praxis. This description of advanced industrial society poses a problem for historical materialism: one-dimensionality is more a form of consciousness or culture than of "reality" (a primary locus of it is positivist thought), yet it seems to be a primary political fact of the modern age. This state of affairs leads members of the Frankfurt school to conclude that in the present period changes in theory and in consciousness must precede political praxis. The primary opposition to the existing order seems to reside in the negativity contained in dialectical thought. Dialectical thought thus becomes a sort of theory-as-praxis. At the same time, this process of thought as negation cannot become a philosophical system, for Marx has permanently discredited philosophy's pretense to ahistorical *a priori* truth. The movement of thought must always be related to the object to be criticized. The Frankfurt school's critical theory, accordingly, is deliberately anti-systematic.

Thus twentieth-century critical theory is based on the claim that self-reflection (in the sense of the dialectic as critique) is, if not a systematic method for liberation, at least a movement toward emancipation. In refusing philosophical systematization, however, these writers also avoid reflecting on the epistemological status of self-reflection, and they must forsake the possibility of an organized emancipatory praxis which would contain a moment of self-reflection.

9. The aesthetic in the Frankfurt school's critical theory of society

The Frankfurt school's focus on dialectical thought as negation and thus as a kind of praxis may be considered an attempt to mediate between German Idealism and Marxism. The fact that this enterprise is, as I have indicated, not resolved is reflected in the ambiguous role that the aesthetic plays in the Frankfurt school. The aesthetic is quite central to their work, yet they interpret it in two different ways. This difference is important in indicating that as long as the central issue of self-reflection is not resolved, attitudes toward the aesthetic will not be resolved.

From its commitment to the interrelation of thought and historical conditions, the Frankfurt school has a commitment to the premise that aesthetic phenomena must be interpreted in connection with their historical period. Given that premise, two alternative interpretations of the aesthetic are possible. First, the aesthetic may be considered to be subordinate to historical conditions. For the Frankfurt school, this subordination is realized in two ways: The aesthetic may be integrated into existing conditions of oppression, as in works of "high culture" which in certain ways reflect and reinforce the maintenance of class divisions; or in the direct integration of the aesthetic into the system of one-dimensionality, as in the sex object or the beautiful machine. At the same time, the aesthetic in its autonomous historical development (as a transcending reflection of what exists) may be forced to self-destruct as what exists becomes so irrational as to be incompatible with beauty. This idea is expressed in Adorno's question, "How can there be lyric poetry after Auschwitz?"

Alternatively, the aesthetic may be seen as containing a moment of transcendance over existing conditions and thereby contributing to the opposition to the status quo accomplished by dialectical thought as negation. In this way art is seen as yielding a sort of dialectical knowledge. By the same token, art remains subordinate to the cognitive value of the dialectic, as it did in Hegel's system.

10. Marcuse: The aesthetic as mediator *(Eros and Civilization, Essay on Liberation, Counter-revolution and Revolt)*

Both the interpretations of the role of art described above revolve around the contradiction between a "bourgeois" conception of high culture and a Marxian conception of the secondary derivation of the realm of the ideal. In this context, Marcuse's writings on the aesthetic stand out as an attempt to revive the emancipatory claim of an autonomous aesthetic.

Marcuse's conception of the aesthetic contains three elements: 1. He accepts Kant's and Schiller's interpretation of the aesthetic as mediating between reason and the sensuous. 2. He retains the Marxian conception of domination as socio-historically conditioned and therefore remediable. 3. He combines these with a depth-psychological perspective that is called for by the recognition that one-dimensional subjectivity is co-constitutive of oppression.

For reasons both of material scarcity and of domination, Marcuse argues, civilization has been organized on the basis of an opposition between sensuousness and cognition, play and work. The advance of civilization has seemed to require the suppression or repressive sublimation of the "lower" faculties of man. An alternative to that conflict and the repression attendant on it, Marcuse claims, has been formulated in philosophy and is exemplified by aesthetic experience and the workings of the imagination. Both reason and the senses participate in the aesthetic without conflict or suppression. Reformulating Schiller's notion of the reciprocity that prevails in the aesthetic, Marcuse speaks of the "de-sublimation of reason and the self-sublimation of the senses" in the aesthetic. The transformation of nature and reason that takes place in the aesthetic indicates that a similar harmonization could occur in the whole of earthly life.

Marcuse sees this mediation between nature and reason as a form of praxis as well as an ideal model, for he interprets the revolutionary praxis of the sixties as based on biological revolt, moral revolt, and aesthetic revolt. Thus while retaining the Frankfurt school's idea that radical negation is the only possible opposition to the existing order, he sees this negation occurring in the form of spontaneous political demands rather than being restricted to the intellectual work of critical theorists. Marcuse's conception of the aesthetic points the way to such an unusual conception of praxis. The linkage of reason and the senses in the aesthetic legitimates, as it were, the fusion of biological and moral protest. At the same time, the idealization and sublimation inherent in aesthetic form serve as a reminder that reflection and cognition must be harmonized with the biological and the moral.

In short, Marcuse takes the notion of the aesthetic as mediator and relates it on a number of levels to the socio-political dimension. His argument, however, suffers to some extent from the same problems as Schiller's. Still lacking a conception of the aesthetic as process, he can describe the biological-moral-aesthetic revolt only as a mysterious spontaneous upsurge; and lacking an understanding of reason as self-reflection, he cannot formulate a relationship between theory and the sort of praxis he describes.

11. Habermas: self-reflection and the emancipatory interest (*Knowledge and Human Interests*)

Habermas has made an important contribution to the understanding of emancipatory processes by exploring the nature of self-reflection. He does this in the context of the Frankfurt school's opposition to positivism as non-dialectical, one-dimensional thought, but he does it more systematically than earlier writers. Habermas reopens the questions of epistemology and philosophy of history that were posed in the late eighteenth century and attempts to resolve them while maintaining certain elements of the Marxist historical-materialist position.

Dialectical thought claims that there is always a relationship between knowledge and interests; positivism denies this relationship and erects a model of objective scientific knowledge. The crux of Habermas' resolution of this conflict is a revised notion of interest which is both material and ideal. Basing himself primarily upon Kant and Fichte, Habermas identifies certain interests which are common to the human species as such and which form quasi-transcendental frameworks within which knowledge is produced in the course of human social evolution. This allows him to differentiate between types of knowledge according to the interests which determine their production. Scientific knowledge serves the instrumental end of mastering nature; cultural knowledge serves the end of maintaining social cohesion. For Habermas, self-reflection also yields a type of knowledge and is governed by an interest: the interest in emancipation from domination. Thus self-reflection is historical—in that it is a reflection on the oppressive aspects of reason's own history and present context—but it is also supra-historical in that it is a process in which humans are capable by nature of participating and which is essential to the life of the species.

Habermas' conception of species interests implies that the subject of history is humans as social beings. The knowledge produced in accordance with these interests is produced within a framework of communicative interaction and must be seen in connection with that framework. Domination may be defined in terms of communicative interaction as systematic denial of the basic nature of human beings as interested and knowledge-producing. These distortions take the form of shared illusions of objectivity (or disinterestedness) which are accepted as given or natural and as such determine communication, consciousness, and actions. Self-reflective knowledge aims at overcoming domination by undoing such distortions.

This theory of self-reflection can be used to solve the residual problems of earlier theories of self-reflection. It obviates the need to postulate an absolute origin of reason in nature, since it postulates a coincidence of species-interests and the activities of reason, and it postulates a self-reflection which has its own history and context as its object rather than one which must create itself from nothing. Furthermore, it reformulates the problem of mediation between nature and reason as a problem of undoing pseudo-natural distortions of reason.

12. Habermas: communication theory and ideology ("On Distorted Communication," Gauss lectures, Princeton University, 1972)

This view of self-reflection as producing emancipatory knowledge within the framework of a species interest in emancipation requires a revision of social theory in terms of communicative interaction. Habermas attempts this in what he calls a "universal pragmatics," or communication theory of society. The central postulates of this theory are:

AESTHETIC EXPERIENCE AND SELF-REFLECTION 95

1. Social reality is constituted through the pragmatics of communication, that is, through speech acts involving truth claims which are accepted by others.

2. This communicative construction of reality is premised on the possibility of full intersubjectivity, that is, of what Habermas calls unconstrained communication. Unconstrained communication would occur in the "ideal speech situation," in which each subject would recognize and be recognized by the other as a separate ego and a competent communicator, that is, a communicator for whom none of the possibilities inherent in the structure of language are blocked off. These possibilities include the mediation of individuality and universality, that is, of individual subject and intersubjective communication; the possibility of meta-communication, in which one communicates about one's own and others' communications; and the possibility of clarifying misunderstandings and subjecting truth claims to discussion.

3. Language in its intersubjective and pragmatic aspects involves a number of reflective and mediating processes. That it does makes it possible for communication to become systematically distorted. Communication may be blocked so as to preclude meta-level communication in some way. Another way of saying this is to say that certain experiential contents may be excluded from intersubjective communication. When communicative competence is blocked in this way, the communicators cease to operate as full subjects. This means that certain aspects of their communication and experience operate as objectified interests which control without being controlled. Ideology and false consciousness may be considered forms of such systematically distorted communication. Distorted communication is of political import insofar as it both alienates power and control and creates the illusion of objectified alienated states of affairs in which agency and communication are not possible.

4. Emancipatory knowledge (knowledge acquired through self-reflection) has the effect of destroying this illusion of objectivity and the correlative illusion of lack of agency and restoring subjects to subjecthood. Such knowledge is achieved through a specific kind of dialogue in which the reciprocity of the ideal speech situation is modified to a therapeutic asymmetry. Habermas considers the interaction between psychoanalyst and patient to be an example of such a dialogue. In the analytic process a number of elements are mediated: a model of unconstrained communication, a general interpretation of

distorted communication, the patient's utterances, and the interaction of patient and analyst. The effect of the process is to restore flexibility of communication in the patient and transform the therapeutic relationship from one of asymmetry to one of reciprocity.

Habermas' theory has the virtue of constructing an intersubjective theory of domination and of one aspect of the emancipatory process. It connects the process of self-reflection with a theory of social evolution and with specific historical conditions, and it provides both for self-reflection as knowledge and for self-reflection as praxis. Where it is inadequate is in terms of the non-linguistic. Although in rejecting an absolute it allows for the existence of non-linguistic (monologic) universals and the non-rational, it does not specifically analyze such areas of experience or discuss their relationship to the linguistic and rational.[3]

III. COMMENTARY ON THE ARGUMENTS

As I have presented them, these arguments form a series which is intelligible but incomplete. They all revolve around a complex of basic issues: problems of mediation, especially between history and reason, nature and reason, and the individual and the universal; problems of priority, in the sense of an absolute, an origin, or authority; and problems of freedom or emancipation and consequently of oppression or domination as well. Attempts to resolve the issues lead the thinkers involved to investigations of the aesthetic or of self-reflection. By the twentieth century the arguments also take the form of attempts to mediate between an idealist and a materialist dialectic. However, neither the issues themselves nor the relationships among them have been completely clarified.

Habermas' work on communication theory in relation to self-reflection provides a new basis for thinking about these issues, but it does not include an interpretation of the aesthetic, and it does not fully consider the claims made for the aesthetic.[4] Thus the new step in the series should be, as I have suggested, a consideration of the relationship between the aesthetic and self-reflection. The first step in such a consideration would be to reformulate the conception of the aesthetic as mediator and harmonizer expounded by Kant, Schiller, and Marcuse, in terms of a conception of reason which incorporates Habermas' theory of self-reflection. Then the communication theory of reason would need to be supplemented with the resulting conception of the aesthetic. The outcome of such a process would provide a basis for a formulation of the dialectic which would transcend the opposition between idealism and materialism. The issues of mediation, priority, and emancipation could then be clarified in terms of such a formulation. In what follows I will attempt to sketch such a mediation between the aesthetic and self-reflection.

Reflection and reciprocity in the aesthetic

In presenting the aesthetic theories of Kant, Schiller, and Marcuse, I pointed out that they could not solve certain problems because their conception of reason did not include its self-reflective moment. Paradoxically, however, their arguments for the aesthetic as mediator or as image of freedom are all based on a recognition of the dialectical structure of the aesthetic, if not of reason. I would like now, primarily through reference to Kant's *Critique of Judgment* and Schiller's *Aesthetic Education,* to show how a reflective and reciprocal structure is a fundamental component of their conception of the aesthetic.

Kant's definition of the aesthetic is obviously dialectical in that it is based on negation and paradox. The aesthetic is defined through negation, in terms of forms of experience which it is not identical to but nevertheless has something in common with. This is how it can be seen as linking the senses and reason. The essence of the aesthetic as Kant sees it is a paradox—subjective universality or *sensus communis.* Furthermore, the basic structure of the aesthetic as Kant sees it is reflective: the aesthetic subject's experience of the aesthetic object includes his reflection upon the state of his own psyche, and the aesthetic judgment is based on the reflective discovery of his pleasure. At the same time the aesthetic subject abstracts from his own position to put himself in the position of a generalized other and judge whether that other would presumably also feel pleasure in this particular object. Thus the aesthetic judgment requires a two-fold reflective movement: a movement from object to subject (which accomplishes the idealization of the object), and a movement from the particular to the general within the subject (from the subject's particular experience to the generalized other). This movement is possible only with the assumption of a *sensus communis,* that is, the assumption that the particulars of subjective sensuous experience are compatible with the universals of reason. It does not, however, result in the subsumption of the particular under the universal concept, as it would if it were a form of knowledge. Rather, it produces a free aesthetic relationship between the idealized particular subject and the idealized particular object. The relationship is not one of subsumption but one of reciprocity.

This idealized reciprocity, which is founded on pleasure and in which subject and object are both universal and particular, forms the basis of Schiller's and Marcuse's conceptions of the aesthetic as well as Kant's. Schiller speaks explicitly of a reciprocity *(Wechselwirkung)* of nature and freedom in the aesthetic. He defines reciprocity as coordinated subordination: in the aesthetic, reason is subordinated to nature in one sense while nature is subordinated to reason in another. As Schiller puts it, in the aesthetic the sensuous ceases to be matter which is determined, and reason ceases to be the agent of determination. Rather, the sensuous becomes an infinitude of particulars, and reason enters into the experience in the form of an enlivened potentiality. Marcuse is referring to the same thing when he speaks of the self-sublimation of the senses and the de-sublimation of reason.

Kant's aesthetic theory also provides the basis for understanding the reflective, reciprocal structure of the aesthetic in terms of communication. Kant begins his presentation of the dialectic of aesthetic judgment by noting that one feels impelled to dispute about matters of aesthetic taste even though it is impossible to settle the disputes, since to settle such a dispute would involve turning the aesthetic into a form of knowledge, in which all particulars may be subsumed under concepts. This is another way of saying, I believe, that aesthetic experience is inseparable from talk about the aesthetic object and from aesthetics. Although this talk can never have the status of scientific knowledge and theory, nevertheless the aesthetic subject tries to mediate linguistically between the particular and the universal. The peculiar characteristic of the aesthetic object, however, Kant says, is that it generates an infinitude of ideas, and it is this infinitude which means that it can never be subordinated to a specific concept. Hence critical discussion and aesthetics as a philosophical discipline remain subordinate in turn to the particular aesthetic object. Thus the reciprocity of the aesthetic also includes a reciprocity of aesthetic experience and critical discussion.

The dialectical structure of the aesthetic and self-reflection as the goal of emancipation

On the basis of this conception of the aesthetic we may compare the aesthetic and self-reflection as emancipatory processes. But in order to do so we need to reexamine the notion of emancipation. As I said earlier, the tradition of thought with which we have been concerned originated when the realization of reason in history was conceived as simultaneously the goal of philosophy and a philosophical problem. Thus the unity of theory and praxis has been involved in critical thought from the beginning. But in some cases this assumption of a unity of theory and praxis has led to a confusion between the structure of reason or the aesthetic and the process of emancipation. Hegel's dialectic offers an example of an explicit equation of the two.

If we suspend the idea of the unity of theory and praxis for a moment, we can distinguish between three aspects of the problem of emancipation (at the theoretical level): the problem of how things are essentially or would be ideally, that is, the goal of emancipation; the problem of what is wrong, that is, the nature of domination or oppression; and the problem of praxis or intervention. Let us begin by considering the first aspect of the problem of emancipation. If we look at the aesthetic as I have just reformulated it, that is, as including moments of reflection and reciprocity, we can see that the aesthetic and self-reflection, considered as models of something both natural and ideal, have in common a structure which is dialectical, reflexive, and reciprocal. To be more precise, if we look at the aesthetic subject in relation to other aesthetic subjects and to the aesthetic object, and at the reasoning subject (reason being understood in terms of Habermas' theory of communication and self-reflection) in relation to other subjects and to the objects of his reason, we see that their experiences have the following logical structures in common:

1. The experience involves simultaneously a reference to an object, a reference to the self, and a reference to other subjects.

2. There is a movement from individual to universal, both at the level of the object and at the level of the subject.

3. The relationships between the object and the subject, the individual and the universal, have in each case the form of subsumption, so that one will be, as it were, embedded within the other; but the

subsumption works in both directions at once, so that there is an overall relationship of coordination. This structure of coordinated subordination I have called, following Schiller, reciprocity.

4. The form of the whole is based on a number of movements, or reflections, all of which have the self or subject as their center. Thus the self has autonomy only through its reflective and reciprocal relationship to its objects and to other subjects.

The reformulation of the aesthetic given above exemplifies all of these aspects. Let me give a few examples from the self-reflection theories. In the ideal speech situation, which Habermas defines as the presupposition of all communication and which recapitulates Hegel's model of mutual recognition, each subject both experiences the uniqueness of his own experience and translates it into universal terms which can be understood by another. Each subject also reflectively recognizes that the other who appears only through those universal terms is also a unique experiencing subject. Another example: in Habermas' description of self-reflection, it is a universal interest of reason that guides self-reflection upon each individual historical distortion; at the same time, it is the necessity of living in a specific historical period that provides the impetus for self-reflection.

The aesthetic and self-reflection as forms of praxis

This model of the logical structure of aesthetic experience and self-reflection allows us to understand the other two aspects of emancipation, namely what is wrong and how to intervene so as to correct it. If aesthetic experience and self-reflection consist of a number of reflective moments with the self or subject at their center, then the very nature of these processes allows for their distortion through blockage of the reflective moments, as well as for their reconstruction or restoration through the renewed activity or intervention of those same moments. The ideal is an image of the natural restored. Further, since the self is the agent of the reflective movements, the self addressed in the theories as the aesthetic or communicating subject is always the implied victim of the distortions and always the potential agent of emancipation.

Of the arguments I have presented, Schiller's and Habermas' provide the best examples of the aesthetic or self-reflection as ideal model, explanation of distortion, and guide to praxis all in one. (Schiller is in fact the only one of the thinkers we have seen to claim explicitly that the aesthetic has not only symbolic but also practical potency). For them, the blockage of the reflective movements which destroys the reciprocal relations between subject and object, and subject and others, and thus also the autonomy of the self is equivalent to domination defined in other terms, thus to false consciousness, ideology, illegitimate authority, etc. For example, Schiller says that what is wrong with his historical period is that nature and reason have each overstepped their (natural) boundaries (as defined by Kant in his critiques), with the result that reason inhibits nature, producing decadence, and nature inhibits reason, producing barbarism. Or Habermas (following the German psychiatrist Lorenzer's book *Sprachzerstoerung und rekonstruktion*) defines systematically distorted communication as communication in which certain contents must be excluded, the result or means of this exclusion being to render the reflective or meta-level of communication inoperative in certain areas. The contents which cannot be drawn into communication then act as *a priori*s, pieces of nature which exercise illegitimate authority. Thus for Schiller the illusion of a conflict between nature and reason is created when the autonomy of each is blocked, and for Habermas certain illusions of legitimate authority and value-free science are created by blockages of self-reflection.

If we look at the way these thinkers conceive the aesthetic and self-reflection as intervening agencies, we see that the intervention consists of natural reflective movements being brought into play. For Schiller, the intervention consists in introducing the detachment and disinterest which characterize the aesthetic; this leap of idealization introduces the reflective distance within which the autonomous functioning of subject and object, nature and reason, can occur. Habermas has explicated the intervention of self-reflection in terms of the therapeutic dialogue (rather than in terms of the activity of critical theorists). In the asymmetrical therapeutic dialogue the self-reflective capacities of one member are applied to the communications of the other within the context of a dialogue, so that the person whose distorted communication is the object of the therapy is restored to full subjecthood. Thus in each case an intervention of reflection results in the restoration of autonomy.

Let us take as an example of such praxis the reciprocal impact on critical theory of the aesthetic and self-reflection, which provides an example of such praxis. Let us think for a moment, as I have suggested, of critical theorists as starting from the problem of nature and reason and becoming tacitly engaged in trying to formulate a theory that will transcend both the idealist and the materialist dialectic. Then we may think of reflection on the aesthetic and reflection on self-reflection as each accomplishing certain redefinitions necessary to the new project. To wit: if we look back at the arguments for the emancipatory power of the aesthetic, we see that they are based on the idea that the aesthetic can liberate man from the domination of reason. Reason in its subsuming, conceptualizing, and problem-solving function is seen as the dominator and destroyer of nature. While this view does reason the injustice of ignoring its self-reflective structure, it has the virtue of redefining and idealizing the area of nature and the sensuous, so that that dimension comes to be seen not as dead matter, passive under the agency of reason, but as the unique and particular which possesses the attributes of form and infinitude. On the other side, although the arguments which claim an emancipatory power for self-reflection derive from the rationalist tradition, which sees reason as liberating man from the domination of nature, they tend to reinterpret this domination as the domination of objectified forms of reason. Thus they involve a reinterpretation not so much of nature as of reason, so that reason is seen as developing, capable of distortion, and capable of transcending its own distortions. To formulate it schematically, we may say that reflection on the aesthetic leads critical theorists to define the area of nature and the sensuous in a way that is reciprocally related to the subject and to reason, and that thinking about self-reflection leads them to redefine reason in such a way that it may be reciprocally involved with the non-rational subject.

As forms of praxis, aesthetic experience and self-reflection have in common the restoration of autonomy and reciprocity through the intervention of a reflective moment. This sort of praxis is distinguished from strategic political action, which, at least since Marx, is what one normally thinks of as praxis, by its ideal character:[5] both aesthetic experience and self-reflection refer directly to a model of the ideal reciprocal relationship between subject, others, and object; and both intervene directly on behalf of potential wholeness and autonomy. Ultimately, I believe, it is the fact that aesthetic experience and self-reflection have this emancipatory process in common that has made them of continuing interest to critical theorists. They are both reflections of the ideal and avenues to it, and they will always be the necessary complements of strategic action.

NOTES

1. This presentation is admittedly more schematic than most of the others. I have not attempted to do justice in any way either to the issue of the early vs. the late Marx, or to the other issues of contemporary Marx criticism. In effect, in my conception of the problem at hand, Marx and Marxism are important principally as a transition between German Idealism and the twentieth-century critical theorists.

2. By the Frankfurt school here I mean especially Max Horkheimer, Theodor Adorno, and Herbert Marcuse. Prototypical for the argument here presented are Marcuse's *One-dimensional Man* and Adorno's *Negative Dialectic,* as well as the early essays by Horkheimer and Marcuse on the nature of critical theory.

3. Habermas has broached this topic in some recent essays, unpublished at the time of this writing.

4. Habermas' discussions of the aesthetic in some parts of *Kultur und Kritik* are largely dependent upon the formulations of earlier writers. He has not integrated those formulations with what is original in his own work.

5. This same ideal character requires that self-reflection and the aesthetic work in an idealized temporal framework, which is why they can complement but not replace strategic political action as forms of praxis.

DEATH AND REVOLUTION: A REAPPRAISAL OF IDENTITY THEORY

KEN O'BRIEN

The thrust of this discussion is that Erich Fromm's contributions to the corpus of the Frankfurt School's critical theory should be reappraised in a more positive light. This task can only be accomplished with a thorough re-examination of his essays between the period 1929 to 1937, as well as a theoretical assessment of his ideas since that period. Our task is to probe the essays of the early period. We will show that when his work is viewed in the context of critical theory, especially in relation to the still largely imprecise non-identity principle,[1] Fromm's contributions are vital. The charge that Fromm's work is revisionist in content and methodology is premature and exaggerated. Nevertheless, this charge has inhibited a continuous critical review of Fromm's contribution, and it has been taken up and repeated by more recent reviewers of the work of the Frankfurt School. Fromm's "populist" and liberal democratic ideas have been more widely disseminated while his more serious theoretical work remains largely unexplored. To this extent such one-sided critique has meant that the dialectical reworking of the substance of Marx and Freud to produce critical theory and negative psychoanalysis remains unfinished and sketchy. Critical theory and negative psychoanalysis with its non-identity principle is only one side of the reworking of Marx and Freud. The other is the convergence of the latter two methodologies to produce a convergent theory along more conventional lines.

The convergent methodology and the non-identity principle are distinct but not separate. They are linked by a critique of establishment social science inherent in both positions.[2] Fromm stressed the specific task of a convergent theory and epistemology. This task is the critique of Freud's legacy or the dissection and critique of the most advanced forms of bourgeois morality. In both Marx and the critical theorists the task of criticism rests on the critique of reification.

Fromm's early work satisfied Horkheimer's criterion (for critical theory) of criticism of establishment social science. Alfred Schmidt observed in his *Introduction* that Horkheimer's influential stamp on critical theory was his assertion that an alternative higher form of scientific practice would involve the elimination of rigid specialized disciplines with their fashionable relativisms and substitution of the central theoretical problem—the exploration of the "connection between economic life, individual psychic development and narrower cultural changes."[3] The question whether Horkheimer's specification is entirely compatible and synonymous with critical theory and negative psychoanalysis as these are presently understood cannot be pursued here, even though it is vital to a definite attribution of Fromm's work among the ranks of the Frankfurt School.

The question to be answered by a thorough re-examination of Fromm's early essays is: Precisely what does subsumption of Freud's metapsychology under Marx's epistemology mean? The answer to this challenges a fundamental principle of the non-identity postulate.[4] The non-identity postulate does not entirely escape an important criticism. This criticism is that the real utilization of "critical repositories" in Marx and Freud does not rest on a treatment of their documents as if their structures of ideas were two uninterrupted "discourses." Numerous works have argued that the ideas of Marx and Freud are characterized by critical interruptions, and that their fragments of methodologies are more vital than their practical sounding conclusions.[5]

Is Fromm's work an integration of Marx and Freud, or an attack on the accepted reasons for convergence?

Fromm's early German essays (1929–1937) are major studies in the sophistry of critical theory. His single most vital thrust is his rejection of Freud's metatheory as ambiguous towards bourgeois tolerance. But more than this Fromm rejected programmatic attempts to integrate Marx and Freud on the metatheoretical level. The first argument had to do with Fromm's rejection of the purported abstractions of man, and of society. The second had to do with Fromm's specific critique of Freud's bourgeois conception of morality and tolerance. His comments on the first ground bear quotation in full:

> The application of psychoanalysis to sociology must be careful to avoid the mistake of wishing to give psychoanalytic answers where economic, technical and political facts give the real and adequate explanation for sociological facts. On the other hand, the psychoanalyst must point out that the object of sociology-society consists in reality of individual people . . . These people do not have some kind of "Individualseele," . . . and alongside of this a separate "Massenseele". . . . There are no two such souls within man, but only one, in which the same mechanisms and laws are valid whether man appears as an individual, or forms a society, a class, a community or what have you.[6]

The most succinct comment which illustrates both Fromm's theoretical and practical attitudes to Freudian psychoanalysis in the period of Fromm's development under discussion runs as follows:

> The psychoanalytic situation is another expression of bourgeois-liberal tolerance. Here one human being is supposed to express to another those thoughts and impulses which stand in the sharpest contrast to social taboos, and this other is not supposed to be startled and angry, nor to adopt a moralizing posture, but to remain objective and friendly, in short to abstain from every critical attitude. This view is only conceivable within the terms of the general tolerance which has developed in increasing measure in the urban bourgeoisie. . . . The tolerance of the psychoanalyst also has the two aspects mentioned above: on the other hand, he shares with every other member of this class the respect for fundamental social taboos and experiences the same antipathy towards the person who breaks them. . . . Freud's writings offer a certain insight into the respect for the social taboos of the bourgeoisie which is hidden behind this tolerance. . . . Certainly Freud took a critical position on bourgeois sexual morality. He was also brave enough to prove that sexual impulses also play a role where other "ideal" motives had been seen before, and even where the acceptance of sexual motives was actually sacrilegious, as in the infant. . . . But even where criticism of bourgeois sexual morality is the issue, in the work entitled "Cultural sexual morality," it emerges that his position is critical, but in no way principally different from that of his class.[7]

The analytical form as well as the developing substantive critique of the two foregoing statements have tended to mould Fromm's earlier and later theoretical stance to psychoanalysis and to the ideological objectives of critical theory. This theoretical stance is neither reductionist (up to 1941) nor supportive of a theoretical strategy for translating psychoanalytic problems into sociological forms. Equally the stance is not revisionist in the sense of emphasizing some ideas of Freud over others.

Fromm's work was an attempt to intersect and so enrich the programmatic task of the integration of theory and praxis assumed by the Institut Für Sozialforschung long before he completed his work on the partial unification of Marx and Freud—which earned him the paradoxical status of fame in North America and estrangement from his earlier colleagues of the Institut. An examination of his essay "Psychoanalyse und Sociologie" indicates that Fromm did not perceive the task of the Frankfurt Psychoanalytic Institute as one of simply providing mediating concepts between individual and society which would somehow reconcile Marx and Freud and therefore theory and praxis. Had this been the sole task for Fromm he would have simply transposed a pared psychoanalytic theory of man's spiritual make up to a materialist theory of social formations, and in this the family would have become the determinate mediating concept in a reconciled theory and praxis.

The consequences of such a theoretical strategy would have been an oversocialized conception of man and society in all of Fromm's subsequent work rather than the concerns with historical evil and death that we see there. Fromm's posture within the Frankfurt Psychoanalytic Institute and his theoretical problematic can therefore be characterized in the following terms:

1. His struggle with Freud's psychoanalysis and a materialist theory (not a Marxist one) was really an attempted sublation of conventional social science specializations.

2. His recognition that the crux of psychoanalysis rested on the function attributed to the family in the development of man's spiritual apparatus as a necessary but not a sufficient explanation.

3. Consequently, the advance of theoretical work rested on distinct analyses in the following areas, among others:

Psychoanalytic contributions to sociological knowledge of the precise extent and ways in which the "spiritual makeup of man has worked as a cause or as a determining factor on the development and formation of society." Economic and technical factors are other determinants.

Questions emerged such as: To what extent changes in the psychological structure of man "—taken as the growth of the ego structure —and with it the rational control of the instinctive and the natural, represent a relevant sociological factor." (The elaboration of this task is taken by Fromm's detractors to be the sine qua non of his work as a whole, but it is not.) To what extent "the family itself is the product of a definite form of society, and to what extent a change in the family itself, brought about by a social change, could be an influence on the spiritual development of the individual . . ." Another example of this would be the significance of technological growth (technik) for the individual psyche through "an ever increasing satisfaction of desires or conversely, the ever decreasing need for denials."[8]

The inference to be drawn from the foregoing is that Freud's psychoanalysis merely opened up these issues for sociology; the problem was to explore them in various ways. What has to be noted is that Fromm extended his own criticism of Freud's ambivalence to bourgeois tolerance to the level of an infrastructural assumption. The existence of this ambivalence within orthodox psychoanalysis was then viewed by Fromm as inhibiting the task of a convergence of Freudianism and Marxism. Fromm's theoretical task became at that point an analytical attack on the prevailing reasons for such a convergence.

In essence Fromm stated that Freud's reality principle also inadvertently accepted death as a human necessity and the goal of human happiness became an impossibility. In Fromm's mind Freud's conceptions of death, as represented in aggression, suicide, and discontent, were really sociologized explanations of evil. Fromm argued in "Die Gesellschaftliche Bedingtheit Der Psychoanalytischen Therapie" (p. 379) that Freud's entire discussion on sublimation was false. Freud chose sexual satisfaction where the choice was between that and neurosis. Nevertheless, for Freud culture as opposed to sexuality was really the nobler and higher road. The inference in Fromm's discussion here is not only that Freud was in this sense ethnocentric— although he does not specify adequately Freud's ethnocentrism—but also that bourgeois culture constitutes a form of death. Implicit in the discussion is also the notion that the context of Freud's dichotomy of culture versus sexuality is a false one. But for all this Fromm never suggests whether Marx's analyses sublate Freud's own analyses.[9]

Fromm's rejection of the Freudian metaphor of death took the theoretically specific form of his attack on the latter's hypostatization of "repression" as caused by the contradiction between sexuality and culture which even as a general case manifests itself in the psychic orientation of the non-neurotic individual. This rejection led Fromm in another direction as well, and that was to question the basic presuppositions about man then held by many "establishment social scientists." Fromm referred to this time and again in his analysis of impotence (1937), as well as in his critiques of the works of Robert Briffault (1933) and of Bachofen (1934). Here he examined the socio-political conditions which conditioned accompanying ideological perspectives on the relationship between theory and action in the modern age. He characterized this relationship as follows:

> There is an extraordinary discrepancy in democracies between the ideological notion that the individual member of society controls, in part, the entire direction of society and the distance that in fact separates the individual from political and economic power.[10]

Another dimension of the connection between socio-political conditions and ideological perspectives is the reification of "authoritarian philosophy." The specific form of this is the reification of impotence to the status of a national law. While the intensification of impotency feelings has its expressions in the neurotic cases of clinical psychoanalysis and its counterpart in normal life in the bourgeois character:

> It has its roots in the entire social constellation and in the spiritual (seelich) situation which is determined by this.[11]

The observation that impotence as an individual experience robs the person of courage to "act" is central to Fromm's analyses of method and the relation between theory and praxis. It is also around this observation that Fromm attempts a partial synthesis of Marx and Freud. But a thorough analysis of this problem of consciousness in its specific relation to theory and praxis requires a scientific orientation, only the outlines of which Fromm believed could be traced at this stage. Nevertheless, we will turn our attention to Fromm's sketch, and its significance for his early formulations.

The conception of impotence as an analogue to
Fromm's critique of non-identity

> *The helplessness of the individual is the fundamental*
> *theme of authoritarian philosophy. (E. Fromm, 1937)*

The foregoing statement is one of the central conclusions of Fromm's essay, "Zum Gefuhl der Ohmnacht." It is an expression of his argumentation that impotence has a socially generalized form as well as specific clinical expressions, and that both are dimensions of passivity. Both are expressions of the inability to act, and the extreme form of impotence is death. The malaise of his age (the 1930s) and culture expressed another side of death in its glorification of method without theory. The practical expression of this glorification was a magical ritualization, a "busyness" in contrast to "activity," the latter expressing a combination of correct theory and method. Fromm's emphasis therefore is on the necessity of "correct theory" as a condition for *action* and social change. It is a Marxist conclusion arrived at by a psychoanalytic route, but one which cannot be disputed today (p. 115).

Fromm's argument attacked orthodox psychoanalysts and other intellectuals as well. He attacked the intellectual posture which asserted that others could not be influenced as a form of rationalized neurotic impotence which failed to distinguish between areas of change within control and areas truly outside control. There is a subtle hint in Fromm's discussion here that tries to establish an analogy between the concepts of impotence and the insistence on non-identity. For throughout this essay (translated as "Some Observations on the Feeling of Impotence") Fromm suggests that theory does not always lead to action while insisting that it is the condition for action. The problem, of course, is that his alternative to impotence is a new awareness; members of society are brought to consciousness through "long work," and his theoretical analogue to this is the principle of "reflexivity" which was later attacked by Frankfurt School members. Reflexivity did not mean for Fromm what it meant for contemporary sociologists such as Gouldner (1970) and Robert Friedrichs (1970). For Fromm reflexivity was to be an essential quality of a special science, similar to psychoanalysis, which would reflect on the operant powers in bourgeois economy and on bourgeois man. He described this intellectual task as the "penetration of facades to discover hidden causal mechanisms," a task asserted by Marx and Freud as well.[12]

The tone of this early formulation cannot be interpreted as revisionist because it did not take the form of a levelling of the contradictions of bourgeois society. Rather this early work represents Fromm's highlighting of specific social and ideological contradictions into a formulation of a new relationship between theory and praxis. Later in this discussion we will show that Fromm's practical concern was with the specific mechanisms through which the administrative "techniques" of the state and the German school system reinforce the hegemony of the petty bourgeois class and ideology, while simultaneous forms of pedagogy and criminal justice guarantee the submission of the majority. Furthermore Fromm suggested that the implications of these "techniques" signify a preoccupation with "busyness" which is clearly discernible within these administrative and political communities.[13] We will restrict our remarks at this point, however, to the problems of theory and praxis raised by his analogy between impotence and non-identity.

One of the most polemical issues of Fromm's intellectual career is his extension of Freud's clinical concept of therapy to the sociopolitical dimension of occidental development. As far as his early work is concerned, it is also one of the most misunderstood aspects of Fromm's work in his attempt to unify theory and praxis. For Fromm's early formulation does not constitute a psycho-history in the tradition of later North American versions. Rather, it was an extension of his critique of the intellectual rationalization of impotence—to which we referred earlier in this discussion—to the prevailing clinical practices of psychoanalysis.[14]

When the critique of impotence is promoted to the status of an ideological category the clinical component of repression can be utilized as a tool for validating assertions about the broad sociological significance of impotence as a consequence of history and socialization. Simultaneously this strategy allows the critical theorist to formulate propositions about the relative degree of impotence in a given society, and of the cross-cultural components of impotence. The exploration of such a connection between the ideology of impotence and the clinical reality of repression was one of Fromm's major tasks in his revision of the problem of theory and action. The exposition begun in "Zum Gefuhl der Ohnmacht" is continued in another essay "Die Gesellschaftliche Bedingtheit Der Psychoanalytischen Therapie,"

(1935). What characterizes both impotence and repression leading to the expression of neurotic symptoms is anxiety in general deriving from the threat of external force, the threat of social isolation, and loss of self-respect derived from the inability to "put across one's own wishes." In the case of the appearance of neurotic symptoms Fromm suggests that the internalization of these "failures" leads to rage and silence in which the individual requires increasing energy in order to maintain the suppressed material beneath the deeper layers of the psyche. It is precisely this ever-expanding repression which makes clinical psychoanalysis a much demanded and lucrative enterprise. What Fromm had to say about therapeutic practice is therefore vital to the task of setting the record straight about the ways in which Fromm extended his critique of Freud's bourgeois tolerance. It is also vital for a partial rebuttal of the allegation that Fromm collapsed theory into therapy in his psychoanalytic revisionism.

"Die Gesellschaftliche Bedingtheit Der Psychoanalytischen Therapie" is a long and rambling essay in which Fromm is less concerned with the collapsing of therapy into theory or vice versa and more concerned with unveiling authoritarian social tendencies in therapy which tend to be masked in the theory itself, that is, tendencies which mask the helplessness of the individual as though it were a metaphysical issue. The method of critique in this 1935 essay is also different in many respects from Fromm's essay four years later, "The Social Philosophy Of 'Will Therapy,' " in which he contrasted Freud's and Rank's conceptions of therapy.[15] While it is clear that in the earlier essay Fromm argued for a specifically more humanist therapy he did so because of his argument against Freud's emphasis on "organic repression," and the inferences which Freud drew from this for the limitations for therapeutic efficacy. Fromm's position on the analytic situation did not resemble that of the "revisionists" such as Ferenczi and Rank for the reasons which his critics would have us believe. He summarized his views of the analytic situation as follows:

> The question of the actual conscious, and, more importantly, of the unconscious attitude of the analyst towards the social taboos whose protection consists in threats of revenge, which have led to repressions now to be uncovered, is therefore of decisive importance to the possibility of therapeutic success as well as the duration of the analysis.[16]

But how can a critical theory validate the claim that important unconscious attitudes of censure against the patient's transcendence of bourgeois social taboos exist within the analytic situation? This is the question which has to be posed and answered before subjecting Freud's claims about the limitations of psychoanalysis to the kind of dialectical somersaults which gave Adorno and his followers the concept of negative psychoanalysis.[17] The question is internal to the methods of psychoanalytic therapy as far as Fromm's early work is concerned, and not ultimately aimed at obliterating theory in the interests of therapy—as Fromm's detractors are quick to point out. The allegation that all so-called revisionism seeks to eradicate the "contradiction" (Jacoby's term) or "discrepancy" (Marcuse's term) which Freud maintained between theory and therapy presumes that that contradiction or discrepancy (though the same meanings cannot be attributed to these terms) was a positive or dialectical force in Freud's work. What is not stated by Fromm's critics is that he was concerned with articulating the ideological and ideational links between repression, which was the key to uncovering the metatheoretical truth of Freud's view of culture and civilization, and "resistance" and "transference," which were therapeutic notions for validating the theory of repression. The aim of Fromm's 1935 essay was to establish that the actual use of the concept of "resistance" is an ideational reflection of a bourgeois ideology of tolerance. Fromm argued this position in another form as follows:

> He [the patient] comes to analysis, the purpose of which is to lift the repressed into consciousness. The anxiety which originally led to the repression, is transferred to the analyst. But this anxiety strengthens or weakens, depending on the personality and behaviour of the analyst. In the extreme case where the analyst takes a critical hostile position towards repressed urges, one can hardly expect at all that the patient is capable of penetrating the resistance to the repressed. If the patient, even if only *dimly* and instinctively, feels that the analyst has the same critical attitude to the breaking of social taboos as other people he met in childhood and later, then the original resistance will not only be transferred into the actual analytical situation, but will be produced anew.[18]

It is clear from Freud's 1915 essay on repression that the theory of repression was not meant to imply that the process of repression is unidimensional or complete at some given point, but that the test of the validity of Freud's propositions was in the clinical observations, to a large extent. The truth value in propositions about repression is

therefore based on the clinical use of the concept of "resistance."
Fromm established this point by stating that

> The resistance is thus a phenomenon occuring necessarily in the course
> of the analysis. If one wished to avoid it, this would mean giving up
> making the repressed material conscious. This is indeed attempted by
> most non-psychoanalytic psychotherapeutic methods. It is the shorter
> way, but the price paid is the giving up of deep change in the spiritual
> structure. The resistance is exactly the most reliable signal that one is
> touching repressed material and not merely moving on the spiritual
> surface.[19]

The discussion which followed the foregoing remarks can be interpreted as Fromm's attempt to probe what can be termed today the
specific class, and indeed racial background, of Freud's notion of the
contradiction between theory and therapy. Fromm was not saying
that Freud's psychoanalytic theory was thoroughly bourgeois or indeed that Freud was racist. He was saying, however, that the specific
use in therapy which Freud made of the concept of "resistance"
provides some insight into an area of "blindness" which made the
viability of psychoanalytic theory not a theory of civilization as a
whole in all respects, but rather one which has ignored non-Judaic-
Christian civilizations precisely by pretending to speak for all civilization. This is an allegation to which critical theory after Freud and
Marx has to respond. Fromm's critics have argued elsewhere that
therapy can be modified on pragmatic grounds, but not in the interests
of a humanism which promises liberation for the individual in an
otherwise unfree society, since the real thrust of therapy is that it
"issues into a social critique and praxis of liberation." Precisely. But
if therapy is not merely a Freudian afterthought, with no systematic
conceptual or ideational link to one or more elements in the meta-
theoretical case, then its uniqueness as a critique has to be penetrated
and developed as well. Otherwise therapy issues into a dangerous
reification and mystification of death and impotence, and theory without a vigorous therapy becomes mere ideological rhetoric. For example, a radical academic critic can today develop a theoretically truth-
ful critique of racism and advanced capitalism while personally and
unconsciously contributing to the further life of institutionalized racism. The variants of this example are many, but the real question then
becomes, "What is 'revolutionary pessimism' in psychoanalysis, and

how is it possible?" This is the challenge to Frankfurt School critical theory. As for Fromm, he put the matter in another form as follows:

> We have already said that Freud ascribed relatively little significance to the actual behaviour and special character of the analyst. This is the more remarkable, *in that the analytic situation, as created by Freud, is quite unusual and unique in our culture and perhaps in general.* There is no situation even approximately similar in which one human being not only "confesses" to another without holding back, i.e. says everything to him which he condemns in himself, but in addition, communicates those fleeting ideas which seem absurd and laughable, and where he pledges to also express all those things which he does not yet know but which could still occur to him, indeed, where he can honestly communicate to the other all the opinions and feelings he has about him, making them the object of dispassionate examination.[20] [Emphasis mine]

We suggested earlier in this discussion that Fromm criticized what appeared to be Freud's leanings towards bourgeois liberal tolerance. Now we see that the forms of this critique require elaboration. First of all Fromm was not in the first instance revising orthodox therapy in the interests of a happy, well adjusted individual monad, or in the interest of the primacy of subjectivity. Rather, the critique of therapy was against the particular weaknesses of Freud's use of the inductive method. The basis of Freud's psychoanalytic induction is the analyst-patient pattern of interaction. "Resistance" is therefore an ideational component of Freud's interpretative inductive strategy as he moved toward his general inferences about the opposition between sexuality and culture. "Resistance" is therefore for Fromm a descriptive notion which in Freud's usage passes into and reinforces the theoretical psychoanalytic opposition between sexuality and culture. Fromm's point is that Freud's usage of "resistance" is as though it were itself a theoretical component of the metatheory of psychoanalysis. As such, he was commenting on the Janus-headed nature of "resistance" in Freud rather than reducing the theoretical opposition between sexuality and culture to a new therapeutic format. In short, before undertaking his own critique of the ideology of tolerance, Fromm made the observation that in orthodox psychoanalysis itself aspects of the metatheory were intentionally passed by Freud into therapy.

> Only in two points does Freud go beyond the purely technical-medical in a positive sense. Once when he demanded, if not from the beginning,

that the analyst be analysed, so as not only to gain theoretically better insight into the processes in the unconscious, but also to become conscious of his own "blind spots" and to be able to control his own affective reactions.[21]

The other point in which Freud recognized the problem of theory passing into therapy had to do with an "objective, unprejudiced, neutral and forebearing attitude" towards everything the patient brings up, but in the interests of tolerance. (Extending on Fromm we can say that tolerance is an ideational component of therapy which while guaranteeing it, in turn passes into theory.) If psychoanalytic therapy had a weakness, an anomaly whereby it unconsciously suppressed its own representation of the individual's plea for aid, and self-clarification in the clinical situation, then Fromm's work was to illustrate that this anomaly of suppression had its roots in the ideological ambivalence of Freud himself, and not in the content of psychoanalytic theory, in the first instance. This was precisely the aim of Fromm's critique, to show that the ideational representation of tolerance in therapy manifested a clear middle class ideology of impotence. It was not yet Fromm's aim to revise the theory of repression, or to signify any priority for individual happiness. In fact, his point is that what appears to be a theoretical, and therefore intellectually acceptable, contradiction between the concept of repression and the concept of resistance in the wider metatheory of contradiction between culture and sexuality is not that at all. In Freud, neurosis had become an intellectual *Ding an Sich,* a thing in itself. It had been presented as a theoretical unity constituted of "resistances" which could be experienced by the analyst in a clinical situation, and at the same time, its opposite, repression, the intellectual hypothesization of the psychoanalytic posture. At this stage Fromm was contesting one aspect of the "thing-in-itself" representation of neurosis, that is, the analytic reconstruction, in which Freud underestimated the problem of tolerance of the particular analyst, as well as of the psychoanalytic posture. If the uncovering of resistances is a viable project, then it implies discovery of knowledge of its real opposite, tolerance, and therefore revelation of repression.

How could "neurosis" be a real phenomenon, a thing in itself, and the unity of a dialectical contradiction, a theoretical principle, at the same time? This is the nub of the issue which the critics of Fromm, and of all psychoanalytic revisionism, have to answer in their assertions that the orthodox positions are part of a social theory which transcends the society in a revolutionary form. Many of Fromm's critics have reacted as though the question was an absurd one, but they have not, nevertheless, come up with an alternative explanation of the relationship between tolerance and the analytic situation which would clarify (more thoroughly) than Freud did the anomalous representations of neurosis.[22]

Fromm did not view the source of this anomaly in the contradiction between theory and therapy so much as in the real opposition between Freud's partial attack on tolerance in his theoretical work while at the same time stopping short of its penetration in his clinical posture. What he detected in the clinical situation was a tolerance for the patient to verbalize his new-found consciousness, but a tolerance which stopped short of encouraging him to act out or upon this consciousness, something characteristic of all nineteenth-century bourgeois tolerance as it manifested itself in reform movements. This is a point that was succinctly made about the posture of science and relativism by Wolff and other writers in *A Critique of Pure Tolerance,* (1969) and it makes the entire notion of theoretical revisionism questionable as far as Freud's work is concerned. The inference which can be drawn from Fromm's view of this limitation is that it weakened the critical thrust of the clinical and theoretical work:

> Certainly he [Freud] is tolerant, and certainly he criticized bourgeois sexual morality because its overly great strictness frequently led to neurotic illness. But even where criticism of bourgeois sexual morality was the issue, in the work entitled "Cultural Sexual Morality . . . ," it emerges that his position is critical, but in no way principally different from that of his class.[23]

Clearly, for Fromm there was a vital distinction between theory and therapy. This distinction which existed in Freud had to be maintained, but not in an unadulterated fashion. Fromm argued that therapy was an incorrect praxis which needlessly extended repression, and therefore reinforced a genetically external, but historical, impotence. Insofar as our interpretation is valid, then, Fromm was adhering to the canons of critical theory established by no lesser figures than Horkheimer and Marcuse when they stated:

> Even in a future society, the happiness of its individuals is no equivalent to the destruction of those now. Theory offers no cure (or healing), to

its adherents, no psychic condition like Christianity. Freedom's martyrs were not seeking the soul's peace: this was not their goal.

And at the end of this paragraph there is a succinct observation as well:

> Philosophy which hopes to find peace in truth has therefore little to do with Critical Theory.[24]

The inference of the foregoing observation means that the non-identity formulation has a paradoxical element. Critical theory cannot be viable without an immanent praxis. Insofar as psychoanalysis is concerned, therapy is an aspect of that praxis (a position that is often ignored by those who hold to the theory-therapy "contradiction"), and therefore cannot be in *dialectical contradiction* (in Marx's sense) with theory. Moreover, one fails to see how the theoretical articulation of an historical opposition between culture and sexuality, as part of critical theory, can be in *real opposition* to therapy. *What one can perceive is a certain confusion among "Frankfurt School theorists" about the distinctions and differences between dialectical contradiction and real opposition* on this point.

A caveat on therapy:
philanthropy versus misanthropy

In the latter portion of his essay on "Therapie" Fromm took up what has since been interpreted as a revisionist support for Ferenczi, Otto Rank, Alfred Adler, and Jung, among others. In fact Fromm's goals have little to do with his later wish for a happy, adjusted subject in an age of repression, but rather are a kind of Damoclean sword over the head of Freud's ideology of impotence. Consider the two following prefatory remarks to Fromm's summary of the positions of Groddeck and Ferenczi in the psychoanalytic movement:

> It cannot be denied that the lack of humility envokes in the analyst of the patricentric character-type an often unconscious hostility towards the patient and that this hostility not only makes every therapeutic success impossible, but also represents a serious danger for the spiritual health of the patient.[25]

In short, to the extent that an unconscious authoritarianism lies behind a conscious outward "tolerance," spiritual ill-health becomes an impotent skepticism which could be adopted by the patient through no independent fault of his own. One of Fromm's goals was a greater insight into the patricentric-authoritarianism of orthodox analysts. He believed that a study of the conflicts within the psychoanalytic movement provides the best sociological data, though indirect, for validating such insight. This second indirect strategy has been adopted by a number of recent critics of Freud. But Fromm made his own position clear in the following statement:

> Together with the way we have taken, i.e., directly gaining a certain insight into Freud's attitude towards the patient from his own statements, there is an indirect way, too, namely by the study of the partly strengthened conflicts within the analytic movement between Freud and his innermost circle on the one hand and the "opposition" analysts on the other.[26]

There are important and still partly unanswered questions as to why Freud and some of his colleagues in his inner circle resisted so ruthlessly the therapeutic revisions of Groddeck and Ferenczi. We cannot hope to examine most of the questions for these conflicts here. But we will summarize the most significant suggestions forwarded by Fromm insofar as they bear on the debate about the identity theory versus the supposed non-identity principle in Freud's work.

Firstly, Fromm suggests that analysts as a rule have the same social interests as other members of their social stratum. Equally, the analyst's understanding of his own drive structure, as well as that of his patient's, has its limits in "his social interests, and in the feelings and insights which are conditioned by these interests." Thus while Freud's attitude was in "contradiction" (the term is Fromm's) with his theory it was logical in relation to his social interests. Ferenczi's therapeutic perspective which advocated the analysis of the analyst as a prerequisite was of limited value because this attitude was in contradiction to the basic structure of his class. What is even more significant, however, is that he was not aware of this contradiction. Fromm put this somewhat dialectical critique of Freud and Ferenczi as follows:

> Freud's personality and the peculiarity of his theory are in the end to be grasped not from individual, but from general social circumstances. Also the fact that a personality like Ferenczi was defeated in the fight makes good sense. Freud's attitude is sociologically seen, the logical one.

Ferenczi was an outsider, in contradiction to the basic structure of his class, and he was not aware of his own contradiction.[27]

Secondly, Fromm suggests that Ferenczi's opposition to Freud was one of principle, a philanthropic versus a deeply misanthropic attitude, and that this was an insufficient basis for opposing Freud. Fromm implies that, to the extent that Ferenczi did not see that the specific social character of taboos is conditioned by the necessity of the internalization of the exterior force over the majority of society, he failed to see the links between the patient's moral conflicts which are not really moral, the bourgeois-authoritarian character of Freud, and the illusions of analysis.

The effectiveness of analysis however rests now precisely on inhibitions being removed which stand in the way of a person following his interests. On the average analysis of the analyst will thus in no way lead to the removal of the bourgeois-character-structure, but rather to its strengthening. And this especially when in Freud's sense the analysis sets up moral taboos and anxieties about breaking them as being biologically conditioned and natural.[28]

In short Fromm's contention is that both Freud and revisionists such as Ferenczi were limited on the question of what constitutes effective therapy. His perspective on the therapists was that neither theoretical insight into the cause of patient anxiety nor analysis of the prospective analysts are fully adequate alternatives. As far as the patient is concerned analytical provision of insight to the patient about his individual childhood anxieties is insufficient because the family is only the "psychological agent" of society, and does not provide insight into real and effective motives of repression.

Given the foregoing, then, what constitutes effective analysis? The answer is simple: "the unconditional affirmation of the patient's right to happiness." Since the peculiarity of bourgeois moral proscriptions rests on its tabooistic character the analyst must have no illusions about proving the concrete circumstances about the biological necessity of rigid and abstract morality, or the specific cause of this or that moral anxiety in a patient, or even earthly wisdom about limiting a patient's claim to happiness.

It [the effective attitude to analysis] is rather to be seen as a life-statement of certain people "under the conditions of their origin and dying out." Without evaluation there is no theory of reality at all, but setting values does not need to be tied to the ideals of idealistic morality. The goal is not the fulfilling of some eternal demands, but the realization of claims to happiness in their different historical forms.[29]

Clearly then insofar as this statement can be said to represent an acceptance of some form of identity principle this does not have the same meaning for Fromm and the Frankfurt Institut members if they reject his formulations. For Fromm viewed morality's tabooistic character as a function of bourgeois capitalism in theory and praxis. This condition has to be exploded in therapy if psychoanalysis constitutes part of a unique response to bourgeois society. What the patient fears in therapy is that the analyst judges him as a person. The patient knows, and according to Fromm accepts, that certain of his actions will be judged by the analyst.

Thus, as far as Fromm was concerned, to reject the possible reformulation of therapeutic praxis was in reality to affirm the externality of urban-bourgeois-tolerance in action whatever one espoused in theory. Fromm then provided for therapy a specific role which he articulated in the latter portion of his essay on "Therapie" (1935). This role emerged from a question which was only clarified fully in "Zum Gefuhl Der Onnmacht" (1937), i.e., what is the function of psychoanalytic theory and therapy in unmasking the feeling of impotence? As he suggested in "Sozialpsychologischer Teil" (1936), the value of a simultaneous focus on the relationship between the structure of authority and its conscious manifestation of impotence in the individual superego is that such a focus reveals the mechanism whereby force is transformed into an internal momentum. Therapy for Fromm provides one of the bases for a "Lebens praxis."

It was specifically in the context of this consideration that Fromm focused on the role of the family, and rejected Freud's claim that the superego is solely the heir of the Oedipus complex, the inheritor of a racial past.[30] We turn now to another dimension of Fromm's critique of impotence as it specially manifests itself in socialization processes and in reformist movements.

Fromm's critique of bourgeois reform movements

In an earlier part of this discussion we suggested that Fromm's early critique did not constitute a levelling of the conscious, intra-subjectivity or the unconscious and their relationship to objective material conditions. Rather, he was attempting to get a handle on the specific conditions under which these operate in bourgeois industrial society. In this section we will summarize three essays, none of which were published in the Frankfurt Institute's journal, in which he set out his ideas in some detail. Between 1930 and 1931, at about the time he joined the Frankfurt Psychoanalytic Institute, his focus of empirical concern was the administrative, ideational, and psychological repression of the contemporary community as this was mediated through education, criminal justice systems, and enlightened reformism. It was within this context that Fromm at first appeared to select Marxist sociology combined with Freudian drive theory as a unique method of complete understanding.[31]

There is no hint in these essays of Fromm's movement towards identity theory. At the same time, however, he did not spell out in greater detail the concept of an alternative "Lebenspraxis" alluded to in his "Socialpsychologischer Teil." What he did was assert particularly in "Der Staat Als Erzieher" ("The State As Educator") that mere criticism of the administrative and psychological techniques of the State's juridical and educative functions and principles which train man into a father-fearing child will not change those principles or functions.[32] The impression given in the review of Bernfeld's work is that if the students' and workers' movements could coalesce to control the "administrative community" this would be the signal for radical social change. But what is this concept of "administrative community," and how is it connected to Fromm's critique of impotence and tolerance?

The concept of "administrative community" was a typification of the specific spheres of activity, within the educational system and the courts, whose functions were co-optation of petty bourgeois students and thereby protection of bourgeois interests in the case of the former; and reinforcement of submissiveness, and deflection and renunciation of drives of the masses, in the case of the latter. Both in the Bernfeld review and in "The State As Educator" Fromm argued that the "educational functions" of these institutions were less important to the ruling classes in modern society than the functions of reinforcing patriarchial authority in its developed form. He therefore argued that radical criticism of the pedagogics of the school (Schulheim in the Bernfeld review was a new type of boarding school) and of the justice system were not vital tasks.

Fromm was saying more than simply that the functions of boarding school and criminal justice really exist behind the rationalized objectives that are presented. For example, in an essay "On The Psychology Of the Criminal And The Punishing Society," published in the "conservative" journal *Imago,* he suggested that the "masses" do not have an awareness of "justice" insofar as the criminal justice system is concerned. They do not have an "inherited lawful moral view." The masses transfer the father-fear from early childhood to the ruling classes, the state and thereby the criminal justice system (p. 247). This maintains social stability, and through repetition makes force unnecessary. The ruling classes are therefore presented to the masses as father through the criminal justice system.

The foregoing argument has, for readers who have interpreted Fromm solely from his later post-Frankfurt writings, a kind of intellectual déja vu. But this is deceptive. In the earlier context Fromm is less concerned with theoretical generalizations of the sort for which he has been much criticized in later writings. In these earlier writings the analysis is more Marcusean—in the tradition of sections of *Eros And Civilization.* In the epoch of advanced industrial capitalism Fromm argued that criminal justice, even in the court room, is concerned with renunciation of drive-satisfying tendencies, and not with fighting crime and rehabilitation (p. 249). Psychoanalytic insight therefore has little practical value as a reformist ideology. He argued that one must remain sceptical. The only positive role delineated for theory was not "judgment" but a "diagnostic" role which would show the operation of combined unconscious factors (such as the satisfaction of narcissistic needs partly mediated through the ego) and economic factors.

Towards a conclusion

In summary it can be argued that while the intellectual context of Fromm is different in each of these three essays discussed above, what they have in common with the writings of the Frankfurt period is the rejection of the division between notions of "healthy" and "neurotic." Fromm made it clear that sublimation is dependent on education which is in turn an economic problem which changes, together with changing cultural and social situations. This general idea provided one of the major bases for Fromm's first use of Marx and Freud. This general conclusion is not based on Fromm's later explanation in

Beyond The Chains of Illusion (1962), which has heretofore been interpreted as a definitive autobiographical statement. Rather our conclusion is based on contextual analyses of the author's earlier statements. Fromm, that is to say, used a combination of Marx and Freud that has not been so far classified as Frankfurt School theory and yet is not clear non-identity or identity oriented in terms of ideology. A re-evaluation of Fromm's early work could provide much needed clarification to salient problems in Frankfurt School critical theory which would suggest that the present non-identity versus identity status of that theory should be re-examined.

From the standpoint of contemporary social theory the single most important thrust of Fromm's early work was the suggestion, perhaps caution, that death and revolution were not incompatible. His critique of impotence is the source of this critique. We have developed this theme at a number of points. We have tried to establish that Fromm's convergence of Marx and Freud—while it may have led to a later accomodation to social democracy—was not primarily identity theory in its early formulation. In attacking Freud at central points Fromm questioned the psychoanalytic notions of praxis (therapy) and action (as possibility) as well. This was Fromm's attack on the ambiguities of Freud's attitudes to bourgeois morality.

In suggesting that Freud's work resonated a certain awareness and yet unconsciousness of bourgeois morality Fromm was de facto attacking one of the major platforms of the non-identity postulate in critical theory. At the same time we have asserted that Fromm was by no means doing so exclusively in the interests of a subjectivist, conformist theory and therapy. This position has been ignored by Marcuse, Martin Jay, and Russell Jacoby but for different reasons in each case. Critical theory unnecessarily narrowed its focus to particular interpretations of Occidental civilization in its uncritical assessment of Freud's contributions of theory and therapy. This insight can be derived from Fromm's detailed argument that Freud's scepticism toward therapy had less to do with his theoretical perspectives and more to do with an authoritarian praxis in his personality and in his ideology. We also argued that the general outlines of such an approach resonate in the works of other critical theorists.

So why is Fromm's work scape-goated as revisionism? A thorough answer to this question would take us well beyond the scope of the present discussion, and into the work of the later Fromm. All we can suggest is that the identity and non-identity postulates are not mutually exclusive positions. What we can suggest is that Fromm in his essay on "Therapie" criticized the positions of the major revisionists such as Ferenczi by suggesting that they attempted to revise therapy on theoretical grounds without understanding that Freud's position was in keeping with that of his class. This cleared the way for Fromm's attack, even though largely inferred, on the notion that "theoretical critique" can be radical in any sense. Fromm was no Marxist. But he was attacking a form of activity that is acceptable in advanced industrial societies.

NOTES

1. A brief summary of the non-identity principle would be the following:

(a) The principle, developed by Theodor Adorno and Walter Benjamin, that Freud's metapsychology cannot be subsumed under Marx's epistemology, on both theoretical and philosophic grounds.

(b) The rejection of the equation of the dialectical materialist-scientific paradigm with an historically higher truth—first specified by George Lukács. This means the rejection of:

(c) The identity principle or the equation of active individual subjectivity in history and objective historical and social conditions realized in the historical mission of the proletariat.

In short, within the context of critical theory acceptance of the non-identity principle means rejection of the idea that historical revolution can be synonymous with the equation of subjectivity and objective historical reality or Hegelianized Marxism. But this meant that the epistemological skepticism of critical theory rests on the refusal to attribute specific place to Marxism in the archaeology of knowledge.

For more on this, see Susan Buck-Morss, "The Dialectic of T. W. Adorno," Telos, no. 14, Winter, 1972, pp. 137–144, esp. p. 143; Martin Jay, Dialectical Imagination (New York: Little, Brown, 1973), pp. 86–118; Russell Jacoby, Social Amnesia (Boston: Beacon Press, 1975), pp. 73–100.

2. It is worth restating that what both positions have in common is the view that criticism of society must start as criticism of the most advanced forms of industrial society, whether bourgeois or not. It is also worth stating that this methodological postulate of "criticism" reminds us of a distinction which is a necessary prerequisite for interpreting Fromm's work, and that is a distinction which has to be drawn between his theoretical and epistemological formulations, on the one hand, and his empirical and historical formulations, on the other. There are some contradictions between the two, but these do not constitute our major focus.

3. Cf. Alfred Schmidt, Introduction to Zeitschrift für Sozialforschung, pp. 29–32. See also Michel Foucault's The Order of Things (London: Tavistock, 1970), pp. 373–375.

4. Ibid., p. 16.

5. See Michel Foucault, The Archaeology of Knowledge (London: Tavistock, 1972), pp. 21–39; Paul Ricoeur, Philosophy and Freud: An Essay on Interpretation (New Haven, Conn.: Yale University Press, 1970), pp. 3–19, 59–76; Martin Nicolaus, "The

Unknown Marx," *New Left Review,* 48, March—April, 1968, pp. 41–60.

6. "Psychoanalyse und Soziologie," *Zeitschrift für Psychoanalytische Paedagogik,* 3, (1929), pp. 268–270, p. 268.

7. "Die Gesellschaftliche Bedingtheit der Psychoanalytischen Therapie," *Zeitschrift für Sozialforschung,* 4, (1935), Heft 3, pp. 365–397, 374–375.

8. All quotations are taken from Fromm, op. cit., "Psychoanalyse und Soziologie," (1929).

9. The tenor of Fromm's critique of tolerance has important similarities in the work of other Institute members. It is the use Fromm makes of it which is different from others.

10. "Zum Gefuhl der Ohmnacht," *Zeitschrift für Sozialforschung,* 6, (1937), pp. 95–119, quotation from p. 114.

11. Ibid., p. 110.

12. See S. Freud, *An Outline of Psychoanalysis* (New York: W. W. Norton, 1949), pp. 35–39. Here, however, Freud goes beyond the archaeological posture of psychoanalysis and suggests that the maintenance of internal resistances is the *"sine qua non of normality,"* a notion which allows Fromm to infer the significance of impotence in mental life, as a general category. Parenthetically, this genetic nature and archaeological posture of the "depth psychology" (Freud's term for the metatheory of psychoanalysis) of psychoanalysis was not asserted as being disjunctive with normal, empirical, cumulative science (in Kuhn's sense). Rather, Freud saw it as part of the "scientific Weltanschauung." See S. Freud, *New Introductory Lectures on Psychoanalysis* (New York: W. W. Norton, 1933), Lecture XXXV, "The Question of a Weltanschauung," pp. 158–182; see also "Some Elementary Lessons In Psychoanalysis," (1938) in *General Psychological Theory,* ed. P. Rieff (New York: Collier, 1963), pp. 218–224. It should be noted that in this connection the relation between theory and therapy is not at all analogous to the programmatic relation between theory and praxis in Marx. There are many references and allusions in the writings of Marx and Engels to a concept of "methodological penetration" of the forms of society to the core of socio-economic relations which conceal the real meanings behind the presented forms. See amongst others the much quoted second edition preface of *Capital,* 1873, Vol. I, Moscow, 1961, Foreign Languages Publishing House, pp. 197–202; F. Engels, *Anti-Duhring,* Part Two (Chicago: Charles H. Kerr, 1935), pp. 148–159. The meaning of methodological penetration is however clearly established as far as a study of Marx is concerned in the foreword to *Grundrisse: Foundations of the Critique of Political Economy (rough draft)* (London: Penguin Books, 1973), pp. 35–37.

13. Cf. E. Fromm, "Die Schulgemeinde Und Ihre Funktion Im Klassenkampf," *Zeitschrift für Psychoanalytische Paedagogik,* 4, (1930), pp. 116–117. (Tr., "Review of Bernfeld's 'The School Community and Its Function in the Class-Struggle,' "); "Zur Psychologie Des Verbrechers Und Der Strafenden Gesellschaft," *Imago,* 17, (1931), pp. 221–251. Fromm's synthesis of "busyness" and its explanation in impotence and non-identity is not entirely unambiguous. For more on the existing situations, what has to be probed is the disintegration of the old conservatism; the failure of bourgeois partisan politicians to consolidate the "new German middle classes" and the established middle classes into a "Staatsvolk" (due to the inflexibility of the existing party system); and finally the internal and external crises of capitalism which destroyed the traditional ideological visions of identity. For more on this see Larry E. Jones, "The Dying Middle Weimar Germany and the Fragmentation of Bourgeois Politics," *Central European History,* 1, March 1972, pp. 23–54; for in-depth analysis of fascism's internal ideological strategic use of impotence, see Ernst Nolte, *Three Faces of Fascism,* Part 4, Ch. 5 (Mentor Books, New American Library, 1965).

14. Cf. Russell Jacoby, *Social Amnesia: A Critique of Conformist Psychology From Adler to Laing* (Boston: Beacon Press, 1975). Here Jacoby puts forward the mistaken view—taken over from Marcuse—that there is a critical tension between theory and therapy in psychoanalysis which is analogous to the tension between theory and praxis in Marxism (p. 37). Jacoby compounds the error with his major point that "The revolutionary edge of psychoanalysis is the refusal to accept social and individual values abstracted from the concrete struggle of men and women against themselves and nature" (p. 37). See also the important summary of the Marx-Freud controversy, and the insightful comment on the Frankfurt School and Marcuse versus Fromm and revisionist polemic in "When Dogma Bites Dogma: Or The Difficult Marriage of Marx and Freud," *Times Literary Supplement,* January 8, 1971, pp. 25–27; M. Jay, op. cit., 1973, p. 109.

15. Cf. E. Fromm, "The Social Philosophy of 'Will Therapy,' " *Psychiatry,* 2:2, 1939, pp. 229–237. It should be noted en passant that our interpretation leads to the viewpoint that to this point (1939) Fromm had not yet assimilated Rank's usage of the theoretical metaphors of life and death fears into his own theoretic and therapeutic perspectives. The assimilation of such metaphors which undoubtedly came later is ultimately central to an explanation of anxiety, guilt, and, therefore, the meanings of neuroses as "clinical problems." For in Rank's and the later Fromm's perspectives the existence of life and death fears is an existential dichotomy which in turn determines historical contradictions such as passivity and impotence. For more on this aspect of Fromm, see K. O'Brien, *The Humanist Perspective in Social Science,* unpublished Ph.D. dissertation, Simon Fraser University, 1972, pp. 50–85 and p. 104. The most recent exploration of Otto Rank's critique of technique and "busyness" as derivatives of life and death fears, and the negative implications of this for psychotherapy, is Ernest Becker's *The Denial of Death* (1974), and *Escape From Evil* (1975) (New York: Free Press).

16. E. Fromm, "Die Gesellschaft Bedingtheit der Psychoanalytischen Therapie," *Zeitschrift für Sozialforschung,* (tr., "The Social Background of Psychoanalytic Therapy"), 4, (1935), Heft 3, pp. 365–379.

17. Cf. R. Jacoby, op. cit., pp. 121–128. See also H. Marcuse, *Eros and Civilization* (Boston: Beacon Press, 1955), pp. 224–226. It is ironic that both the somersaults and the social histrionics—the allegations that Fromm is revisionist and therefore pretheoretical and bourgeois—are carried out by left writers under the aegis of what are obviously pages of multi-national, corporate, capitalist publishing media.

18. E. Fromm, op. cit., (1935), p. 369.

19. Ibid., p. 366.

20. Ibid., p. 370.

21. Ibid., p. 371.

22. Cf. S. Freud, "Neurosis and Psychosis," (1924), in *General Psychological Theory: Papers on Metapsychology* (New York: Collier, 1963). See also H. Marcuse's explanation of neurosis as rebellion of the Id in *Eros and Civilization* (Boston: Beacon Press, 1955), pp. 224–225.

23. E. Fromm, op. cit., p. 375.

24. M. Horkheimer and H. Marcuse, "Philosophie und Kritische," *Zeitschrift für Sozialforschung,* VI, 3 (1937), pp. 625–647, p. 631.

25. E. Fromm, op. cit., p. 385. It should be noted that there is an important footnote in the original text at the end of this second statement quoted. Here Fromm makes it clear that he recognizes a distinction between the works of Groddeck and Ferenczi whose differences with Freud centered on the therapy, and the works of Adler, Rank, Jung, and Reich who gave up decisive features of the theory in favour of their own schools of thought.

26. Ibid.

27. Ibid., p. 394.

28. Ibid.

29. Ibid., p. 395.

30. Ref. E. Fromm, "Sozialpsychologischer Teil," in *Studien über Autoritat und Familie*, Schriften Des Institut für Sozialforschung (Paris, 1936), pp. 77–135. We cannot explore in this discussion a thorough examination of "Authority and the Family." Suffice it to say that Fromm's project at this time was based on the thesis that the family under bourgeois capitalism has become the "agent" of external physical force, the latter being an insufficient but necessary basis for authority in class society. The super ego is therefore contradictory, expressing a conscious need for love of external authority, and unconscious fear of that authority. This latter is a more reliable basis for society. This is a vital essay insofar as it represents his first attempt to demythologize personality formation in class society, by taking the concepts of masochism and sado-masochism out of the previously exclusive realm of clinical psychoanalysis and placing them within the realm of society. It is the much criticized "sociologization" of psychoanalysis. Another problem which cannot be fully explored here, again for reasons of brevity, is Fromm's exploration of the problem of impotence via the anthropological bases of matrilineality and matricentrism. While this writer does not deny that Fromm sought a convergence between ethnology and social psychology theory, it was one only to the extent that he developed a dialectical materialist analysis of the genesis of matriarchal and contemporary patricentric structures. It is in this connection also that Fromm's work pursued the ontological rather than the methodological status of Marx's concept of "Nature." This synthesized materialist conception of history (which is only one aspect of his work) led in more recent writings both to a search for the historical bases of inequality, and evil, a conception of man's possibilities which has been criticized elsewhere. Our point is that it is a mistake to view his writings out of context. For more on this see E. Fromm, "Die Sozialpsychologische Bedeutung der Mutterrechtstheorie," *Zeitschrift für Sozialforschung*, iii, 1934, pp. 196–227, edited by Max Horkheimer, Paris, Librairie Felix Alcan, 1970 (1935), (tr., "The Theory of Mother Right and Its Relevance for Social Psychology,") in *The Crisis of Psychoanalysis* (New York: Holt, Rinehart, Winston, 1970), pp. 84–109; "Robert Briffault's Werk über das Mutterrecht," in *Zeitschrift für Sozialforschung*, 2, 3 (1933), pp. 382–387. For one of the clearest analyses of the specific weaknesses of Fromm's later utopianism in relation to his use of ethnographic data, see Alfred Schmidt, *The Concept of Nature in Marx*, (tr. by Ben Fowkes) (London: New Left Editions, 1971), esp. pp. 156–163.

31. Cf. E. Fromm, op. cit., 1930 and 1931; also Fromm's review of Siegfried Bernfeld, "Die Schulgemeinde und Ihre Funktion im Klassenkampf," (1918), in *Zeitschrift für Psychoanalytische Paedogogik*, 4, (1930), pp. 116–117. See especially the final paragraph of this review. My interpretation of this aspect of Fromm's work differs somewhat from Martin Jay's. His chapter, "The Integration of Psychoanalysis," has tended to supplement the general impression of others that Fromm's so-called convergence of Marx and Freud stemmed from a combination of religiosity, naturalism, and ethnographic interpretation of Marxism. My own interpretation is that this is possibly a later formulation. But the three essays under examination indicate a different focus for Fromm's early concern with Marx and Freud. See M. Jay, op. cit., pp. 88–89.

32. E. Fromm, "Der Staat Als Erzieher," op. cit., p. 9.

BEYOND IDENTITY THEORY

PAUL PICCONE

One of the ironies of critical theory in the 1970s is that, although practically defunct in Germany, its birthplace, it is alive and well in the English-speaking world.[1] This is all the more striking since during their American exile the "founding fathers" were so skeptical about the possibility of their work ever taking root in America that they rarely wrote in English, and their journal, the *Zeitschrift für Sozialforschung,* continued to appear in German almost up to the time when it ceased publication in 1941. What is even more ironic is that, while critical theory is catching on in North America and England with a whole new literature developing in the wake of the translation of most of critical theory's classical texts into English, in Germany it is precisely the American social science rejected by the new converts that increasingly reigns supreme. Obviously, the grass is always greener on the other side. Yet, it would be a mistake to seek an explanation of this phenomenon merely in terms of shifting intellectual fads: more substantial political and socio-economic conditions account for this seemingly abnormal state of affairs. An investigation of its historical roots, moreover, will throw considerable light on the very character of critical theory now practically in its third generation of theoreticians.

The question concerning the differences in the development of political consciousness and Marxist theory in Europe and in the New World is, of course, still very much an open one. Whatever the reasons for these historical differences, however, they certainly have nothing to do with America being "so barren of theoreticians that it is under the illusion that it has escaped Marxism."[2] As Camporesi has convincingly shown, the theoretical contributions of Louis B. Boudin, Ernest Untermann, Robert R. LaMonte, and other American Marxists at the beginning of the century are no less rigorous than those of Kautsky, Luxemburg, and Labriola, while the debates and discussions in Charles H. Kerr's *International Socialist Review* are not much below those found in *Die Neue Zeit* or *La Critica* during the same period.[3]

While the theoretical level of American Marxism compares favorably with its European counterpart, the same cannot be said of political consciousness. As Werner Sombart indicated as early as 1905, this state of affairs can be roughly explained in terms of higher American wages, the lack of sharp class differences between the working class and middle classes, and the ready presence of the frontier as a "safety valve" for social discontent.[4] Although Sombart's work has fallen into disrepute due to his subsequent support of Nazism, as Irving Fetscher points out, if one adds the constant influx of immigrants to the presence of a still subservient Black population and the resulting upgrading of the "resident" working class, plus the privileged international position of American capitalism, then one has a fairly accurate account of the situation.[5]

All of this, however, is still insufficient to throw light on the tortuous genesis and development of critical theory on both sides of the Atlantic for, as Sombart himself readily recognized, in terms of the logic of his own explanation, the differences were only *temporary* ones and therefore due to disappear in time.[6] What is crucial here is that World War I was fought in Europe where the resulting devastation provided the framework for the rise of Hegelian Marxism and critical theory: *the workers' councils.* To the extent that in America the war brought no devastation but, rather, proved to be a major stimulus to industrial development, there was no major *post-bellum* socio-economic collapse as in much of Europe. The absence of the subsequent council experience also meant the lack of any need for a theoretical reflection concerning the failure of this council experience—hence no necessity to reconstruct Marxism along Hegelian lines. Furthermore, to the extent that opposition remained fairly well under control in America, unlike most of Europe where the shift from entrepreneurial to oligopolistic capitalism had to be violently mediated by brutal forms such as Fascism, Nazism, or Stalinism, the shift was postponed until after the Great Depression, and then smoothly carried out by means of the New Deal.

Thus, to understand the middle-European roots of Hegelian Marxism and critical theory, along with the series of events which in the 1970s make it relevant in America, it is necessary to examine briefly the history of Hegelian Marxism in the 1920s, the heritage it bequeathed to the original critical theorists, as well as the various internal problems confronted by this tradition throughout its short history.

* * *

All three leading Hegelian Marxists of the 1920s were intimately involved in the various council movements around 1919: Lukács was minister of culture in Budapest,[7] Korsch was a member of the Socialization Commission in Berlin,[8] and Gramsci was the major theoretician of the Turin councils.[9] All three had also become socialists in the process of seeking solutions for the social, economic, and cultural problems of pre-World War I Europe. A closer examination of their main theoretical contributions readily reveals how deeply rooted they were in European culture and to what extent they saw their socialism as the ideal culmination of Western civilization. Because of this, all three aimed their most violent polemics against their fellow social-democrats for having vulgarized and de-activated the doctrine of socialism into a set of slogans unable to provide real solutions to contemporary socio-economic problems and, consequently, unable to organize the masses concretely for their historical revolutionary task.

Pre-World War I social-democracy, from the 1891 Erfurt Program to the beginning of the war, presented socialism either as the historically necessary outcome of the logic of capitalist development whereby the shift of property relations would automatically solve all social problems, or as an ethical ideal to be implemented in order to fulfill those promises of the French Revolution which capitalism could not fulfill.[10] Both accounts systematically ruled out subjectivity and the dialectic since within the determinist model socialism was unavoidable, so that nothing needed to be done except to wait for its arrival, while for the voluntarist model an ethical ideal arbitrarily chosen was to be realized within a fundamentally static context.[11] What had happened to Marxist theory was that it had itself fallen prey to that logic of reification which it otherwise denounced. Thus, it had been reduced to the level of a contemplative theory of being, unable to affect a reality which it could only, at best, passively affirm.

In many respects, the very genesis of Hegelian Marxism already corroborates one of the recurrent themes of Adorno's thought: the autonomy of theory. Lukács', Korsch's, and Gramsci's contributions were not the result of their immediate political efforts, but of the reflection on that work and its failure. The theory of reification, cultural hegemony, and of the unity of theory and practice elaborated respectively by Lukács, Gramsci, and Korsch, inherited as much from the neo-idealist tradition from which all three men came, as from what passed at the time for Marxism and socialism.[12] What made their work so original was that they were able to re-constitute Marxism by synthesizing in the process all of the best achievements of bourgeois culture. Only through such a dialectical synthesis can the part truly grasp the possibilities of the totality and seek to transcend the onesidedness historically bestowed on it by the fragmentation of the bourgeois world.

Thus, Lukács' originality was not in introducing the theme of "alienation" which had already become widespread through the existential writings of Nietzsche and Kierkegaard or the sociological works of Georg Simmel—or even through Lukács' own earlier works such as *The Soul and the Forms*—but in analyzing it in terms of the division of labor and the resulting objectified conceptual forms. It did not take much social insight to realize that "authentic existence" was impossible at the turn of the century. Thomas Mann's *Buddenbrooks* successfully captured the essence of an age when cleverness and unprincipled expediency had systematically displaced traditional protestant values. Benjamin Franklin's life-style so well described and theoreticized in Weber's *The Protestant Ethic and the Spirit of Capitalism* was clearly a thing of the past. The resulting split between culture and life was further intensified by the extension of "formal rationality" not only within the productive process, but to most facets of everyday life. By identifying this development with the Marxist theory of commodity fetishism, Lukács was able to provide a thorough-going critique of almost every cultural aspect from philosophy to economics —or even to social-democracy which had not managed to escape the fate of the rest of society. The framing of alienation within the logic of capitalist production, and the re-interpretation of Marxism through the Hegelian dialectic of whole and part, produced a theory which could locate the proletariat as the historical agency of change and its political aim as the reintegration of that hopelessly fragmented cultural whole typified by commodity fetishism.

Gramsci's account of the problem of cultural hegemony had a

roughly similar intent. In explaining the revolution's failure to come about in terms of the proletariat's lack of awareness of its own objective interests, and the geographical stratification of the labor force in an industrial North and a peasant South, Gramsci focused on the cultural dimension as the primary domain of political struggle. As in Lukács' case, the proletariat's social revolution was to be primarily a process of spiritual reintegration and cultural rebirth, ushering in a new epoch, and at the same time fulfilling the millenarian emancipatory goal of Western civilization. Socialism was to be not just a re-structuring of property relations or of the productive process, but the massive politicization and acculturation of large groups hitherto excluded both from politics and culture.

Approached differently by Korsch, the problem of revolution also boiled down to bringing about a society of self-conscious subjects. In fact, the problem of ideology was circumvented precisely by differentiating between *theory* and ideology in terms of what concretely mediates human activity. Ideology is reduced to those ideas which are not, and cannot be, actualized. The problem with earlier varieties of Marxism, according to Korsch, was that they did not really provide an alternative to the predominant contemplative bourgeois consciousness and actually prevented any genuine emancipation by camouflaging the socialist alternative as nothing but a streamlined variety of the existing state of affairs. The problem of revolution was located squarely in the development and success of self-conscious subjects running their own lives free of determination from above for the first time in history. This is why, after 1926, Korsch did not hesitate to condemn even Bolshevism as a form of capitalist domination lacking emancipatory content.

What was common to all three independently developed accounts was the Hegelian framework which combined the themes of proletarian emancipation and cultural reintegration in the development of a *collective subjectivity,* representing an historical leap into a new age as well as the fulfillment of dreams that humankind had dared to dream from its very beginning. Lukács' identity of subject and object reintegrating the *active* part with the passive remainder of its own creation, Gramsci's "modern prince" understood as that transitional organization embodying the aspirations of the masses and catapulting them for the first time into the historical scene, and even Korsch's violent polemic against all forms of political manipulation, posed the coming of socialism as the solution to the cultural and economic problems of pre-World War I Europe.

This problematic, however, exhausted itself when capitalism began, after the aborted thrust of the council movement, to alter systematically the objective conditions conducive to collective subjectivity. The introduction of the assembly-line and of the "scientific" organization of labor checkmated the possibility of self-management in the productive sphere, while the explosion of the culture industry reinforced that social isolation whose imminent elimination had been the *leitmotif* of Hegelian Marxism. Compounded with massive state intervention in all facets of everyday life, these post-World War I processes of social reconstruction meant the *definitive* defeat of the council movement and the growing irrelevance of all radical social theories presupposing those historically transcended social conditions.

Councils' self-management is only possible in a context where production is organized in such a way that the workers themselves can fully grasp the nature of the process and autonomously run it.[13] Furthermore, it presupposes a highly skilled labor force whose political consciousness is the direct expression of their objective experiences. The introduction of the assembly-line and of the "scientific" organization of labor had much more to do with politically defusing such an explosive social phenomenon by dequalifying the labor force, thus preventing it from ever taking over management functions no longer fully understood or directly experienced, than with increasing efficiency or rationalizing the productive process. The resulting robotization of labor, centrally planned and administered by the new state apparatus of Fascism, Nazism, Stalinism, or even the Keynesian New Deal, had, as its cultural counterpart, the introduction of the mass media which marked pre-packaged forms of social consciousness in a context where reified working experiences had no chance whatsoever of being translated into an awareness of the dynamics of the whole.

Thus, the decline and fall of Hegelian Marxism was not the result of intrinsic theoretical deficiencies—which also abounded—but of an altered socio-historical context and of harsh authoritarian mandates. Given the rapid rise of Fascism and Stalinism, it is not altogether surprising that within a short span of a couple of years Lukács accepted the Third International's ultimatum either to stay in line with "official policy" or be purged, Gramsci was imprisoned and slowly killed by the Fascist apparatus, and Korsch was eventually expelled in 1926 from the German Communist Party.

That the fundamental socio-economic contradictions were not resolved by the re-structuring of the productive process in the 1920s can be readily seen by the coming of the Great Depression after an initial boom period fueled by the reconstruction of a destroyed central Europe. Ultimately, the post-1930 development of massive state apparatuses in advanced industrial societies—whether liberal, Fascist, or Communist—to administer the new robotized masses so well depicted as the cheerful idiots of socialist realist art or of World War II North American productivist propaganda, drove the last nail in the theoretical coffin of Hegelian Marxism which subsequently survived in esoteric archives or in the disillusioned memory of those few who managed to stay alive and sane through it all. Forgotten by the consumerist amnesia of the post-World War II era, this early wave of Hegelian Marxism had to wait until 1968 to be rediscovered and appreciated by the student movement. But by that time it was too late: its moment had passed and it could resurface only as revolutionary nostalgia.

Given this state of affairs, it is not surprising that the new generation of Hegelian Marxists in the 1930s took as its point of departure the objective impossibility of collective subjectivity, and sought to preserve whatever free space had been created for the bourgeois individuality that the system increasingly seemed to rule out. In carrying out this theoretical retreat, the new Hegelian Marxists in the 1930s called themselves "critical theorists" and concentrated their analyses on culture and on the psychological dimension. Not only were they developing new conceptual forms for new historical contents, but they found themselves doing so in a new continent. The rise of Nazism and the accompanying anti-Marxism and anti-Semitism made it impossible for the Frankfurt School to work in Germany. So they were confronted, in the American exile, with a full-blown product of a process of social transformation which in Germany was still developing. In spite of its language and constant references to European culture, critical theory came into being in the late 1930s and early 1940s specifically as a theory of American society. Although it still spoke German and had no initial impact in the U.S., critical theory had irrevocably moved beyond its European origins.

While in Germany and Italy working class opposition had to be violently dealt with in order to re-structure the process of capitalist accumulation, in America the lack of the traumatic experience of the workers' councils made the shift much easier to carry out without having to resort to authoritarian means. Thus, the integration of internal opposition provided by the traditional working class as a *regulatory* mechanism to replace the rapidly disappearing market required no storm-troopers.[14] The displacement of the competition and anarchy of the productive sphere by the relatively well-planned vertical and horizontal integration of oligopolistic capitalism also meant the obsolescence of the spontaneous generation of that constructive negativity which Hegelian Marxists had taken as the foundation of socialism. The systematic impoverishment of the quality of labor within the "modernized" productive process[15] and the parallel colonialization of consciousness by the growing culture industry[16] became the two sides of that social reality that critical theory sought to apprehend. It is a society so characterized that the Frankfurt School tried to deal with, and, in so doing, reconciled European theory with the American experience in a world where regional and national differences were rapidly becoming meaningless. Before returning to the different problematics in Germany and in America, however, it is necessary to examine the nature of the theoretical synthesis carried out by critical theory.

*   *   *

The objective historical impossibility of realizing the collective subjectivity postulated by the first generation of Hegelian Marxists meant that a subjectless revolutionary social theory dealing with the dynamics of the totality could avoid instrumentalization by the ruling administrative apparatus only by becoming increasingly more abstract and utopian. The politicization of the productive process and the industrialization of culture not only instrumentalized political opposition within the logic of the false totality, but also defused revolutionary theory so that it could only assist in the counterproductive function of legitimating and regulating the new administrative machinery. Thus, Adorno's critique of identity theory sought as its target all affirmative theoretical efforts which, consciously or unconsciously, legitimated and therefore occluded the new forms of domination. Yet, as we shall see, the new theoretical synthesis was not fully carried out, with the result that Adorno's critical theory itself fell prey to its own critique. The shock of Auschwitz and Siberia intensified the pessimism concerning emancipatory possibilities which in *The Dialectic of the Enlightenment* had extended the critique of capitalist society to cover all of Western civilization from Odysseus to the atomic bomb. Worse yet, it ended up ruling out the consummation of that process of enlightenment whose arrest and reversal into myth was seen as representing the source of the new computerized barbarism.

In order to understand both the incompleteness of the synthesis attempted by critical theory as well as possibilities which it thereby unwarrantedly ruled out, it may help to consider briefly the most fundamental structures of Marxism at the different levels of living activity, theory, and meta-theory. As all Hegelian Marxists have stressed, Marx's claim that the proletariat is the heir of classical German philosophy represents the historical specification of a longing for emancipation which, in various forms and at different times, has permeated all of Western civilization. Such a *telos* obtains at the level of meta-theory which can only be conceptually articulated through the historically grounded theory that it generates as the mediation meant to facilitate the satisfaction of those intersubjective needs constituted in the process of seeking emancipation. Thus, although every historical specification of the meta-theory is constituted by the conceptual framework provided by the theory through which it is articulated at any given time and tends to become indistinguishable from it, unlike the theory itself, the meta-theory is trans-historical and, precisely because of this, it can guarantee the historicity of concrete social theory. Furthermore, whereas the very temporal grounding of theory already presupposes its built-in obsolescence, whether it succeeds in mediating the social reality at which it is aimed (thus changing the objective conditions whose teleological articulation constitutes its concreteness) or fails to do so (thus revealing its abstractness and inadequacy to the task for which it is meant), the meta-theory's trans-historical character provides precisely those criteria without which it is impossible to re-constitute theory once the realization of its unavoidable obsolescence finally comes. Independently of its categorical formulations—which are necessarily contaminated by the very historicity of the theory within whose framework it is intellectually articulated—the meta-theory can only exist as *faith*.

What eventually happens to Adorno is that he loses faith. He no longer believes in the possibility of a universal history[17] and must reject the Hegelian teleology to fall back on an abstract Kantian moralism which can neither explain itself nor realize its ethical ideals. The theoretical retreat from the unrealizable collective subjectivity of earlier generations to bourgeois individuality is not itself historicized and dialectically articulated within the logic of the false totality, but merely considered a refuge to an increasingly obsolescent social space that precludes any meaningful practical outcome. Although his passionate defense against the students' charges just before his death concerning the autonomy of theory, the counterproductive nature of terrorism and violence, etc.,[18] is generally sound, the essential point is silently granted: critical theory has become socially impotent.

Such a tragic outcome of one of the most brilliant philosophies and social theories in the twentieth century is not unavoidable. In fact, on a closer inspection, it turns out to be primarily the result of the incomplete synthesis originally attempted in the 1930s. When the social scene is characterized by a radical rupture between social being and social thought, the search for collective subjectivity must retreat to bourgeois individualism; and when, in the administered society, there is a diminishing free space, the dialectic itself must become historically specified in order to avoid deterioration into its ever-present trap of abstractness and idealism. This historicization of the dialectic within such a context needs a *phenomenological foundation*.

In fact, from the very beginning of the century the relation between social being and social consciousness had been systematically tackled by Husserl's phenomenology—from the *Logical Investigations* up to the attempt to ground meaning in the *Lebenswelt*. Yet, critical theory never developed an appreciation for any type of phenomenology. Although Marcuse, in one of his earliest published works, sought to develop a "phenomenology of historical materialism"[19] in order to re-constitute a radical social theory adequate to the tasks posed by the new capitalist phase, and even Adorno, while still a student, met Horkheimer when the latter was giving a course on Husserl, to subsequently write a thesis on phenomenology,[20] nothing constructive came out of it. While up to 1934 there was a certain ambiguous attitude toward phenomenology, after that date it became one of open hostility. In 1936 Marcuse attacked phenomenology as "the last bourgeois theory of knowledge,"[21] and Adorno's own arguments in his *Zur Metakritik der Erkenntnistheorie* are strikingly similar to the ferocious attacks by the old Lukács who saw it as a step in the intellectual preparation for Fascism in his *The Destruction of Reason*—a work that the Frankfurt School generally rejected as the destruction of Lukács' own reason.[22]

The year 1934 is crucial: it is the time of Hitler's consolidation of power and, what is more important for our arguments here, the year of Heidegger's collusion with the new order. In retrospect, it is difficult to appreciate fully the devastating impact of these developments on the second generation of Hegelian Marxists. Even before the horrors of Auschwitz, it was clear that Nazism was a reversion to barbarism and, moreover, a monumental default on all the emancipatory promises of Western civilization. Those intellectuals who reached intellectual maturity between World War I and the early 1930s never recovered from the shock which fills the pages of their works. The older Lukács went even so far as to indict all of German thought from 1850 on as a gradual preparation for Nazism consistent with the period of decline of entrepreneurial capitalism. Both in Adorno and Lukács, phenomenology is reduced to a moment in the development of totalitarian consciousness, while retreating to the Hegelian dialectic as the highest expression of Western thought. What probably prevented the Frankfurt School from any further serious consideration of phenomenology, as the foundation for a Marxism rendered obsolete by changed objective conditions, was an interpretation of Husserl's own work as a preparatory step to Heidegger's ontology. The latter's ultimately reconciliatory character was hidden by a veil of "historicity" and "authenticity" which seemed to provide a path to salvation in the context of progressive cultural disintegration. But the existential moment had the upper hand, and the promised salvation turned out to be a privileged result of an exceptional act of intellection possible only for the chosen few. Coupled with resigned acceptance of the unavoidable degeneration of mundanity, the Heideggerian solution ruled out *collective* salvation as well as the very possibility of qualitatively changing the human predicament. Whereas the young Marcuse had sought to historicize this predicament as the determinate expression of a certain phase of capitalist development, Heidegger's existentialism could allow only for the displacement of one mode of degenerate mundanity by another through their respective historicization, while hypostatizing the unavoidability of this degeneration to a structure of being. In so doing, Heidegger falls into line with traditional bourgeois thought for which the ahistorical not only takes logical precedence over the historical, but also relegates the latter either to the past or to irrelevance.

But the Frankfurt School's periodization of phenomenology was premature: it rushed to a judgment *before* Husserl's own work had reached its conclusion, thus short-circuiting the possible assimilation of the phenomenological problematic to deal with the shattered relation between social being and social consciousness. Only in 1936 did Husserl publish part of his work on *The Crisis of European Sciences* (whose full text appeared only in 1954 because of the Nazis' doubts about the purity of the author's blood), after the Frankfurt School had already relegated Husserl to the secondary position of a precursor of Heidegger. A short review of this published section by Marcuse in 1936 fails to catch the originality of Husserl's later work, and although thirty years later the evaluation improves considerably, the generally negative appraisal remains.[23] As Adorno put it, phenomenology as a "first philosophy" comes at the time of the last philosophy, thus providing another anachronistic form of positivism.[24]

The problem with this interpretation is that it focuses solely on Husserl's early work where the stress is mainly on the relation of essence to appearance, and the essence itself is left not only uninvestigated in its logical primacy, but altogether severed from the sociohistorical context within which it obtains. Only later did Husserl systematically emphasize the life-world as that historically constituted dimension which as the beginning and ending of all activities provided both the determinations as well as the foundation for the alienated life that theory was to apprehend in order to change. In so doing, Husserl provided the only genuinely *materialist* theory of knowledge adequate to the new phase of capitalist development.

The Frankfurt School's premature rejection of Husserl left Adorno and Marcuse with the old Hegelian dialectic and all of its traditional problems which were recognized but not remedied—and the resulting lacerated theory itself was subsequently presented as the only adequate one for a lacerated world.[25] The problem of identity theory according to which the concept exhausts the object, thus violating its particularity and, extended to people-as-objects, reduces them to the manipulable statistics of the "totally administered society," is, first and foremost, the problem of the Hegelian dialectic. Similarly, the resulting *reconciliation* with the status quo was also one of the most striking features of the Hegelian dialectic. No one more than Adorno and the critical theorists is more aware of such a quandary. Yet, the solutions proposed do not thereby become satisfactory. The tactical return to Kant provides only epistemological "first aid," leaving altogether unsolved the fundamental problem of radical social theory: the rupture between social being and social consciousness. Thus, when Adorno criticizes other theories—including phenomenology—he continually resorts to a sociologism which uncritically pairs forms of being with forms of thought without being able to articulate the intrinsic relations between the two, other than through a subtle variation of the theory of reflection that he had successfully devastated in "orthodox" Marxism. Holding fast to the *logic of the essence,* Adorno loses sight of those appearances without whose complementarity this very logic ends up as another ideological mystification occluding the processionality of the real. Furthermore, from his privileged position of the logic of the essence, he not only can throw critical thunderbolts at the reified phenomena of the administered society, but can also nail all other theories down as frozen images, and hence as accomplices of that same administered society. Far from being constantly mediated by the phenomenal immediacy of which it claims to be the essential movement, Adorno's dialectic itself remains a frozen expression of a pre-World War II reality stopped in its tracks by Auschwitz and Siberia.

All of Adorno's fundamental themes are brilliant elaborations of the logic of entrepreneurial capitalism. Thus, identity theory—his philosophical *aqua regia* which dissolves all theoretical reifications—is presented as the essential structure of a capitalist reality where unequal exchange at the workplace between capital and labor (which is presented as an equivalence occluding the underlying institutional exploitation) functions as the fundamental model of bourgeois thought. Yet, his own social analysis has already shown *exploitation* to be a special case of *domination* while the logic of late capitalism is not primarily concerned with necessary accumulation, but with the retention of existing relations of domination. Thus, the destruction of particularity and otherness—which was Adorno's basic analysis of anti-Semitism and racism in general—is the historically specific task of an earlier phase of capitalism, whereas in its late monopoly stage it is precisely the retention of this *otherness* and particularity which guarantees the continued viability of the system of universal domination.

In this respect, the Frankfurt School remains historically located in the 1930s—notwithstanding the fact that most of the main works on critical theory were written much later. Its contribution remains the highest expression of radical social theory between the two wars and, to the extent that post-World War II thought has not really gone beyond it, a contemporary heritage yet to be critically appropriated.

* * *

The incomplete theoretical synthesis carried out by Adorno's critical theory thus stands to the transition phase from entrepreneurial to monopoly capitalism in the same way that the Hegelian Marxism of the 1920s stood with respect to entrepreneurial capitalism. In many respects its incompleteness captures the very character of the transition period which critical theory sought conceptually to apprehend. Furthermore, this explains the paradox mentioned earlier whereby critical theory is dead in Germany while thriving in America. To the extent that West Germany is still passing through the technocratic stage of the transition from entrepreneurial to monopoly capitalism, it exhibits all the features of that one-dimensionality postulated by critical theory. Thus, not only is all "otherness" still being annihilated as was the case in the American 1950s, but critical theory does not seem to provide any radical political leverage for those seeking concrete conceptual mediations against administrative repression. In the American context, however, where the technocratic transitional phase is over and the new monopoly capitalism reigns supreme, the system is rapidly discovering that it is *too repressive* for its own good. Its effectiveness, in fact, can be guaranteed only by critical watchdogs that had earlier almost entirely been eliminated. As a result, not only are official organs of repression dismantled *from above,* but some free space is artificially created to allow for the growth of the needed critical dimension. In a situation where no *other* meaningful radical social theory is available, it is not surprising to find critical theory thriving—even if only by default. From the perspective of those being thrust into this artificially created free space, however, the most immediate task is to move beyond identity theory and investigate concrete alternatives for realizing the often defeated yet irrepressibly present emancipatory need.

NOTES

1. For a brief account of this state of affairs, see Martin Jay, "Some Recent Developments in Critical Theory," *Berkeley Journal of Sociology,* vol. XVII, 1973–1974; and Fred R. Dallmayr, "Critical Theory Criticized: Habermas' *Knowledge and Human Interests* and Its Aftermath," in *Philosophy of the Social Sciences,* vol. 2, no. 2, 1972.

2. Raya Dunayevskaya, *Marxism and Freedom,* 3rd ed. (London, 1971), p. 270.

3. Cristiano Camporesi, *Il Marxismo Teorico negli USA, 1900–1945* (Milan, 1973), especially chapters 1 and 2. One need only to run through the list of both original contributions as well as of translations published by Charles H. Kerr & Co. in Chicago before World War I to realize how theoretically sophisticated and up to date American Marxism was at that time.

4. Werner Sombart, "Study of the Historical Development and Evolution of the American Proletariat," in *International Socialist Review,* vol. VI, no. 3, 1905, pp. 129–136. The argument is better developed in his *Warum Gibt es in den Vereinigten Staaten keinen Sozialismus?* (Tübingen, 1906). Selections from this book are now available in English in Werner Sombart, "American Capitalism's Economic Rewards," in John H. M. Laslett and Seymour Martin Lipset, eds., *Failure of a Dream? Essays in the History of American Socialism* (Garden City: Doubleday, 1974), pp. 593–608.

5. Cf. Irving Fetscher's "Comment" on Sombart's essay in Laslett and Lipset, eds., op. cit., pp. 618–624.

6. Sombart, *Warum Gibt es,* p. 141 ff.

7. Cf. David Kettler, "Culture and Revolution: Lukács and the Hungarian Revolution of 1918," in *Telos,* no. 10, Winter 1971, pp. 35–92; and Rudolf Tökes, *Bela Kun and the Hungarian Soviet Republic* (New York, 1967). Lukács' writings during this period can now be found in his *Political Writings 1919–1920,* trans. Rodney Livingstone (London, 1972).

8. Cf. Gian Enrico Rusconi, "La Problematica dei Consigli in Korsch," in *Annali Feltrinelli, 1973* (Milan, 1974), pp. 1197–1230. Korsch's writings during this period can now be found in his *Schriften zur Sozialisierung* (Frankfurt, 1969); and his *Arbeitsrecht für Betriebsräte* (Frankfurt, 1968).

9. Cf. Carl Boggs, Jr., "Gramsci's Theory of the Factory Councils: Nucleus of the Socialist State," in *Berkeley Journal of Sociology,* vol. XIX, 1974–1975, pp. 171–188; Alastair Davidson, "Gramsci and the Factory Councils," in *Australian Left Review,* no. 45 (October, 1974); and John M. Cammett, *Antonio Gramsci and the Origins of Italian Communism* (Stanford, 1967), and chapter 4: *"Ordine Nuovo* and the Italian Soviets," pp. 65–95. Most of Gramsci's writings during this period are now in his *Scritti Politici,* Paolo Spriano, ed. (Rome, 1967).

10. This is how Arthur Rosenberg presents the problem in his *History of Bolshevism* (New York, 1942).

11. For an excellent analysis of these problems, see Andrew Arato, "Re-examining the Second International," in *Telos,* no. 18, Winter 1973–74, pp. 2–52. Cf. also Lucio Colletti, "Bernstein and the Marxism of the Second International," in his *From Rousseau to Lenin: Studies in Ideology and Society,* trans. John Merrington and Judith White (London, 1972), pp. 45–108.

12. Andrew Arato, "The Neo-Idealist Defense of Subjectivity," in *Telos,* no. 21, Fall 1974, pp. 108–161. Here, Arato gives an analysis of the neo-idealist heritage of Hegelian Marxists, especially in Germany.

13. Cf. Sergio Bologna, "Class Composition and Theory of the Party," in *Telos,* no. 13, Fall 1972, pp. 3–27; and Mossimo Cacciari, "Sul Problema dell' Organizazione, Germania 1917–1921," in Gyorgy Lukács, *Kommunismus 1920–1921* (Padova, 1972), pp. 7–66.

14. For an elaboration of the logic of this process, see Mario Tronti, "Workers and Capital," in *Telos*, no. 14, Winter 1972, pp. 25–62.

15. Cf. Harry Braverman, *Labor and Monopoly Capital: The Degradation of Work in the Twentieth Century* (New York, 1974).

16. Cf. Stanley Aronowitz, *False Promises: The Shaping of American Working Class Consciousness* (New York: McGraw-Hill, 1973), chapter 2, "Colonialized Leisure," pp. 51–134.

17. Theodor W. Adorno, *Negative Dialektik* (Frankfurt, 1966), p. 315.

18. Cf. Theodor W. Adorno, *Stichworte, Kritische Modelle 2* (Frankfurt, 1969).

19. Herbert Marcuse, *"Contribution to a Phenomenology of Historical Materialism (1928),"* in *Telos*, no. 4, Fall 1969, pp. 3–34.

20. The title was "Die Transzendenz des Dinglichen und Noematischen in Husserls Phänomenologie." For an historical account of the events surrounding this, see Martin Jay, *The Dialectical Imagination: A History of the Frankfurt School and the Institute of Social Research 1923–1950* (Boston, 1963), chapter 1.

21. Herbert Marcuse, *Negations: Essays in Critical Theory*, trans. Jeremy J. Shapiro (Boston, 1968), p. 154.

22. For a critical comparison of the two works, see Guido Neri, *Prassi e Conoscenza* (Milan, 1966), chapter 9, pp. 136–148.

23. Cf. Herbert Marcuse, "On Science and Phenomenology," in Robert S. Cohen and Marx W. Wartofsky, eds., *Boston Studies in the Philosophy of Science*, vol. II (New York, 1965), pp. 279–290.

24. Theodor W. Adorno, *Zur Metakritik der Erkenntnistheorie* (Frankfurt, 1972), p. 47.

25. Adorno, in fact, goes so far as to attack as ideological any theory that does otherwise. See Theodor W. Adorno, ed., *Der Positivismusstreit in der deutschen Soziologie* (Neuwied and Berlin, 1969).

THE SLIME OF HISTORY: EMBEDDEDNESS IN NATURE AND CRITICAL THEORY

JEREMY J. SHAPIRO

For Susan Starbird

Human freedom, the intentional and generative capacity to create the future, finds itself held back by the weight of the past. Sartre has captured this experience in his description of the slimy:

> It is horrible in itself for a consciousness to become slimy. This is because the being of the slimy is a soft clinging, there is a sly solidarity and complicity of all its leech-like parts, a vague, soft effort made by each to individualize itself, followed by a falling back and flattening out that is emptied of the individual, sucked in on all sides by the substance. A consciousness which became slimy would be transformed by the thick stickiness of its ideas. From the time of our upsurge into the world, we are haunted by the image of a consciousness which would like to launch forth into the future, toward a projection of self, and which at the very moment when it was conscious of arriving there would be slyly held back by the invisible suction of the past and which would have to assist in its own slow dissolution in this past which it was fleeing, would have to aid in the invasion of its project by a thousand parasites until finally it completely lost itself. . . . The horror of the slimy is the horrible fear that time might become slimy, that facticity might progress continually and insensibly and absorb the For-itself . . .[1]

The experience of the slimy as the domination of the past over the present and future is the material of myth, symbolism, and philosophy. It is elaborated in the idea of karma, in the cycle of *hybris* and *nemesis,* in the Biblical notion that the sins of the fathers are visited upon the sons unto subsequent generations, and in the idea of original sin. Sliminess is both individual and sociohistorical, ontogenetic and phylogenetic. In the individual, the slimy manifests itself in the repetition compulsion through which the past continually re-enacts itself, forcing the potential novelty and challenge of life into the constraints of unresolved conflicts and unreleased pain. In the species, sliminess manifests itself in the historical transmission of domination, impeding human emancipation by absorbing even the moments of greatest historical change into the oppressive forms of the past. In Marx's words, "The tradition of all dead generations weighs like a nightmare on the brains of the living."

Of course, the power of the past over the present and future is never complete for either the individual or society. As long as there is anything that can still be called human, there is some element of transcendence of the past, of being in the present and generating the future, however weakly. Indeed, it is only in view of this transcendence that it is possible to experience and speak of sliminess at all. It is only a consciousness that is launching forth into the future that can experience itself as being held back by the invisible suction of the past. The most complete victory of the slimy still presupposes what is a constitutive factor of human existence and human consciousness: the synthetic activity through which humans continually create for themselves a present that is differentiated, however slightly, from the past, and a future that always has the possibility of being different from the present. Any inventory of what makes human beings human must include this synthetic activity through which time is constituted and the past transcended. Human beings are not only subject to time but its creators as well:

> Time is thought of by us before its parts, and temporal relations make possible the events in time. Correspondingly it is necessary for the subject not to be himself situated in it, in order to be able to be present in intention to the past as to the future. Let us no longer say that time is a "datum of consciousness": let us be more precise and say that consciousness unfolds or constitutes time. Through the ideal nature of time, it ceases to be imprisoned in the present.[2]

At the same time, the inventory of human nature would have to take account of the concrete reality in which this imprisonment exists nonetheless. The ideal nature of time is no guarantee of human freedom. The transcendental subject that constitutes time is itself the result of an empirical genesis, one that contaminates the transcendental subject with the traces of a real past, an unfinished past of unfreedom and suffering that seems to seep continually into the present and drag the transcendental subject down into the mire of repetition that constitutes its prison: the road to hell paved with the good intentions of the transcendental subject. It is because of this imprisonment in time and repetition that the historically new, the acts of liberation, occur in history through the cunning of reason: not merely in spite of the domination of the past but through it—through its forms and its essential sliminess. This sliminess I should like to refer to as *embeddedness in nature*. The dialectic of human freedom is that its transcendence is embedded in nature.

The concept "embeddedness in nature" stands for the German *Naturwüchsiqkeit* which Marx introduces and discusses in *The German Ideology* as well as in the *Grundrisse*.[3] The term itself denotes the quality of unplanned, spontaneous growth in uninterrupted continuity with nature—being rooted in or embedded in nature. The concept refers to the fact that human beings have the capacity to act freely and create the future through the use of their rationality and agency, and yet are held back, both individually and collectively, by their immersion in the past and in nature. An implication of Marx's use of the concept is that human beings, through their very nature, have the capacity to control the course of history itself, and that the actual course of history can be comprehended only in the light of this possibility of controlling it.

According to Marx, embeddedness in nature has dominated the entire history of the human species as the domination of the past over the present through (1) the domination of the conditions of labor over the capacity for abstract labor, and (2) the domination of the division of labor over the existence and self-consciousness of the individual.[4] Marx sees the historical significance of capitalism in its (1) setting abstract labor free as a force of production through the process in which labor creates its own conditions, and (2) freeing individuals from their identification with particular social roles allotted to them by the social division of labor, which occurs as their work existence becomes contingent to their personal identity.[5] For the first time, individuals can freely associate with one another as individuals, and they can do so under conditions that enable them to know themselves as the ultimate productive force. Thus they can create a rational and humane society and achieve the domination of the present over the future (and past), bringing the historical process under control. They can insert the free and chosen use of reason among equals into the previously uninterrupted continuity between nature and history.

Communism is for Marx the end of embeddedness in nature as domination of past over present. In the *Communist Manifesto* he writes that "in bourgeois society the past rules over the present, in communist society the present rules over the past." That is why socialist revolution involves a different relation of past, present, and future than any that has previously existed:

> The social revolution of the nineteenth century cannot draw its poetry from the past, but rather only from the future. It cannot begin with itself before shedding all superstitious belief in the past. Earlier revolutions required world-historical memories, in order to numb themselves to their own content. The revolution of the nineteenth century must let the dead bury their own dead, in order to arrive at its own content.[6]

What enables communism to shed all superstitious belief in the past and draw its poetry from the future is its termination of embeddedness:

> Communism distinguishes itself from all previous movements by overturning the basis of all previous relations of production and interaction and consciously treating, for the first time, all naturally embedded presuppositions as creations of previous human beings, stripping them of their embeddedness in nature and subjecting them to the power of the associated individuals.[7]

This social revolution involves not only new relations of production and interaction but a new mode of existence for the individual. For embeddedness in nature affects the existential structure of each individual human being. That is why communism severs "the umbilical cord of the individual's natural connection with the species."[8] In the *Grundrisse*, Marx describes the mode of existence of the individual once the umbilical cord of embeddedness has been cut:

> In fact, however, if the limited bourgeois form is removed, what is wealth except the universality of the individuals' needs, capacities, en-

joyments, productive forces, etc., produced by universal exchange? The full development of human control over natural forces, those of so-called nature as well as of its [the human being's] own nature? The absolute realization of its creative endowments, without any other presupposition than the preceding historical development, which makes this totality of development, that is the development of all human powers as such, into an end in itself, not measured against a pre-given standard? Where it does not reproduce itself in a particular form but rather produces its totality? [Where it] no longer seeks to remain something that has become what it is but exists in the absolute movement of becoming?[9]

In the state of post-embeddedness depicted by Marx, the individual has ceased to become the object of uncontrolled forces and is instead entirely self-created, ceaselessly going beyond its own limits by means of its creativity, and continuously participating in the movement of its own becoming. The individual has completely escaped from embeddedness simply by casting off the "limited bourgeois form."

Marx accounts for the existence of embeddedness in nature in terms of a peculiar and incomplete self-transcendence of nature that came about with the emergence of the human species. In the human being, nature gave rise to a being that could relate universally to itself, its conspecifics, and its environment—it is in these terms that Marx describes the human species-being.[10] At the same time, this capacity comes into existence in a situation that systematically limits it. Marx describes the first forms of society and ideology as resulting from what he calls the "limited connection" between the human being and its conspecifics and environment.[11] That is, owing to the lack of development of the productive forces, production relations, and division of labor, human beings do not experience the constitutive role of their own synthetic activity in the structuring of the natural and social world. They consequently experience themselves as being dominated by society and nature, even though these are in part their own product. Through this limited connection with other persons and things, their universal generative capacities are restricted. The dialectic of history is the result of the contradiction between the human species-being (universality) and its limitation.

The dialectic of history is resolved through completion of the self-transcendence of nature that occurs when embeddedness in nature is overcome and human beings bring the historical process under control. This self-transcendence is at the same time the "resurrection of nature," because it ends the conflict of nature with itself that was manifested in embeddedness and the abstract contradiction between universality and its limits. The consummation of the dialectic is effected by capitalism because it is the nature of capitalism to end all limits to human interaction and the human relation to the natural world. It thus liberates the universality of the human species-being from its "limited connection" and makes it possible for human beings to posit their nature for itself and for themselves. The human essence exists in itself at the origin of history—but it does not yet exist for itself. Under conditions of embeddedness in nature, there is a contradiction between human nature in itself and for itself, manifested in the contradiction between its limited existence for itself and its potential total existence for itself. To the extent that human beings cannot become aware of their total interdependence, there is an incompleteness in human nature. A species-being for itself is one that recognizes its own essence as a social being and consequently recognizes that its own interest is what is in the interest of the species: the individual and general interest coincide, not merely in reality, but in self-consciousness. It is capitalism that produces this recognition and this identity of the individual and the general interest.

Marx himself did not provide a concrete explanation of the genesis of the human species-being. For him it was an irreducible fact of nature. With the modes of historical explanation available to him he could not formulate materialistically and concretely the idea of a self-transcendence of nature.[12] Consequently he employed the dialectical contradiction in his theoretical framework without being able to provide it with an ultimate foundation. Nevertheless, there are several features of Marx's conception that can serve as essential guidelines in the construction of such a foundation on the basis of present knowledge.

The first such feature is Marx's use of a two-stage model of the genesis of human nature. Stage one is the birth of the human species-being at the origin of history; stage two is its consummation in the communist revolution. The second feature is the notion that human nature is not fixed. That is, while the underlying stratum of human nature is structured by the universality of the human species-being, its empirical manifestation is deformed by embeddedness in nature. Consequently communism involves the transformation of human nature. Revolutionary practice is for Marx not merely a method of social change and a principle of cognition but a method for the self-genesis of human nature in which humans bring their deformed nature into accord with their species-being. At the same time, their species-being is liberated toward new forms that were impossible within embeddedness. Through the overcoming of embeddedness in nature, the species-being becomes something other than it was when deformed. The third useful feature of Marx's model is its teleology. Marx's conception is teleological in the most legitimate, "cybernetic" sense of the term. The *telos* of history operates not as a metaphysical mode of causality but rather as a feedback mechanism. Once human species-being has originated, it can be consummated (as communism) if and when the right conditions have been created, as they have been through the development of the productive forces and modes of production up to the final differentiation of abstract labor under capitalism. History is a search strategy for the projection of conditions under which the species-being can be realized.[13] But this strategy is the fortuitous one of variation and selection, in which the species-being acts as a constraint.[14] It is precisely this process that constitutes history as the self-alienation of human species-being. Here "alienation" has lost all theological connotations and can be interpreted in a strictly cybernetic manner—as the species-being's inability to overcome embeddedness in nature until (unless) social evolution brings about the right conditions. That is why there is no mechanical necessity in the transition from capitalism to socialism but only the first realistic possibility of overcoming embeddedness and liberating the species-being. For Marx it was, of course, indubitable that human beings, presented with this possibility, would choose it.

Because of his rationalistic assumptions, Marx underestimated the depth at which embeddedness is rooted in the individual's psychic and organic existence. He tended to think of embeddedness as consisting entirely in the underdevelopment of productive forces and division of labor external to the individual, such that progress in these two areas would lead automatically to the surfacing of human rationality. Thus he did not comprehend that embeddedness in nature at the sociohistorical level is thoroughly mediated with the existence of the individual. Marx did realize that the end of embeddedness meant the severance of the umbilical cord of the individual's natural connection with the species, but he did not see that the umbilical cord grows through the intra-psychic and intra-organic existence of the individual. At this level it is an independent variable. For in reality the drama of each individual existence is lived in the struggle between embeddedness and its transcendence. This has been well described by Ernest Schachtel, who points out that "the fundamental situation of embeddedness is the intrauterine situation . . . where no separation from shelter and from the sources of energy supply (food, etc.) has taken place."[15] From birth onward each individual, depending on circumstances, emerges to some extent from embeddedness and yet remains to some extent caught in it:

> Man is also embedded in the countless patterns of routine, convention, more or less automatic behavior on his own part and the part of others. He is embedded in his family, his home, his work, the circle of his friends, his town, his language, his culture, and his country. These publicly or privately "institutionalized" patterns, while created by man and changeable by him, in a way take the place of the instinctive behavior in which animals are embedded. The embeddedness function of these patterns plays a large role, psychologically, in the conservative tendencies of man, in his fear of new individual as well as social ways of life.[16]

Embeddedness is not merely the result of the state of the productive forces and mode of production: it has strong roots in the disposition of the human organism. Anxiety itself is fundamentally an emotion of distress about the loss of embeddedness, and in this form it militates against the free use of rationality and the ability to transcend the past toward the future:

> Man's anxiety in leaving embeddedness is the one most powerful antagonist of his world-openness. It wants to confine him in the embeddedness of the familiar so that he will not experience the awe and wonder of the infinitely new and unknown.[17]

Of course, human beings are not defined exclusively by embeddedness. The human's world remains open

> to the extent to which time and again he can transcend such confinement in acts of object-centered interest and love, because only in such acts does he actually encounter the world and people around him, in their own right, without being blinded by the strength of his embeddedness needs.[18]

In comparison with other animal species, the human capacity for the transcendence of embeddedness can be clearly seen. Reflective consciousness makes possible taking charge of development toward emerging from embeddedness. Schachtel points out that the human species has symbolized, in such figures as Christ and Buddha, its belief in the human potentiality for a full emergence from embeddedness.[19] But this emergence can only occur from within and in the face of all the psychic and organic pressures toward embeddedness, not as a mere by-product of social revolution.

Marxism is the first world-historical formulation of the belief in emergence from embeddedness as a practically oriented theory. But in Marx's original formulations, the theory of embeddedness stops short of focussing on its psychic and organic prerequisites. That is because Marx saw these as consequences of two forms of institutional embeddedness: the family and the nation. For Marx, such features of embeddedness as conservatism, being closed to novelty, fear of change, attachment to limited social groups, and dependence were the offshoots of archaic institutions, principally the family, the feudal system, and the nation. The emergence of a revolutionary proletariat was tied for Marx to capitalism's destruction of these institutions. Hence in the *Communist Manifesto* proletarian revolution is linked to the prior abolition of the family and the nation:

> In the conditions of the proletariat those of old society at large are already virtually swamped. The proletarian is without property; his relation to his wife and children has no longer anything in common with the bourgeois family relations; modern industrial labor, modern subjection to capital, the same in England as in France, in America as in Germany, has stripped him of every trace of national character.[20]

Marx also speaks in the *Manifesto* of the "practical absence of the family among the proletarians" and asserts categorically that "the workingmen have no country." These ideas were of great importance to Marx. They were part of the justification for his belief that capitalism was ending embeddedness in nature and thereby making possible its definitive transcendence. For it was clear to Marx that interrupting the continuity of embeddedness in nature depended on the simultaneous ending of embeddedness in the individual and the species. Only in this case could the "freely associated individuals" themselves become the basis of a new social order grounded in their rationality and agency. Thus it was essential to locate historical forces that eliminated embeddedness simultaneously for the individuals and the society (in this case the working class). Hence Marx's emphasis on the destruction of the family and the nation under capitalism, since they seemed to underlie the psychological traits of embeddedness.

It is here that Marxian theory has been most inadequate. For the structures of authority, dependence, and individual motivation and belief connected with the nation and the family have persisted with great strength in advanced capitalism (and "socialism"). And it is clearly these same structures that operate as the limiting factors to the emergence of a rational, democratic, socialist solution to the problems generated by the world capitalist system. A characteristic description of this situation can be found in Robert Heilbroner's survey of the present world crisis. Heilbroner argues that there are two general tendencies of human nature that militate against such a rational, democratic, socialist solution: the tendency to submit to authority and the tendency to identify with limited social groups, such as the nation, instead of with the species as a whole—"the traits of obedience and the capacity for identification."[21] Heilbroner derives both of these traits from human childhood and its structuration by the family, particularly the child's powerlessness and dependence on adults, and its original identification with its own family in distinction from any other entities. He argues that these traits form insuperable limits to the overcoming of embeddedness:

> For the capacity for survival must reckon with the need for—perhaps the ultimate reliance on—welcomed hierarchies of power and strongly felt bonds of peoplehood, to the discomfiture of those who would hope that the challenges of the human prospect would finally banish the thralldoms of authority and ideology and foster the "liberation" of the individual. Our analysis provides a warning that these hopes are not likely to be realized, and that the tensions immanent in socio-economic trends must be worked out within and through the political elements in "human nature."[22]

Far from being abolished by advanced technological civilization, the "hunger" for political authority and the "fantasy" of political identification are employed by contemporary capitalism *and socialism* for their own sustenance and for the erection of more stable and total systems of domination. If capitalism and technology have not eliminated embeddedness in nature as it affects individual existence, then there is no possibility for human freedom and rationality in the integral sense envisioned by Marx, unless there is a discernible evolutionary trend toward the overcoming of embeddedness despite the persistence of the family and the nation, and unless there is a discernible or at least conceivable political practice that can attack embeddedness at the individual and social levels simultaneously. If there is no such trend and no such practice, then Heilbroner's conclusion of hopelessness regarding the human prospect is justified.

The critical theory of the Frankfurt School has always been governed by the concern for overcoming embeddedness in nature. That is because it has always been concerned with the crucial issue of Marx's philosophy of history: the possibility of rational human subjects. From the beginning, critical theory has focussed on the conditions favoring or disfavoring the emergence of the subjects who are to accomplish the crucial break with the past. Accordingly it has turned its attention to social phenomena previously considered by Marxism as part of the "superstructure" or as ideology: personality, family, and authority structures and the realm of aesthetics and mass culture. The common object was the ability of capitalism to destroy the preconditions of critical, revolutionary consciousness, particularly by making use of elements of the dynamic of embeddedness at the individual level. This meant arriving at a sophisticated awareness of the depth dimension in which social oppression sustains itself. It is for this reason, too, that critical theory has focussed on the philosophical foundations of Marxian theory and the dialectical method. For the sliminess of history asserts itself even within Marxism and socialism as the inability to grasp the historically new and the tendency to grasp it as the mere repetition of existing social structures and social conflicts. Hence the resistance of critical theory to the reduction of the dialectical method to either a scientific or a structuralist method. For it is the essence of the dialectic that historical reality is constantly generating new forms that can be negated only determinately, that is, in terms of their specific structure. This does not mean that critical theory can dispense with structural models and scientific procedures, but rather that the latter's significance must be mediated with a process of historical self-reflection.[23]

Critical theory has, in short, addressed itself to the question of the nature of embeddedness, the trends that reinforce or reduce it, and the preconditions for a political practice that would take it into account. But in perceiving that Marx's structural and evolutionary models were inadequate to the abolition of embeddedness and were becoming accessories to it, critical theory tended to deny the possibility of such models and thus of accounting for critical theory itself. If rational subjects had been eliminated from history, how could critical theory itself have any basis in historical reality? It was this question that underlay the alleged "idealism" of the Frankfurt School. And it was not clear what practice followed from a theory that showed how deeply in the human psyche social oppression is rooted. Except for some of the projects of Wilhelm Reich, it is only quite recently that the possibility of synthesizing individual liberation and radical politics has even become conceivable. Thus critical theory has tended to shy away from attempts at a practice based on its own conceptual framework, remaining far closer to orthodox Marxism than is suggested by the insights of critical theory itself. The recent development of critical theory in the direction of a communication theory of society, however, has laid the foundations for a new evolutionary theory of embeddedness in nature and its transcendence that also accounts for critical theory as part of the evolutionary process and suggests the direction of a new political practice.[24]

Homo sapiens evolves through the cultural transmission of information from one generation to the next by means of socialization into cultural systems, and these systems themselves learn, evolve, and become reflexive as the learning mechanisms enter awareness and become governable. This mode of evolution occurs through the emergence of language and its far-reaching consequences. Rationality is rooted in language. For all human communications implicitly claim a theoretical truth and normative validity that can be verified only through rational argument or discourse.[25] Moreover, the possibility of discourse is rooted in a particular and indeed peculiar social precondition: what Habermas calls the ideal speech situation. All discourse implies the possibility of a rational consensus, which presupposes an equal, symmetrical, and uncoercive distribution of opportunities to engage in discourse: asking questions, giving interpretations, and making recommendations.[26] The existence of this ideal speech situation must be presupposed for any communication to be possible. Yet it is only feebly realized in human society. Since cultural learning advances most efficiently under conditions of rationality, and cultural evolution favors actualization of the optimal conditions for cultural evolution itself, human evolution is quasi-teleological, tending towards the realization of its own rational *a priori.* This would lead to the institutionalization of discourse, so that all claims to validity in human communication, including ethical and political norms, would be subject to systematic, as opposed to haphazard, rational examination; the establishment of political, social, and economic democracy as the foundation of the institutionalization of discourse; and an increase in personal autonomy within relations of increased interdependence, to guarantee the human capacity to participate in the two prior conditions.

In this perspective, emancipatory thought, of which critical theory is one part, is not just a current in the history of ideas, or an ideological reflection of class struggle, but part of the process of sociocultural evolution itself. Critical theory is a component of what could be called the emancipatory subsystem of sociocultural evolution, whose differentiation into a separate subsystem marks a turning-point in world history. This differentiation occurred in the context of the industrial and democratic revolutions at the end of the eighteenth and the beginning of the nineteenth centuries. From the point of view of intellectual history, it can be dated as beginning with Kant, whose critical philosophy founded the distinctive emancipatory method that was developed in the Hegelian and Marxian dialectic. The specific function of the emancipatory subsystem is the control and direction of the evolutionary process itself. It articulates and makes reflexive the capacities for such control that are given in human nature but emerge autonomously only with the emancipatory subsystem. If the main obstacle to human freedom and rationality is embeddedness in the past, then we can say that the emancipatory subsystem is a cultural learning mechanism for trying to solve the problem of escaping from and overcoming embeddedness. Once the direction of emancipation is understood as the institutionalization of discourse, the history of emancipatory thought, and of critical theory in particular, can best be comprehended as a progressive attempt to penetrate to deeper and deeper layers of the roots of embeddedness in nature in order to make possible free action and the instauration of rationality. Each stage of theoretical development finds itself confronted with embeddedness and develops a theory and practice to overcome it. The failure of this unified theory and practice poses the problems to be faced by the next stage of development, which must generate a new theory to account for the elements of embeddedness that have not been dealt with despite the previous efforts of emancipatory thought and practice. In other words, the overcoming of embeddedness operates as a practical *a priori* that turns into the knowledge-constitutive interest of emancipatory knowledge.[27] Perhaps the significance of the cultural symbolism of embeddedness and its transcendence, as in the image of the slimy, is in formulating the tasks and problems of emancipation before they have been conceptualized at any given stage of emancipatory knowledge.

This evolutionary perspective sheds light on the current situation of critical theory and embeddedness in nature. For we can now see the two-stage emergence of human nature described by Marx, with the attendant embeddedness in nature, in terms of the lag between the emergence of intersubjectivity and the ideal speech situation on the one hand and the organization of society and behavior on the other. We know that the emergence of the biological nature of the human being occurred through a complex feedback process in which the development of language reacted back upon brain and behavior, with the modified brain and behavior then favoring increased development of language (and the associated forms of co-operation).[28] The attainment of the intersubjectivity and co-operation involved in human language, that is, of the minimal formal requirements of the ideal speech situation required for linguistic functioning, occurred within the social system of hominid society and the nervous system of its members, and generated contradictions within both the social and nervous systems. The social system was hierarchical with a rigid rank order and an inherited basis for behavior based on dominance and submission. And the development of complex forms of social behavior among the primates and hominids favored the increasing use of emotion as a form of behavioral regulation, since emotion made possible the stabilization of learned behavioral patterns and their occasional revision, thus reducing the necessity for innate programming of behavior.

It was into this system that the formal imperatives of human intersubjectivity, the ideal speech situation, and rationality were introduced. On the one hand, and in the long run, language made obsolete both hierarchical social organization and the regulation of behavior by emotion, since both impede the learning process grounded in intersubjectivity and the rationality of discourse. Accordingly it created a selection pressure in favor of social democracy and the regulation of behavior through self-reflective rationality. The process of evolution in two stages is one in which social structure and behavioral regulation are "catching up" with the initial evolutionary advance.[29] On the other hand, and in the short run, language reinforced both hierarchical social structure and emotional dominance. For the development of the linguistic capacity increased the authoritarian components of human behavior through the prolonged infantile dependence that accompanied the genesis of the human brain and social learning and the use of the internalization of authority for the establishment of social behavior patterns. And it intensified the employment of emotion for the regulation of the motivational and identity structures that grounded human behavior.

Human culture dealt with these contradictions by reorganizing the social and behavioral system to make use of the adaptive advantages of the linguistic learning system while incorporating the remnants of the hominid social order and mode of behavioral regulation as limits upon the operation of pure intersubjectivity: the emergence of language erected the order of distorted communication based on psychic repression that has governed the history of civilization as embeddedness in nature. Each social order has institutionalized particular forms of distorted communication which, because they were anchored in the repressive character structure of individuals, resisted alteration from the inside. Here we can see the evolutionary meaning of Marx's conception of prehistory as embeddedness in nature. For the dialectical contradiction between distorted and undistorted communication corresponds to Marx's contradiction between "limited connection" and "universality."

Seen in this way, the contradictions generated within hominid society and nervous system have not yet been resolved. For, understood in terms of embeddedness in nature, the evolution of the human species is still incomplete: the forms of human interaction have not yet caught up with the initial emergence of linguistic learning through intersubjectivity and discourse and the possibility of a discursive, consensual mode of conflict resolution and need gratification. It is the comprehension of human evolution as an incomplete process that distinguishes critical theory from traditional theory: in Nietzsche's words, "the human being is a rope tied between animal and superman."

If the current project of critical theory is revising the theory of evolution in order to account for embeddedness in nature in a more

complete and complex fashion than classical Marxian theory, its practical task is to devise a political practice that can confront and eliminate embeddedness.[30] The latter exists as a system of constraints at
three interlocking levels: over-all social and economic structure, inter-
personal relations, and personality structure. The repressive structure
at each of these levels supports that of the others. That is why the only
effective strategy for overcoming embeddedness must deal with all of
them simultaneously. Otherwise each level finds itself accepting as
given the elements of repression stabilized at the other levels. In the
past, movements of radical political change have been limited by
acceptance of the motivational structures and behavior patterns of
repressed individuals as well as oppressive patterns of interaction
among them (such as sexism), so that radical change is threatened by
what Marcuse calls "psychic Thermidor": the resurgence of the repressive need for domination. But psychoanalysis and other forms of
therapy aiming at undoing individual repression have been limited by
their acceptance of a normative identity that includes adaptation to
and acceptance of irrational and repressive social norms, and small-
group, communicational change methods have been limited by communicational constraints deriving from irrational individual behavior
on the one hand and repressive social structures on the other. At the
present time, critical theory's practical goal is the integration of radical change at these three levels. New developments in the theory and
practice of change favor such an integration.[31] The institutionalization
of discourse requires not only the elimination of social and economic
inequality and injustice. It requires also the institutionalization of
methods for continuously undoing distorted communication and
emotional distress, and the liberation of the creative and transcendental faculties of the human mind. These are the prerequisites for rationality becoming a continuous, synthetic, chosen achievement rather
than an automatic mechanism that is subverted by its own automa-
tism and rigidity. The institutionalization of discourse is impossible
without the institutionalization of reflection. Only through eliminating the roots of embeddedness in nature, which exist in the system
constituted by world capitalism, distorted communication, and deformed identity, can the human species hope to escape from the slime
of history into the realm of freedom.[32]

NOTES

1. Jean-Paul Sartre, *Being and Nothingness,* trans. Hazel E. Barnes (New York: Washington Square Press, 1966), p. 778.

2. Maurice Merleau-Ponty, *Phenomenology of Perception,* trans. Colin Smith (London: Routledge & Kegan Paul, 1962), p. 414.

3. Marx's concept of embeddedness in nature is discussed in detail in Jeremy J. Shapiro, *The Concept of Embeddedness in Nature: Marx and the Self-Reflection of History* (Ph. D. dissertation. Waltham: Brandeis University, 1976). The term is unfamiliar to English and American readers because the standard translation of *The German Ideology* usually translates *naturwüchsig* as "natural." References to English-language editions of *The German Ideology,* consequently, are not helpful. The term *Naturwuchsigkeit* appears throughout Part One ("Feuerbach") of all German editions of *The German Ideology.* It has also reappeared in several recent works of Jürgen Habermas and his associates. See, for example, Jürgen Habermas, *Toward a Rational Society* (Boston: Beacon Press, 1970), p. viii.

4. The first point is a primary theme of the *Grundrisse,* the second of *The German Ideology.*

5. The first point is from the *Grundrisse,* the second from *The German Ideology.*

6. Karl Marx, *Der 18. Brumaire des Louis Bonaparte,* ed. Herbert Marcuse (n.p.: Insel, 1965), p. 12 f.

7. Karl Marx, *Die deutsche Ideologie,* in Karl Marx, *Die Fruschriften,* ed. Siegfried Landshut (Stuttgart: Kroner, 1964), p. 399.

8. Karl Marx, *Das Kapital* (Berlin: Dietz, 1961), vol. I, p. 85.

9. Karl Marx, *Grundrisse der Kritik der politischen Ökonomie* (Berlin: Dietz, 1953), p. 387.

10. Marx's concept of the human species-being and its universality is discussed in Herbert Marcuse, "The Foundation of Historical Materialism," in his *Studies in Critical Philosophy* (Boston: Beacon Press, 1972). The human being's ability to relate universally to its environment, its conspecifics, and itself resides in several human capacities that derive from human tool use and language: humans can relate to objects as such, they have world-openness, they have ontological preunderstanding (knowing Being *as* Being), they achieve reciprocity of perspectives with other human beings, they possess self-awareness and self-reflection, they possess rule-governed generative competences.

11. *The German Ideology,* loc. cit. (Landshut edition), p. 357.

12. This could not be accounted for adequately in either Darwinian or Hegelian terms. A conceptual scheme that can account for the self-transcendence of nature is presented in Karl Popper, "Evolution and the Tree of Knowledge," in *Objective Knowledge* (Oxford: Oxford University Press, 1972).

13. On search strategies, see Herbert Simon, *The Sciences of the Artificial* (Cambridge, Mass.: M.I.T. Press, 1969), pp. 67–72.

14. The construction of Marx's theory given here is, of course, not found in Marx in this form. It is an attempted reconstruction of Marxian theory in accordance with recent theory of revolution, particularly Popper's model referred to in note 12 above.

15. Ernest G. Schachtel, *Metamorphosis* (New York: Basic Books, 1959), p. 49.

16. Ibid., p. 52.

17. Ibid., p. 53.

18. Ibid., p. 54.

19. Ibid., p. 52.

20. In Karl Marx and Friedrich Engels, *Basic Writings on Politics and Philosophy*, ed. Lewis S. Feuer (New York: Doubleday Anchor, 1959), p. 18. Marx's idea of a class whose interest was general emancipation and the implications of this idea for critical theory are discussed in William Leiss, "Critical Theory and Its Future," *Political Theory*, II (1974), pp. 338–343.

21. Robert Heilbroner, "The Human Prospect," in *The New York Review of Books*, Jan. 24, 1974, p. 30.

22. Ibid., p. 31.

23. See my "The Critical Theory of Frankfurt," in *The Times Literary Supplement*, Oct. 4, 1974.

24. Much of the following is based on the work of Jürgen Habermas. See, in particular, the following works: *Toward a Rational Society* (Boston: Beacon Press, 1970); *Knowledge and Human Interests* (Boston: Beacon Press, 1971); *Theory and Practice* (Boston: Beacon Press, 1973); *Legitimation Crisis* (Boston: Beacon Press, 1975); *Theorie der Gesellschaft oder Sozialtechnologie* (Frankfurt am Main: Suhrkamp, 1971); *Kultur und Kritik* (Frankfurt am Main: Suhrkamp, 1973); *The Communication Theory of Society* (Gauss Lecture, Princeton University, 1971) (typescript); "Zur Entwicklung der Interaktionskompetenz" (mimeo); "Toward a Theory of Communicative Competence," in Hans Peter Dreitzel (ed.), *Recent Sociology No. 2* (New York: Macmillan, 1970); "Toward a Reconstruction of Historical Materialism," in *Theory and Society*, II (1975), pp. 287–300; "Zur Rekonstruktion des historischen Materialismus" (mimeo); "Wahrheitstheorien," in Helmut Fahrenback (ed.), *Wirklichkeit und Reflexion: Walter Schulz zum 60. Geburtstag* (Pfullingen: Neske, 1973); and, with Dieter Henrich, *Zwei Reden* (Frankfurt am Main: Suhrkamp, 1974).

25. Habermas, *Theorie der Gesellschaft oder Sozialtechnologie* and *The Communication Theory of Society*.

26. Habermas, "Wahrheitstheorien," p. 255 f.

27. One aim of the theory of embeddedness in nature is to provide a more concrete foundation for Habermas' conception of the knowledge-constitutive interest of emancipatory knowledge. See *Knowledge and Human Interests*, part three.

28. See Edgar Morin, *Le paradigme perdu: la nature humaine* (Paris: Seuil, 1973).

29. This conception is based on Popper's model of genetic dualism in "Evolution and the Tree of Knowledge." See note 12 above. Popper distinguishes between the behavior-controlling and executive parts of an organism and proposes their independent mutation in the following manner: "Once a new aim or tendency or disposition, or a new skill, or a new way of behaving has evolved in the central propensity structure, this fact will influence the effects of natural selection in such a way that previously unfavourable (though potentially favourable) mutations become actually favourable if they support the newly established tendency. *But this means that the evolution of the executive organs will become directed by that tendency or aim, and thus 'goal-directed.'* " Op. cit., p. 278.

30. This is, strictly speaking, a simplification undertaken for reasons of space. Embeddedness cannot be completely "eliminated." The pathos of idealism comes precisely from denying that element of embeddedness which is inherent in homo sapiens. However, embeddedness can be surmounted and rendered inoperative through a process in which the acceptance of the ineradicable component of embeddedness is an essential part. See the reference in note 32 below.

31. See, for example, James H. and Marge Craig, *Synergic Power: Beyond Domination and Permissiveness* (Berkeley: Proactive Press, 1973); Harvey Jackins, *The Human Side of Human Beings* (Seattle: Rational Island Publishers, 1965) and *The Human Situation* (Seattle: Rational Island Publishers, 1973); Jay Haley, *Strategies of Psychotherapy* (New York: Grune & Stratton, 1963); Bert Somers, "Re-evaluation Therapy" (type-

script); Sally Hufbauer and Shierry M. Weber, "A Co-Listening Manual" (typescript); Branko Horvat, Mihailo Marković, and Rudi Supek (eds.), *Self-Governing Socialism* (White Plains, N.Y.: International Arts and Sciences Press, 1975), 2 volumes; Thich Nhat Hanh, *Zen Keys* (Garden City: Doubleday Anchor, 1974); and Oscar Shaftel, *An Understanding of the Buddha* (New York: Schocken, 1974).

32. An attempt to provide an integrated critical approach to practice integrating all three levels in my *Zen Socialism* (Boston: Beacon Press, forthcoming). Many of the ideas in the present paper have been developed in collaboration with Shierry M. Weber.

CRITICAL THEORY AND HERMENEUTICS: THE DEBATE BETWEEN HABERMAS AND GADAMER

DIETER MISGELD

The critique of social heteronomy, of modes of social organization and of beliefs sustaining them, which subject individuals to universal regimentation by anonymous social processes, is intrinsically linked to the emancipatory intentions of theorizing activity in critical theory. It has inspired its studies on authority and its critique of the institutions of bourgeois life. It has ultimately guided its indictment of technology and science as vehicles of a progress so irresistible and beyond the reflective control of those carried along by it, that progress appears as irresistible regression and makes communal reflection and decision about the direction of such progress impossible.

Its diagnosis of the time is that a natural and confiding relationship to authority has become impossible and a cultivation of the contents of prescientific and humanistic culture cannot take place without resentment and in a spirit of urbanity. Advocates for a withdrawal from the social and epistemological position of the autonomy of reason and of the critically and autonomously reasoning intellectual have been the targets of determined Frankfurt school critique. This is the more so since conservative critics of progress at times have recommended subjection to the imperatives of industrial-technological production and a blindly obedient acceptance of the attendant processes of authoritarian social mobilization.

It amounts to a major reorientation of critical theory, then, when Juergen Habermas adopts heremeneutical reflection as a viable orientation in the logic of social science, and enlists its support for a critique of the objectivist features of empirical-analytical social science, thus developing the theme of a "critique of instrumental reason" with more clearly methodological intentions. For Habermas enlists Hans-Georg Gadamer's *Wahrheit und Methode* in support of his critique of the objectivism resulting from adherence to the natural scientific paradigm in social science. Yet Gadamer introduces as a theme of his hermeneutics the "rehabilitation of authority and tradition." He criticizes the enlightenment, not for its reversion into mythology, the mythology of total control over nature, ultimately leading only to the control over men, which is Adorno/Horkheimer's position in *Dialectic of Enlightenment,* but for its abstract opposition of reason, authority, and tradition, as if all tradition and all authority were unreasonable. Gadamer even proposes that hermeneutics take an ontological turn and not just be a doctrine of method. He pursues Heideggerian motives, taking the existence of what is as a guiding theme for an analysis of interpretive understanding in its historicity and a theory of language. Due to his ontological orientation, Gadamer's scepticism about objectifying knowledge extends even beyond science to the reflective consciousness of our social situation which critical theory intends to achieve.

Habermas' interest in Gadamer can best be understood, I claim, in terms of a shift in the orientation of critical theory: the critique of ontology, while still a requirement for critical theory, no longer has priority equal to that of a critique of science and technology as ideology. Adorno's position, as well as the later Heidegger's, indicates the lack of resourcefulness of the metaphysical tradition, Hegel's philosophy included. Heidegger's philosophy is inarticulate and mystifies the historical facts of technology and science as a fate of being *(Seinsgeschick).* Adorno confines himself to the posture of the "philosophizing intellectual,"[1] refusing to elaborate a theory and the methodological relationships required by a critical theory of the present age with practical intentions. An injunction against organising knowledge in a systematic form bars Adorno from developing both a stringent argumentative basis for the validity of critical theory qua theory and a clarification of a socially emancipatory praxis required by the theory. A combination of hermeneutics, emancipatory reflection and causal analytical knowledge can provide a new basis for critical theory, imposing a critical limit on the absolutism of a knowledge of society, really only gained self-reflectively, as in Adorno's case, and therefore solipsistically.

Gadamer pursues a critique of the epistemological subject's role in historical understanding which shows how the subject, even if he is armed with the methods of science, is not able to extricate himself from the very traditions which he attempts to study, as if he, e.g., as a historian, was fully independent from them. The resourcefulness of historical understanding, Gadamer argues, cannot be affixed to the employment of an objective method, making events and ideas of the historical past the object of an explanatory science—just as nature.

His critique of the autocracy of scientific method is linked, however, with a critique of the Cartesian model of self-certainty and its effects in the epistemology of historical understanding and comprehension. Historical understanding is described by him as a communicative understanding achieved in the medium of speech. It cannot be properly comprehended in terms of a model of self-reflective knowledge, aiming at self-certainty rather than opening oneself to what the other or a subject matter "says." Hence, Habermas' interest in Gadamer's hermeneutics cannot merely result from a superficial fascination with the analogy between, on the one hand, Horkheimer/Adorno's frequent critical references to the solipsistic posture of bourgeois individualism in its epistemology, as represented by the Cartesian heritage, and, on the other hand, Gadamer's critique of the autonomy of judgment which the historian presumes to possess vis-a-vis the historical past. It may rather be motivated by the insight that critical theory was not capable of developing its critique of "bourgeois" individualism by making an implicitly thematized idea of communal reflection a central topic. Habermas, it seems, noticed that hermeneutical reflection on historical understanding had faithfully described the origin of understanding in the practice of communication and had, therefore, made communal reflection thematic. It had also discovered the practice of understanding as a social practice, that of interacting individuals, and in doing so, it had left the contemplative attitude behind, which Horkheimer/Adorno had named as a distinctive feature both of metaphysical and philosophical thought and of science.

Habermas however still feels that he is in a position to describe Gadamer as a conservative. This is so because Gadamer rehabilitates authority and tradition when he claims that true authority does not have to present itself in an authoritarian way, and describes recognition of authority as an invariant feature of historical understanding. The recognition of authority is an essential feature of an understanding not solipsistically certain of itself and dependent on the tradition context of language. It is a voluntary recognition due to the finite nature of understanding, and occurs, in hardly politically suspicious forms, whenever we affirm that a text of the historical past says something to us which we could not quite have learned in our contemporary environment or simply by discovering it on our own. It occurs as well whenever we find that we cannot conceive of ourselves without reference to a given order of social life (such as the state or the family), in spite of all its disorder. This is so even if the recognition of such order is usually tied to the recognition of the authority of those representing it. As provocative as Gadamer's theme of a rehabilitation of authority and tradition, in reaction to its enlightenment critique, may sound to Habermas' ears, it does not seem to warrant a mobilization of political invective. Habermas recognises too well that Gadamer's views follow from an intricate methodological position and an impressive analysis of the process of *Verstehen*. In this sense Gadamer's work represents the model of the critique of progress, to which critical theory must address itself. Today it is to surpass the fixed juxtaposition of the enlightenment's dedication to the pursuit of emancipation and social progress and of its counterpart—the *Gegenaufklaerung* or reaction-formation to enlightenment-critique and rationalism—which has dominated German philosophical consciousness from Hegel to Heidegger.

Habermas implicitly credits Gadamer with insights capable of focusing the perceptiveness of critical theory (for mere semblances of progress) and sees himself in a position to assimilate the elements of the critique of progress which hermeneutics brings to light. Habermas must share some aspects of Gadamer's conviction that our understanding of our historical past cannot be described as the linear and cumulatively proceeding acquisition of knowledge. Nor can communicative interaction and the reaching of understanding in it be defined in such a way. Being absorbed in the attempt to understand a subject matter is a feature of interpretive understanding. Consciousness of one's involvement as an ego is not required for succeeding to understand. But to be absorbed in one's task of understanding to the degree of self-forgetfulness is only possible where something tells us something such that we cannot refrain from listening. It "proves" its authority in this sense. Not all things, institutions, texts, or persons in the world can lay a similar claim to our attention and there is no class of items in the world, be they institutions or not, which we can single out in advance as having of necessity the "right" to expect the surrender of understanding and of reflection. The surrender rather occurs in the process of understanding.

Thus the "rehabilitation of authority and tradition" results from a reflection on the process of reaching an understanding. It is Gadamer's transcendental position which makes him interesting for Habermas and a transcendental orientation cannot *a limine* preclude any role for critical reflection. In giving an account of heremeneutical reflection Gadamer assimilates the theory of action to that of communicative interaction. The latter orientation gives rise to his particular critique of instrumental reason and to a *methodological* foundation for the rehabilitation of authority and tradition.

The following are six considerations in terms of which Gadamer's hermeneutics could become relevant to Habermas' redesign of a foundation for critical theory:

(1) If critical theory is no longer certain of its ability to comprehend "the logic of history" and if it cannot resign itself into merely formulating the experience of the irrationality of its course (Adorno), a clarification of its logical and epistemological status becomes urgent. Critical theory, interpreted by Habermas as a philosophy of history with political intentions, is to take notice of a theory of historical understanding which (a) is distinct from a theory of historical explanation as it occurs in history as a science, and (b) describes the role of interpretive understanding in social practice. Hermeneutics takes account of both these considerations, because it takes historical understanding to be a practice of life and describes the practice of life as the practice of speech, which articulates our historical existence in communicative interaction.

(2) Critical theory is concerned with the critique of instrumental reason. Critical theory takes itself as the reflective element of social practice. It will find a theory appealing which sees itself as belonging to a practice as well. Hermeneutics is the reflective element of the

continuous appropriation of tradition in which we engage as historically existing beings.

(3) Critical theory has become a critique of instrumental reason. If technology and science have become a background ideology under present historical conditions, the critique of political economy is to be superseded by a critique of those modes of collective interpretation of our social situation which prevent us from perceiving it as a situation to be practically solved and not merely technically mastered. Hermeneutics builds on the distinction between praxis and techné. It also attempts to describe interpretive understanding as distinct from the objectifying methods of the sciences. Hermeneutics can help critical theory clarify what the difference is between solving practical problems of the kind encountered in communicative interaction (e.g., all those involving social norms), and those to be solved with the assistance of scientifically instructed techniques of instrumental control. Hermeneutics, which is heir to the late Husserl's and the early Heidegger's phenomenology, can help achieve this, since it represents something like the "linguistic" turn of phenomenology. A theory of "ordinary language communication" is required to delineate clearly the boundaries of communicative experience over against scientifically objectifiable data of experience.

(4) Critical theory has become increasingly critical of the "objectivist" features in Marx's philosophy of history. Marx could not develop the idea of a critique of ideologies, of "objective" illusions, so the criticism goes, because he equated critique with natural science and thus distorted reflection naturalistically. He also assimilated communicative interaction to socially organized labour. In doing so, the connections between the critique of illusion and a theory of interaction became obscured. Hermeneutics implies the outline of a theory of communicative interaction. Its concentration on dialogue with the "eminent" philosophical and poetical texts of the historical past assimilates our past history to interaction. As such it is a counter-model to Marx. Critical theory will have to place itself between or above both a materialist and a language interpretive theory of history.

(5) Gadamer clearly designates the limits of scientific method over against a reflection on communicative interaction. In Habermas' words: "I take Gadamer's authentic achievement to be the demonstration that hermeneutical understanding, with transcendental necessity,

is referred to the articulation of a self-understanding, which provides orientation of action."[2]

This is accomplished, for Gadamer, by seeking out experiences of truth transcending the controlling sphere of scientific method. In them we understand ourselves in such a manner that our own being comes into question. In confronting our historical heritage, we learn to face conceptions of how we are to be which may question what we are. Here the very own being of the one who knows comes into play. The words we use to express such self-understanding are the words in which we express the orienting effect which experiences have. They are, then, not stripped of historical content, nor organized by a theory. They do not have the form of propositions asserting facts. They are not like science-words which so objectify "experience that it no longer contains any historical element."[3] We may learn to risk our preunderstandings and prejudgments in acquiring an openness for new experience in which we experience ourselves as transformed and changed. The methodical exercise of scientific research may prove to be the pursuit of an illusory insulation from experience, if the truth discovered in it is the only one to which we are committed. We are then trapped in the historical logic of instrumental reason, in which we become as alien to ourselves as to our historical tradition. In this sense, hermeneutics is a critique of instrumental reason.

Critical sociology also has an interest in defending the claim to truth which may arise out of communicative experience. The latter is not an object of "scientific method." It is better described as a participatory relation of the understanding subject to the subject confronting him *(alter ego)*. Here the "understanding subject must invest a part of his subjectivity"[4] in order to acquire the truth of the other as subject. The dialectic of recognition does not correspond to the logic of objectifying statements and controlled observation. In particular types of participatory understanding, e.g., the therapeutic dialogue, one may even realise a particular truth-claim, e.g., a claim to authenticity. Here the suffering surrender of self-deceptions clearly is not only a result to be achieved by scientific method, or the result of a technique instrumentally applied. I must have become a question for myself, in order later to claim a more authentic relationship to myself. In this sense, critical theory is a critique of instrumental reason like hermeneutics.

(6) This is not all, however, for (a) the empirical social sciences

mostly do not allow for a participatory understanding of data in which access to data via the understanding of meaning can be achieved. A critique of the empirical social sciences is required in order to extend the hermeneutical critique of "instrumental reason." It must ensure a "communicative access" to the data of social science and explain the validity of comprehending society in historical terms. (b) Critical theory is not hermeneutics: it aims at a critique of society and of our history. It is oriented toward emancipation from our historical past, in so far as this history can be seen as a history of the exercise of domination and repression. Here critical theory joins forces with science against hermeneutics. Science is to provide us with new means of control over our natural condition. Critical theory must incorporate science if it is to be a critique of tradition. The vantage point justifying this critique, however, cannot be derived from the rationality of scientific discourse. Such discourse does not point toward a more rational form of life. It can be engaged in monologically and does not require a participatory understanding of others, as realized in dialogue. Yet the notion of emancipation, in the name of which critical theory turns against tradition, implies reference to a shared form of life in which we have come to an understanding with one another which need no longer be revoked. It is with regard to the possibility of formulating such a notion of an ideal form of life that hermeneutics will take its final critical stance over against critical theory.[5] Against these objections critical theory must prove itself viable.

But we must first consider how the hermeneutical project is assimilated by Habermas and what he leaves aside in doing so. Critical theory and hermeneutics both envisage a critique of instrumental reason as the major task confronting them under present historical conditions. Yet they approach the task in different ways. This can best be seen by noting how Habermas approaches Gadamer's hermeneutics and then by pointing to features in Gadamer's work which are not easily fitted into the location designed for hermeneutics in Habermas' metatheoretical reflections.

Habermas proposes to make use of Gadamer's systematic reflection on interpretive understanding in the context of a theory of interpretive procedures in the social sciences.[6] These are to be seen as supplementing explanatory methods in the social sciences. In opening access to meaning generated in communicative interaction as the basic "datum" of social science, hermeneutics can help remedy an instrumentalist distortion rampant in the social sciences. It can rectify their concern with objectifiable and technically instrumental knowledge, their interest in a knowledge controlling experience by making it schematically accessible and repeatable. Yet hermeneutics is relevant to the project of a critical social science in an even deeper sense. It provides a mode of reflection which makes it possible to diagnose the state of the social sciences as suffering from the said instrumentalist delusion. And in doing so, it also lets the will to intervene in the practical context of life, still typical of critical theory even in its most sublimated form, become more problematic for itself. However, this latter aspect is not openly acknowledged by Habermas, nor is it clear what his position is on this matter even now. There seems to be no reason to believe that the preconception with which Habermas entered into the debate with Gadamer has ever fundamentally changed, in spite of significant alterations. Habermas is convinced that hermeneutical reflection upon the interpretive nature of textual comprehension and speaking must be so transformed as to become effective within the sciences or not at all. It must be severed from its all too strong ties to the tradition of *Geisteswissenschaft.*

What makes it possible to conceive of hermeneutics as a critique of instrumental reason? In *Truth and Method* Gadamer takes the *Geisteswissenschaften* and methodological reflection upon them as his point of departure. He argues against Dilthey's view (standing for those of many others) that "what is called 'method' in modern science is everywhere the same."[7] He says: "What makes the human sciences into sciences can be understood more easily from the tradition of the concept of *Bildung* than from the concept of method in modern science."[8] He proposes a refashioning of what we think is peculiar to the understanding of one's heritage in literature, history, and the arts, and what is typical of the appreciation of art and of faithfulness to custom and tradition. Since Kant, philosophers have told us that such understandings, unless supported by some sort of scientific method or theory, cannot be called knowledge. The consequence could be, however, that we no longer can account for the way in which the reading of literature, the experience of art, or historical tradition are "humanizing" influences and make us civilized. Denied their legitimacy in losing the dignified status of items and modes of "knowledge," these experiences are relegated to a subordinate role in our scheme of things and what we take the world to be. They thus become elements of a practically irrelevant subculture. For Gadamer, therefore, all those dimensions of our historical experience, where strict methods do not yet play an exclusive role, are to be rehabilitated as a kind of knowledge. Only then can we hope to recover their moral and practical relevance. We require this for a critique of instrumental reason. Hermeneutics cannot merely be a "doctrine of method," not even for the *Geisteswissenschaften*. If there are experiences of truth transcending the sphere of control of scientific method, interpretation is to be seen as an element of all "prescientific" experience, and the phenomenon of *Verstehen* and of adequate interpretation is not just a special problem for a doctrine of method in the *Geisteswissenschaften*. The hermeneutical phenomenon is basically not a problem of method at all.

Gadamer builds on Heidegger's existential analytic. Interpretive understanding designates the basic movement of human existence, which constitutes its finitude and historicity, and hence encompasses the whole of its experience of the world. The movement of understanding is encompassing and universal. This we take to represent the "ontological" posture of hermeneutics, as opposed to the notion of interpretive understanding as a set of procedures peculiar and restricted to the humanities. They, rather, "are joined with modes of experience which lie outside science: with the experience of philosophy, of art, and of history itself."[9] The authentic claim of hermeneutics is a philosophical one for Gadamer: what is at issue "is not what we do or what we ought to do, but what happens to us, over and above our wanting and doing."[10] The concerns of hermeneutics are distinct from epistemological or methodological ones. They are "ontological." The process of understanding, understood ontologically, is co-extensive with an experience of our world and history, in which we are not masters of either or both. This, indeed, is the meaning which experience mostly conveys to us. Becoming experienced, then, does not have the sense of acquiring a skill and successfully exercising it. It means that one has learnt how to live, possibly without being able fully to account for it. Knowing how to live is a form of wisdom and does not always and necessarily imply mastery of the conditions of life. It may imply a recognition not only of what one cannot change, but even more an insight into what one ought not to attempt to change. It follows that meaning can be present, even where we do not expect it: "I maintain that the hermeneutical problem is universal and basic for all interhuman experience, both of history and of the present moment, precisely because of the fact that meaning can be experienced, even where it is not actually intended."[11]

Gadamer takes interpretive understanding to be an element of all activities of human life. As such, hermeneutical reflection on the interpretive element in practices of life is not restricted to the analysis of phenomena of reflective appropriation of meaning. Not only what we can be conscious of as our motives for action and for the application of interpretive procedures in every day life counts as a hermeneutical phenomenon. Subjective meaning-intentions, which we can explicitly ascertain as our own and objectify, only describe a limited range of those meanings, in which we *participate*. What we participate in, be it a "form of life," an institution, a social role, or a tradition, we know about somehow, but we cannot account for it by giving an objective account of it of a kind that would not require or even *a limine* forbid the use of personal pronouns. We may not be able to express it at all in some form of conceptually organized knowledge. What we participate in, in a most fundamental way, is language. We can never account for language by reference to principles of a reasoning activity which is initially conceived as outside or beyond language.

We participate in language, Gadamer says, by "belonging" to it. And we can say that in speaking we appropriate meanings of words, without being able to account for them merely in terms of our own meaning-intentions. History, as mediated by language, gains supremacy over our individual consciousness, expectations, and practical intentions. Hence we speak of the *tradition-context of language,* as that to which we belong. And this is so, not because language in the sense of our capacity to speak is a generic characteristic of human beings, true of them in all their history, but because in language, our use of it, tradition speaks, or our heritage. Language *is* our heritage, but it speaks as the historical past to which we still belong. Gadamer describes our belonging to the tradition context of language (qua speech) as analogous to the manner in which we are conscious of participating in a game. "We have seen that a game has its being, not in the consciousness or actions of the players, but, on the contrary, it draws these into its own realm and fills them with its spirit. The player experiences the game as for him an overpowering reality . . ."[12] Hermeneutics takes the totality of our experience of the world to be like this and therefore turns toward ontology, taking the experience of language in speaking as its guiding theme. It finds that our having a world is dependent upon the availability of language and the experience of the world in language is absolute. The hermeneutical problem reveals itself as universal. It reaches as far as our practices of speaking, universally occurring interpretive processes and activities, and is as broad as our modes of experiencing whatever is. In all of this, language remains essentially the language of dialogue. It "acquires its reality only in the process of communicating and of reaching an understanding." Thus it is not "a mere means of communication."[13] Our relation to our past is of such kind, as long as the "tradition" of speaking continues, in which we speak out of the tradition context of language. And we will always do so, since we cannot objectify or transcend the "tradition" context of language toward, e.g., the material conditions of factual history, as if we could look at language as a tradition context from outside it. Language is always ahead of our understanding it, as is history.

Gadamer perceives the insight into the ontological nature of the hermeneutical problem and its universality to be of critical importance for a continued anchoring of human life in the preservation, assimilation, and continuation of a heritage, and for the disciplined carrying-out of these concerns in the humanities, if not elsewhere as well. Hermeneutics is to gather critical force over against the technological enmity to history. Practical motives emerge for his concern with historical tradition and the interpretive procedures of everyday life communication, in which a heritage becomes part of contemporary forms of life. Technology, scientific method, and even the rationalism of the tradition of critique in philosophy from Kant to Hegel, Marx, Husserl, and the Frankfurt School have something in common, in Gadamer's view. They either aim at presuppositionless objective knowledge and ignore the historical embeddedness of those modes of knowing which convey self-understanding, or they aim at knowledge having the practical effect of making societal and historical actors totally rational. Both lend themselves to a fateful combination of technological and political utopianism, since both aim at the substitution of historically evolved institutions and mores by more rationally organized ones. Usually political utopianism and the idea of emancipation from circumstances, which are there by "nature" or historically grown conventions, attempt to find support by using scientifically objective methods in order to evince factors from the context of social life, which stand "behind" the actors, and are not part of their self-understanding, but which are the really "determining" ones. In all these cases the parameters of our self-understanding, implicit in the common prephilosophical formation of it, are ignored. Standards of rationality standing outside or beyond our historically structured experience of interaction situations are applied to these situations. The tradition context of language then appears as a source of continuous misunderstandings. Gadamer states: "Is the phenomenon of understanding adequately defined, when I say: Understanding means avoiding misunderstanding? Isn't there rather in truth something like a 'supporting' consensus?"[14] Thus, although the disciplined process of interpreting tradition is only necessitated because of "the lack of immediate understandability of texts handed down to us historically," ultimately every successful "appropriation of tradition is dissolved into a new and distinct familiarity, in which it belongs to us and we to it."[15] Understanding and consent are not only in question, says Gadamer, they are also underlying elements.

A difficulty lies in an appropriate explication of the manner in which "consent" underlies. Gadamer seems to indicate the following steps toward its solution. The interpretive appropriation of, let us say, a historical text, cannot simply suspend nor can it ever completely overcome the prejudgments, in terms of which we formulate our initial understanding. They are unavoidably part of a "preunderstanding." This is the more so, since preunderstanding is the essential element in what Gadamer calls *wirkungsgeschichtliches Bewusstsein,* a "consciousness of the effectivity of history within understanding itself."[16] History is ever at work in our consciousness of our own situation, so much so that we can never place it in front of ourselves, and Habermas' suggestion to link "tradition" to other structures of the social life-world, as "labour" and "domination," has a constructivist ring from this point of view, giving it the appearance of an idealist delusion. This is why Gadamer says that *wirkungsgeschichtliches Bewusstsein* is more being than consciousness, and that being is never fully manifest. The being that is never fully manifest might even encompass the basic order of our being, which is not susceptible to volitional interference and cannot be "produced." It rather is to be respected.

Once more Gadamer's ontological (rather than "methodological") accentuation of hermeneutics becomes visible and the limits which he sees for any emancipatory practice are more obvious. There seem to be for him some "fundamental" realities of human life, which must remain inviolate or will simply remain so on their own accord. It is not possible, however, to state unequivocally which they are, or whether they are institutions such as the family. Applied to scientific progress, this means: "Whatever science is able to achieve, it will not be able to transcend a limit, which perhaps no one knows and which, however, is placed before everything." In this sense, obviously, Gadamer does not correspond to the stereotype of a conservative critic of progress. Some fundamental "orders" of human life, which function as such limits, are mentioned: "Birth and death, youth and age, home-country ("Heimat") and alien world, commitment and freedom."[17] Nowhere do his remarks provide illustrations of real historical concreteness, and we cannot infer that particular systems of government, values, the major religions, the monogamous family, or even philosophy, constitute such boundary conditions to historical change. Biological-physiological factors like "birth and death," but also moral ones like "freedom and responsibility" are not to be taken as anthropological constants, defining human nature without any reference to historical interpretations of them. They are rather boundary lines for a commonality of understanding which is constantly built up and maintained throughout history. What they "mean," one might say, is dependent on interpretations, provided by the members of society themselves, acting and interacting historically by reference to them. In this sense we cannot "define" them as such. They can be described only in terms of the interpretive procedures actors and understanding individuals apply to them.

Hermeneutics remains phenomenology, in the sense of employing the method of "intentional analysis." But it also asserts that "meaning can be experienced even where it is not actually intended." The more fundamental the orders referred to are, the less it seems they can be intended, and the more they assert themselves on their own accord, with a power of persuasion which cannot be broken by reflection. It is not just the order of a common language Gadamer has in mind here. And of it we can easily say that it asserts itself without coercion and cannot merely be viewed as an order of force or rule. There are sociologically and historically more concrete conditions of our self-understanding as well, of which we cannot dispense in understanding and which exert a normative force. This is why Gadamer proceeds to rehabilitate authority and tradition, as he puts it polemically.

In *Wahrheit und Methode* this has its place in the context of the critique of historicism. It is again aimed at describing limitations to a rationalist conception of understanding, and in this case the discreditation by the enlightenment of both prejudgment and authority is under attack. On it historicism builds. If the model of "self-reflection" established by Descartes is joined with scientific method, the contrariety of reason and authority results. The authority of reason alone makes all claims to authority based on the continuity of tradition appear false and invalidates all prejudgments based on considering oneself as dependent on this continuity. The method of universal doubt takes the place of a historical understanding which initiates into the normative traditions of a culture. Tradition is operative on us by forming our personal and social preoccupations before we can even pass judgment on the manner in which they are operative. There are legitimate prejudgments and the prejudgments (preoccupations) of the "individual, far more than his judgments, constitute the historical reality of his being."[18] Universal self-reflection cannot be the vehicle for universal emancipation, because it is not attainable. Our dependency on the continuity of traditions of understanding is a fact which has been kept repressed from modern historical consciousness. This repression makes us assume a greater temporal distance between the modern epoch and its historical predecessors than is warranted and is possible for us to cope with. Gadamer agrees with Hegel when he considers our humanity to have been brought forth historically. And understanding ourselves as belonging to such a history becomes a norm of interpretive understanding, simply because this is the norm in terms of which we have historically learnt to understand what constitutes humanity. There are no ahistorical social norms. "Long before we understand ourselves through the process of self-examination, we understand ourselves in a self-evident way in the family, society, and state in which we live." This is the demonstrable meaning of the following metaphor, putting the issue emphatically. "The self-awareness of the individual is only a flickering in the closed circuits of historical life."[19]

What is the view of social institutions indicated by Gadamer? Family and state would seem to be supra-individual aspects of historical life, to which the individual finds himself subordinated in any case. But even the historically more variable and contingent constellations of factors, in which we may encounter family or state, display much more mutual consistency, continuity, and resiliency to change than we are usually willing to attribute to them. We are victims of a perspectival illusion, so to speak, if we conceive ourselves as able to achieve emancipation from tradition and a history, which, from the scientific point of view, may appear as a faulty experimental design. The prevalent attitude toward authority is an example in turn. Concrete forms of authority are meant, such as those of parent, teacher, or expert. These are "authorities" which we all not only have in fact always recognized and do recognize, but their recognition is "unavoidable." In other words, it is inconceivable that we could, e.g., ever make sense of a process of education, even if described in terms of a process of "self-formation," as by Habermas, without attributing some legitimate role to such "authorities." This is the critical insight which Gadamer consistently turns against Habermas' defense of the critique of tradition, authority, and prejudgment. Gadamer of course realizes that the Enlightenment was concerned with a particular kind of authority, against which it pitted its demand that the "authority of reason" replace faith in "merely" historical authority. It intended the substitution of "mere" authority by one's own judgment. However, when we construe the relation between reason and authority as one of absolute incompatibility, we do not allow for the possibility of all those actually occurring cases where authority is recognized, not on grounds of blind obedience, but from an insight into its justification. There is authority which is freely recognized and seen as "natural." It does not have to present itself in an authoritarian way, says Gadamer. It can best be compared to the unassuming authority of an expert, who is consulted to provide advice within the range of his expertise and does not venture beyond it.

Gadamer believes traditions, customs, and mores to manifest their authority in a similar way. They are "freely" adopted by us, although we cannot create them out of our independent insight. The hermeneutical reflection on methods in the humanities therefore makes Gadamer conclude that the interpretation of texts and other works cannot simply be divorced from historical experience and the manner in which we conduct ourselves toward the past in life. In it the real concern is not distantiation and freedom from what is inherited. "Rather, we always stand within traditions—and this is no objectifying process, i.e., we do not conceive of what tradition says as something other, something alien. It is always part of us."[20] Gadamer then aims at an overcoming of the abstract opposition between a most natural, inadvertent appropriation and preservation of tradition and historical research. Such research comes to be seen as the merely more deliberate carrying out of a reflective appropriation of tradition, which our pretheoretical preservation of it already is engaged in. Hermeneutics, therefore, does not propose the suspension of all claims to our attentiveness emerging from this ongoing process of assimilation and transformation. It does not pursue the chimera of "unprejudiced" science.

Gadamer's rehabilitation of authority and prejudgment should be taken as an illustration for the dependency of our schemata of interpretation on the tradition-context of language. Preunderstandings of historical texts, brought to a reflective presence in hermeneutical insight, never can be put aside once and for all. They issue in new preunderstandings or in our being "preoccupied" with something meant in novel ways. In this sense we must speak of an objectivity which is proper to language over against the speakers and their naturally acquired communicative competence. The issue of the universality of hermeneutics reveals itself then as that of the extent to which knowledge is dependent on the tradition-context of language. Gadamer therefore does not develop a theory of interpretive understanding in order to rectify the course of the social sciences. Nor does he propose that interpretive understanding be joined with explanatory procedures in the social sciences.

Habermas, in adopting the latter view, must deny the claim to universality of hermeneutics. Yet critical theory for him is to share Gadamer's insight that interpretive understanding, a disciplined art developed in the interpretation of texts and the experience of discourse, is an historical and communicative practice. It issues in the application of what is understood to the situation of the one who understands. Unless hermeneutical understanding is thoroughly self-applicative, there is no understanding. Hermeneutical understanding is as reflective, in this sense, as critical theory is to be, in Habermas' design. A communicative access to the data of social science implies, according to Gadamer, the recognition of the dependency of theorizing on the modes of understanding embedded in social practice, where they are always at work. The critical theory of society will have to begin with them and return to their context. Every theoretically or methodogically secured insight from an abstraction from communicative experience is to be retranslated into this context, where there are no privileged knowers: "In a process of enlightenment there can only be participants."[21]

Yet critical theory makes a further claim. Habermas concedes that language can be described as functioning in the manner of a "metainstitution, on which all societal institutions are dependent. For social action only constitutes itself in ordinary language communication."[22] However, Habermas also sees that language as the context of tradition revealed in speech must also be seen as dependent on societal processes which do not manifest themselves completely *in* language. Apparently, the relation of such societal processes to language as a "metainstitution" is to be conceived analogically to the role of "unconscious motives" in our understanding of our own (individual) motives for action. Such processes, and, as we should add, structures, are "labour" (mode of production and productive forces) and "domination" (in the sense of institutions controlling or legitimizing means of coercion and power). "Labour" and "domination," we must assume, consist of sets of infralinguistic conditions, which "determine" the constitution of social action in communicative interaction, by providing for it objective conditions. In these conditions the constraints of reality reveal themselves as external nature, to be rendered controllable and to be reflected in the procedures of scientifically instructed technical control, and as the coercive and compelling nature of drives, reflected in societally approved modes of repression. This is why we must comprehend social action in terms of an objective context, which consists of language, labour, and domination.

Thus critical theory demands the self-limitation of the hermeneutical approach on behalf of critical reflection, which cannot be thought of but as taking an interest in its own generation by emancipating itself from tradition. For it, reaching reciprocal agreement in the discursive examination of reciprocal and competing truth claims is a normative concept. A frame of reference is to be discovered which allows us to transcend the context of tradition as such. Only then tradition can also be criticized.

But Habermas anticipates the possible hermeneutical objection: "How shall such frame of reference be legitimated if not itself by the appropriation of tradition?"[23] Critical theory thus has complicated matters further for itself. If it is to adhere to the view that in a process of enlightenment there cannot be any privileged knowers, how can it wish to transcend the context of tradition as such? For in doing so, assuming it can be done, must not new privileges accrue to the one developing the "frame of reference" which permits the projection of a freedom from tradition? And must he not rely on a conceptual equipment not available to ordinary communicative competence? Thus, would he not encounter the hazards of having to translate back into contexts of communicative experience a theory formulated on the basis of abstracting from this experience? Habermas' problems arise because he aims at an all-inclusive theory of the contemporary age. Yet he also wants to retain a linkage with praxis, which he himself understands as not capable of being fully guided by a theory. For praxis has its own grounds of intelligibility, independent from a theory making it the object of comprehensive reflection.

I suggest that Habermas' subsequent work is to be interpreted in terms of this dilemma. The theory of communicative competence and the project of a universal pragmatics is to establish the basis for a communication theory of society, in which the data base of social science is secured in such a way that the social scientist is found to be one of his own data, in effect constituting them as a speaker of a natural language. The project of a theory of social evolution, focussing on the logic of worldviews, as well as the theory of crises in late capitalism, is to be viewed as an attempt to transcend the boundaries of what can be understood by merely reflecting upon natural language communication. It is claimed that then it becomes possible to explain how historically specific modes of communication originate, and how their distortions are systematically organised. Yet the ability to decipher them as distorted cannot issue from mere reliance on historical reconstruction or a reconstructionist theory of the pragmatic universals of speech. It also, at least, requires that one risk one's preunderstanding as an act of practical discourse, and that one engage in a communicative action denying, in its accomplishment, its own communal basis. Such a rupture, opening a cleavage in communally shared understandings, cannot be secure of its own groundedness no matter how elaborate the theories instructing it. It remains a practical, situated activity. In this sense, critical theory may still be seen as dependent upon a hermeneutical element, the impossibility of securing intersubjective understanding before we have entered into a situated discourse with others about the specific matters at hand in this very situation. Here critical theory will once again encounter tradition. It can no longer maintain itself on the level of tradition transcended. Thus the very confrontation between a hypothetical anticipation of possibilities beyond all known traditions (and societies) and the reality of tradition will take place within a tradition-bound situation. Reflection transcending tradition will either have to learn to appraise itself as involved in the formation of tradition or forego the possibility of becoming practical. It is not altogether clear yet whether Habermas is willing to recognize the priority of practice in this sense.

NOTES

1. This is the title of an essay by Habermas in: *Philosophische-Politische Profile* (Frankfurt: Suhrkamp, 1971), dedicated to Theodor W. Adorno.

2. J. Habermas, "Zur Logik der Sozialwissenschaften," in *Philosophische Rundschau* (Tübingen: Mohr) vol. 5, p. 174.

3. Hans-Georg Gadamer, *Wahrheit und Methode,* 3rd ed. (Tübingen: Mohr, 1972); English trans. *Truth and Method* (New York: Seabury Press, 1975), p. 311.

4. Habermas, *Theory and Practice* (Boston: Beacon Press, 1973), pp. 10–11.

5. Cf. Gadamer, in "On the Scope and Function of Hermeneutical Reflection," Chicago, *Continuum,* vol. 8, 1970.

6. Habermas approaches Gadamer in terms of these issues in "Zur Logik der Sozialwissenschaften" in pp. 149–176. His careful review of *Truth and Method* initiated the debate whose stages have been collected in *Hermeneutik und Ideologiekritik* (Frankfurt: Suhrkamp, 1971).

7. Gadamer, *Truth and Method,* p. 9.

8. Ibid., p. 18.

9. Ibid., Introduction, p. xii.

10. Ibid., Preface to 2nd ed., p. xvi.

11. Gadamer, *Continuum,* vol. 8, 1970, p. 87.

12. Gadamer, *Truth and Method,* p. 98.

13. Ibid., p. 404.

14. Gadamer, "Die Universalität des Hermeneutischen Problems," in *Kleine Schriften I* (Tübingen: Mohr, 1967), p. 104.

15. Gadamer, *Continuum,* as quoted, p. 83.

16. *Truth and Method,* p. 267.

17. In "Über die Planung der Zukunft," in *Kleine Schriften I,* p. 178.

18. *Truth and Method,* p. 245.

19. Ibid.

20. Ibid., p. 250.

21. Habermas, *Theory and Practice,* p. 40.

22. "Zur Logik der Sozialwissenschaften," as quoted, p. 179.

23. Ibid., p. 176.

THE PROBLEM OF SENSE: HABERMAS V. LUHMANN

FRIEDRICH W. SIXEL

In recent years, Jürgen Habermas and Niklas Luhmann have fought out a literary controversy on sociological theory which has gained the attention of experts on both sides of the Atlantic. It began when Luhmann suggested that sociology badly needed to reconsider its basic concepts.[1] He further proposed to treat the notion of sense as most fundamental in this connection, since social objects are not simply what they are, but rather what they mean (p. 11); it is constitutive to them that they are understood, i.e., make sense. Therefore sociology cannot do without a theory of sense. So far, Habermas agrees fully with Luhmann (pp. 142–145). But that is about all they can agree upon. In almost every other respect they differ fundamentally, be it regarding the strategies of building up a new sociological theory, its emerging structure, or its purpose. Their views on these issues are diametrically opposed to each other, as reflected in the title of the joint publication which contains the bulk of their dispute: *Theory of Society or Social Technology.*

Those among us who knew the differences in philosophical orientation between Habermas and Luhmann had expected that their controversy would boil down to a repetition of the positivist dispute or "Positivismusstreit" in the early sixties between Adorno and Popper. This, however, is not the case at all. There are at least two remarkable differences. While the older dispute found hardly any literary response, the more recent quarrel has stirred up a considerable number of publications, not only in sociology, but in a few adjacent disciplines too.[2] Secondly, it has been noted[3] that the Habermas-Luhmann debate is far from being the kind of trench warfare that the Adorno-Popper controversy certainly was. While in the sixties the two discussants tried mainly to demarcate their positions against each other, Habermas and Luhmann make every effort to listen to and to learn from what the other has to say.[4]

This leads to a kind of agility in their discussion which adds to its attractiveness as an intellectual game. But since both Habermas and Luhmann use in the course of their debate what they learn from each other, the observer also has the pleasure of being witness to significant developments and modifications of the two traditions involved. Thus Habermas's dialectical and Luhmann's systems-theoretical sociology differ at the end from what they were at the beginning.

Of course, this agility implies that the meaning of concepts employed changes as the discussion proceeds. This has earned the two discussants the objection of being imprecise and vague.[5] It would seem to me, however, that such a complaint, though not unfounded, would lose considerably in strength among those who read the text with the same willingness to learn as these two authors. Modifications of views are clearly spelled out and presented step by step. This remains the case, even if one includes Habermas's *Legitimation Crisis* in this discussion, and thus stretches its duration from 1968, when Luhmann delivered a first portion of it as a seminar paper, to 1973, when the *Legitimation Crisis* was first published. This book of Habermas's is to be included not only because it allows its author to respond to Luhmann's previously presented rejoinder and thus makes the number of shots even, but also because it presents its views by adopting a systems-theoretical idiom like Luhmann's. It is doubtlessly part of the controversy.

The adoption of a systems-theoretical language increasingly influences Habermas's way of arguing in the debate,[6] while in turn Habermas's attack on Luhmann's notion of complexity forces the latter to reformulate the meaning of that concept as the argument goes on. It seems to be obvious that semantic changes of this nature, of which I name only these two, make it inadequate just to represent the "result" of this debate. An attempt has to be made to convey the dynamics of it, at least in its major streams of thinking. Such an intention, however, will not aim at presenting a sheer reflection of the debate. As is always the case in human speech where total feedback is impossible, it will be my appropriation of this debate which I shall present. It will, nevertheless, be my hope that the discussants themselves can still detect the sense of their encounter in what I try to make out of it.

Briefly outlined, I intend to proceed like this: first, I deal with what I take to be Luhmann's position and then Habermas's views up to a point. In a second part, I would like to compare those aspects of their positions to each other where a head-on confrontation is most conspicuous. I plan to do this by putting the different arguments point by point against each other. Needless to say, the whole presentation will be permeated by my own critical views.

Luhmann, like Habermas, departs from the firm result of transcendentalism that the object depends on the cognitive faculties—Kant speaks of categories—of the subject. At the same time, he is aware of the difficulties that emerge with the definite formulation of these categories. Attempts of this kind imply one monological subject into whose horizon a solitary world of objects implodes (pp. 26–27). On this basis, differences among and changes of subjects and their worlds, as they occur in social life, would be closed off. In a combination of Edmund Husserl's phenomenology and modern systems theory, Luhmann hopes to find a way out of this dilemma.

Husserl, though he holds on to the transcendental dependence of the object on cognitive terms of reference, tries to dynamize what Kant called categories by pointing out that every concept contains its own transcendence. This is to say that whatever sense is being made in terms of which further cognition can take place, there is necessarily other sense which is excluded from it and which thus transcends the horizon of the sense actually at hand. In order to distinguish itself from sense not being made, any kind of sense necessitates a consciousness of what is not immanent to it. This is the meaning of Husserl's notion of "transcendence immanent to consciousness." It is adopted by Luhmann, because of the intentionality[7] that it implies and because it allows one to conceptualize cognitive change (p. 30). Luhmann points out that Husserl's dynamization of the categorical framework of cognition turns the idealistic determination of the world of objects into a mere contingency relation (p. 11). This is to say that the world still depends on cognizing categories, but these can vary in their structure. They are what they *happen* to be, without requiring a particular structure with logical necessity. Also, Luhmann bears in mind that "sense" is of course not a monolithic unity in Husserl's thought but an ordered cluster of meanings (Husserl's "Sinnzusammenhänge"). At this point, Luhmann turns his attention to systems theory. He observes (pp. 10–11) that systems theory has undergone considerable changes over the last decades. A trend in these modifications can be identified. It leads from the old ontological definition of systems in terms of parts and wholes via notions like balance and interference to functionalist conceptualizations focussing on interdependences between system and environment. The openness of systems leads in cybernetics to the idea of an overcomplex environment to which the systems' own complexity has to respond by selection. Cybernetic systems thus have a quasi-transcendental relation to what is external to them.

It takes Luhmann only two more steps, and the marriage between Husserl's philosophy of sense and systems' theory is consummated. First, he has to distinguish between "information" as used in cybernetics and the concept of sense in Husserl's philosophy. He does this by defining sense as a strategy of selecting information (p. 12). Now, selection does not mean elimination of external complexity, but its reduction in terms of the systems' internal structures. Secondly, Luhmann reformulates Husserl's "cluster" of sense into "system of sense." Now both streams of thought can come together: systems of strategies for the selection of information have in the reduction of external complexity a transcendental relation to their environment. Out of this marriage a dynamic systems theory can be born.

First, we have to note that what was, philosophically speaking, contingency of the world, is for Luhmann now the dependence of that world on a logically arbitrary complexity of a system of sense. Change in sense systems is conceptualized as being initiated by information that the system cannot incorporate. Though communication is always a dosage of surprise (p. 43), some information may be so grossly surprising and alien to the system that this information can only make sense in a system different from the one at work. The intrinsic need of a sense system to make sense of whatever complexity emerges in its environment compels any sense system that is impotent to process the new pieces of information to alter its own reductive structure (pp. 45–46). Change is a reflexive act. When a sense system realizes the difference of the sense mediated to it through new information, it synthesizes its own structure with the sense system from which the new information comes to it (p. 31). Thus Luhmann concretizes the dynamics that he found philosophically formulated in Husserl's notion of "transcendence immanent to consciousness."

The basic shape of Luhmann's theory obviously owes its peculiar features to the special nature of sense systems. They must not be confused, though, with other types of systems. Among those other systems, Luhmann seems to see a hierarchy leading from mechanic, organic, cybernetic, via psychic to social and then sense systems. Adaptational ability seems to increase somehow on the way up this hierarchy and is greatest in sense systems.

From what has been said, it seems to be clear that the concept of sense systems implies the concept of evolution. "Formation of systems [of sense, F.S.] is on one hand the premise of evolution, and on the other hand, a functional aspect in evolution" (pp. 368–69). Differences and distinctiveness of sense systems from each other are thus a condition for evolution. Their clear separation guarantees that they find other sense systems external to them. In this distinctiveness lies the potentiality of the internal restructuring of sense systems if there is information mediated among them. This restructuring, of course, takes place on the basis of the existing sense structure. Thus the notion of continuance is no longer a problem in the theoretical explanation and analysis of change (p. 22). This is so far the most important gain flowing from Luhmann's introduction of self-transcending sense systems into sociology. Even completely negated sense is not "garbaged out," as might happen to complexities in cybernetics. Instead, it is virtualized as different sense and thus remains as a piece of storage within the horizon of possible interpretative schemes (pp. 33–34).

Luhmann's theory is not intended as a philosophy but as a framework for an empirical science of sense. As such it needs concrete references in psycho-organic and social systems (pp. 29–30). It is important that these references are not confused with sense systems as such. They are merely the substrata of sense, resting ultimately on material systems. This makes it understandable that to Luhmann the environment of sense systems is made up by nothing else but other sense systems, mediated to each other through information. Other types of systems become related to sense systems only in terms of the sense by which they are identified.

Having a second look now at the concept of information we should note that as a system's output it is defined by Luhmann as action.

Insofar, it represents a system's reductive activity on the basis of its own internal structure. Receiving information, or, as Luhmann puts it, experiencing, is a system's intake of what is reduced by another system (pp. 75ff). This constitutes communication as the peculiar type of interaction among sense systems. Provided that the communication does not involve too many problems of reduction the system could continue without changing its structure. Communication to Luhmann is thus, on one hand, actualization of shared sense (p. 42), though it may also lead, on the other hand, to a change of sense, if action and experiencing encounter difficulties. As far as sheer sense systems are concerned, in principle all sense is possible. This is a heritage from Husserl's notion of the logical arbitrariness of cognitive categories. It involves considerable risks in Luhmann's view, however (pp. 61–62). Since man is organized on the basis of a material system, he has to depend on other material systems of the world which he does not produce but only interprets. Therefore these interpretations are threatened by potential disappointment. Luhmann seems to imply here that these threats, ultimately that of death, could be received as frustrating information by the system of sense. Such surprising information may also initiate a change of the sense system or lead merely to a negation and virtualization of the meaning behind the threatening information. By defining the relation of subject and sense this way, Luhmann has little problem in moving on to the notion of intersubjectivity (pp. 51–52). Intersubjectivity emerges simply out of the mutual encounter of different sense systems and not of human subjects who are both sense and body. These different systems of sense develop a communicative compatibility with each other that is to be seen as an integrative system of sense. From here we can turn to Luhmann's view on the relationship between wider social systems (e.g., kingroups, bureaucratic organizations, or sports teams) and sense. With some simplification, we might say that these systems are also constituted by sense and not the other way around. Enriching his edifice by the familiar idea of systems nesting in each other, Luhmann can suggest that more specific systems of sense stand in the relationship of subsystems to superordinate systems of sense. These systems vary in their degree of complexity and integrative potential for communication. Luhmann does not, of course, deny that social systems (like human subjects) also exist on the basis of material substrates.

At this point, I would like to emphasize that it is only through the introduction of such a sharp difference between subject and sense that Luhmann manages to move from a notion of subject to that of inter-subjectivity. For Habermas and others it remains to be seen whether a conceptual separation between the concrete human being and sense is tenable. Later on in the discussion, Luhmann drops the notion of the human subject altogether.

Before we study how the concept of the human subject drops out of Luhmann's system, let us see what role he assigns to society. As may be expected, society constitutes sense as little as other social systems do. It too *is* constituted by sense. The conceptualization of an overarching system of sense leaves Luhmann the problem of how to segregate societies from each other. His reasoning in that connec-tion runs like this: empirical observation shows that societies deter-mine, on the basis of their sense systems, which kind of complexity is to be negated as non-reducible (p. 24). This clearly threatens the philosophically postulated arbitrariness of sense. As a sociologist, Luhmann pays due respect to this, but argues further by saying that though valid strategies of reduction are arbitrarily determined, they do not, once adopted, allow for arbitrariness in further development and change (p. 383). Thus societies as intersubjectivities differ from each other depending on choices of sense previously made; their past determines their present. Moreover, this difference is reinforced since subsystems of sense, "down" to those which constitute the individual subject, differ from society to society regarding their ways of interac-tion, or better, of communication (p. 52). On the basis of previous choices and also of the nature of their internal communication, soci-eties segregate themselves from each other. From here, Luhmann draws a major conclusion regarding the function of society. Its inter-subjective sense is the steering system of the society's further evolution (p. 99). Progress in society will take place to the extent to which its sense system can produce alternatives. Therefore Luhmann can say that change, progress, and/or evolution, which have ceased to exist as theoretical problems in his view, are in reality problems of society (pp. 20–21). For this and other reasons soon to be explicated, Luh-mann's sociology cannot give up the concept of society, though it can eventually drop the concept of subject.

Society usually delegates the job of taking leadership in evolution to social subsystems and the systems of sense "behind" them (pp. 16, 84). The kinds of subsystem which assume this task vary in the evolution of society. Luhmann thinks, more or less, of the following sequence of subsystems in this respect: kinship, religion, politics, economy, and science, moving from the past to present. These subsystems, in the course of evolution, increasingly differentiated from each other and from the wider society on both the level of social organization and that of sense and produced the kind of thought that sets the terms of reference for thinking in the whole society. They also harness alternatives in the horizon of virtualized sense. In doing so, they bring about structural changes which may mean progress if they increase the reductive abilities of the system. New sense, as a structurally new strategy of explaining the world, will spread throughout the existing intersubjectivity and thus through the society as a whole social system. The notion of leading subsystems not only implies that the society decides through them which thoughts are to be negated. It also means that these subsystems determine the degree of complexity that people in that society have to endure (p. 16).

According to Luhmann, it is science which determines in modern society how the world is to be seen. Of course, such determination takes place in interplay with other sense systems in that society, but science holds the position of leadership. In view of this historical role of science, sociology as a subsystem of science has to determine its own function (p. 86). It is quite obvious that Luhmann assigns to sociology as the empirical science of sense systems (pp. 29–30 and p. 59) crucial importance. On one hand, this discipline has to investigate the sense practically at hand and at work in society, including, of course, the organizational forms through which it operates. On the other hand, it is part of sociology's task as a theoretical discipline of sense to propose alternatives to the sense "behind" the existing praxis. It is implied in such a conceptualization of sociology that its epistemological framework is based on the praxis of society. Its terms of reference are capable of describing the meaning of ongoing reality because they are developed in view of it. At the same time, sociology as a sense system itself has to do more than descriptive work. It is part of its theoretical task to know that this dependence on the meaning of ongoing life is a contingent one (pp. 25–26). Society and thus sociology could be different from what they are. As a sense system sociology can step outside of praxis and thus it can come to know its own transcendence as a horizon of virtualized possibilities. Suggestions coming out of this storehouse and put to social reality have the potential of changing that praxis, thus offering sociology a new reality for study. Reflexive awareness of the contingency of its framework secures sociology the kind of generality for its theory (p. 37) that is adequate to the concrete historical stage of the society in which it exists. This way, according to Luhmann, sociology gains insight into the basically hypothetical character of its truth. Search for ultimate truth cannot possibly be its purpose. Sociology knows "that the positivity [of truth, FS] is nothing else but the structural variability of that system in which it tries to find truth" (p. 86). As a theory of action (à la Parsons), sociology cannot arrive at such conclusions, since its concept of sense as a strategy of understanding is not dynamic enough.

The awareness of its own historicity separates Luhmann's sociology from that of Parsons, as Habermas also points out (p. 142–143). A social theory to which the idea of dynamic sense systems is central can only understand itself in direct correspondence to a concrete particular society. It is for this reason that Luhmann's sociology cannot possibly drop the concept of society as it eventually eliminates the idea of the human subject as the agent of life. This grounding in concrete societies also precludes the buildup of general and ultimate epistemological frameworks universally applicable in the study of any society whatever. If attempted, as in the case of Parsons, these frameworks are, nolens volens, mere elaborations of culture-bound thought. Luhmann simply takes it seriously that this is the "fate" of all sociological endeavors. Luhmann's conceptualization of sociology as the theory of social praxis brings him, at first glance, surprisingly close to Marx. This is also seen by Habermas (pp. 142–143) and is certainly among the reasons why Luhmann's thought evokes his interest. That he rejects it after close examination has to do, among other reasons, with Luhmann's concept of the relationship between theory and praxis, as we shall see.

We noted that, to Luhmann, praxis as the existing complexity of the world is the reference point of theory (e.g., p. 94). On its structure, theory ultimately rests. Thus complexity of real life becomes the key concept in Luhmann's social theory[8] and the key mover of progress. To him it is not man who makes history but praxis, since it is from praxis that theory gets the necessary material for its function as a creator of transcendent alternatives. Man seems only to execute what sense systems have to offer. By enacting sense, man becomes what he otherwise would not be: a subject.

Although the primary status of complexity in Luhmann's theory is presently the focus, another important aspect of his thinking comes to mind again: sense systems depend on real man so that they can be thought. Luhmann does not leave any doubt on this, though as an obvious point he does not elaborate on it. It is just another aspect of his idea presented above that a theory of sense systems needs concrete references for having the rank of an empirical discipline. Also the function of sense which aims at transcending the *status quo* of praxis cannot take place without real men thinking the necessary conceptual processes. But these processes have their origin in the existing sense, i.e., the socially practiced strategy of thought, and in the human subject. As such, this sense of praxis provides man with the terms of reference for his thinking. In the terms of this same praxis, i.e., in the terms of his ongoing society, man comes to understand his own existence. Thus, he is what he means to himself. This is another way of saying that the subject is constituted by sense and not the other way around. Again—and we return now to our particular context—complexity as offered by the horizon of life reveals why it deserves, in Luhmann's view, the status of the key concept in sociology, especially if it wants to understand change and evolution.

Having presented Luhmann's systems' theory of sense in society up to this point, it seems to be appropriate to turn now to Habermas's views. His criticisms of Luhmann's theory as a basis for sociology are doubtless spurred by his fear of its implicit political consequences. As a scientific mechanism that produces alternatives for praxis and thus guides progress, it also produces the reasoning for its proposals. Thus, this kind of sociology has to Habermas the latent function of delivering legitimation of whatever nature for the political power of experts. Bringing into the open Luhmann's conceptual mistakes is seen by Habermas as his main task. "Only this way, I may hope to learn from Luhmann . . . what one can learn at any rate from such a comprehensively formed and surprising mind" (p. 145). Even though Habermas concentrates on what he considers to be Luhmann's conceptual mistakes, the controversy nevertheless deals also with the potential consequences of their theories for political life.

Habermas, who appreciates the utility of systems' theory and has himself employed it, rejects Luhmann's theory of sense systems because it constitutes an unmediated relation between theory of society and the praxis of society. This danger is particularly imminent when modern science becomes the leading subsystem and social theory sails in its wake (p. 143). Habermas's criticism might briefly be introduced like this: as a scientific mechanism for the reduction of sense and the selection of alternatives, Luhmann's theory tries to lay down the foundation for a sociology capable of assuming the role of the leading subsystem in society. In its rationality, however, it hardly pays attention to human will. Therefore, this proposal need not and does not reflect carefully upon the relation of will to norms. Both are taken for granted. How their interplay responds to social values *(Sollwerte)* and motivation is also outside Luhmann's considerations. Therefore his theory need not and does not sell itself to praxis via legitimation nor does it reflect on it. It argues for its own validity only in terms of functionality. Habermas, however, will try to establish that only if values, motivation, norms, and will are also reasoned about in praxis and theory can theory legitimize its own propositions.

It is implied in Habermas's views on Luhmann's theory that it can only understand itself in connection with a praxis that does not exist or, rather, does not yet exist. Will, norms, values, and motivation do play their role in society as it exists right now. Therefore, a sociology à la Luhmann might present an alternative to existing reality, but it is of scientistic nature. Only as such can a leading subsystem prescribe to society that future style of praxis of which it presents itself as the theory already.

It should be admitted that Habermas does not quite choose this way to demonstrate Luhmann's mistakes, but it seems to me to be implied in the arguments which he presents. He does point out that a prescriptive role is intrinsic to Luhmann's theory, even though it claims to be rooted in life praxis. This has to do with the way by which a sociology which has an insufficient or no concept of legitimation feeds back its proposals to society. Here lies the dilemma in Luhmann's theory. Its peculiar relation to praxis implies that its application in real life would have immediate political consequences. Therefore Habermas has to speak to Luhmann about politics too, although he wishes to concentrate on conceptual mistakes. The way he actually chooses to do this is by examining Luhmann's concept of sense. Since it functionalizes truth, in Habermas's opinion it abolishes the difference between the dichotomies of correct/wrong on one hand, and of true/false on the other (pp. 228–229).

Habermas's interpretation of this difference leads to an understanding of the human subject which is fundamental for his rejection of

Luhmann's theory. It is not only important to remember that Husserl had significant difficulties with the vital role of the subject in political economy, but it has also to be pointed out that Luhmann completely ignores the dialectical tradition of the nineteenth century (p. 143).[9] It is only in reaction to Habermas that he takes it up. By ignoring the claim of dialectical materialism that man is part of nature and that thus matter is a constitutive factor in cognition, Luhmann constructs his theory of sense as a theory of abstract sense. To sense abstracted from matter, the material body of man is of course merely a source of information and thus a potential risk, as Luhmann in fact thinks (p. 61).

Although the formulation of a historical-materialistic theory of cognition is yet to be completed,[10] its basic structure is certainly there. Originating in Marx's first thesis on Feuerbach and leading up to the well known endeavors of the Frankfurt School of sociology, there is a stream of thought that is aware of the "a priori of the body" (Leib-a-priori) in cognition, if I may use K. O. Apel's well known phrase. Man being a citizen in the world of matter and of mind depends for the construction of his reality on both material production and the sense-ful organization thereof. Modes of production, and not just leading systems of sense, constitute or, better, reproduce the human subject who in turn conceives of the world in the terms "behind" the existing mode of production (pp. 276–279). In principle, Habermas accepts Kant's distinction between the world of nature ("pure reason") and the world of ethics ("practical reason"), but he "schematizes," i.e., confronts man's cognitive "categories" with the reality of both worlds in a way quite different from Kant (p. 209). Differing with Kant, he sees the two in relation to each other. This move, reminiscent of criticisms of Kant launched also by Habermas's dialectical ancestors, changes the meaning of the "categories." Although Habermas also appreciates that understanding of nature aims at its control and that acting ethically aims at social order, he has learned from Marx that control of nature always requires social order so that these two interests nest in each other. Social order is based on consensus, i.e., rests on human communication. Agreeing with Luhmann in a limited way, Habermas knows that shared sense provides the "categories" for understanding the world in its totality. This implies that principles of controlling manipulation and consensual agreement can be applied to nature *and* society. Thus their distinction in Kant's philosophy is overridden by Habermas's post-Marxian thinking. From here he deduces two types of rationality as strategies for understanding: one, *instrumental rationality,* aiming at manipulation of the world in both its material and social dimensions, and the other, *communicative rationality,* related to maintenance of consensual agreement. As the first aims at success it calls for functionally correct selection of means; and as the second aims at order it is based on integrative truth.

However, there is an area in which man's rationality, i.e., his way of making sense, has to be correct and cannot just be judged under the criterion of true conviction. This is the realm of nature of which man himself is a part and where he definitely depends on the success of his instrumental means. Here a logically arbitrary choice of sense, despite Luhmann, is out of the question. In this world of sheer correctness, arbitrary revisions of sense would not help (pp. 219–220). This consideration does not devaluate the principle of truth to Habermas since organization of the social control of nature still depends on consensus. But this consensus has to be in keeping with correct understanding and ways of harnessing energy from nature. It is this consideration which leads Habermas to the insight of the importance of making a distinction between "true" and "correct." Luhmann's cybernetically influenced notion of sense, however, knows only of the functionality of sense, expressed in its success in reducing a complex world of whatever information. Thus, it cannot introduce into its conceptualizations (among other sociological concepts) the notion of communicatively established values *(Sollwerte)* (pp. 148–149).

Of course, to Habermas, social order, however communicatively maintained, has to serve survival too. It has also to be used instrumentally for that purpose. This insight is conceptually fundamental for potential partiality in the use of the communicative order. In as much as this partiality threatens communicatively attained convictions on the form of society or production, the dysfunctionality of instrumentally applied means is a condition for initiating change primarily through what Habermas calls *discourse.* In discourse, people do not act on nature, give orders, learn what they have not known, etc., i.e., they do not produce but reconsider the principles of production, regardless of whether they relate to their understanding of nature or of society; the form of production and possibly also the understanding of nature come under revision. Out of this type of communication a new view of the world will emerge if previous partialities and dysfunctionalities in praxis are overcome. Thus discourse is constitutive to Habermas's historical materialistic theory of cognition and its dynamization (pp. 195–201); indeed it is vital to his whole thinking.

Taking up and going beyond ideas from Wittgenstein (pp. 178–179), Habermas points out that in *discourse* thus conceived human subjects do not react towards each other just as dry systems of reductive rules. Intersubjectivity here emerges out of the encounter of real men as they acknowledge each other as beings of sense and body. Of course, they are historical men, thinking in terms of the existing praxis, but for the transcendence of that praxis they need not be reduced to mere carriers of sense. Instead, Habermas's theory of cognition returns to the human subject in his totality and historical concreteness.

Habermas cannot accept Luhmann's claim that a cybernetically derived sociology should take the position of the leading subsystem in society. If he were to agree to the notion of leadership for theory at all, then it would only be for a kind of social theory that engages in discourse with praxis (p. 276). Under the modern conditions of the division of labor, this certainly requires expertise, but of a kind that thinks in terms of the existing praxis, makes its contradictions visible, e.g., between repression and universalizable interests, and seeks a way out of them in consultation with praxis. Such theory would be mediated to praxis through the terms of the discourse. Therefore Habermas's theory leads to the political process as the form through which society solves its problems. It understands itself as the basis for a theory of praxis, i.e., a *theory of society.* Luhmann's theory, however, advocates, in Habermas's view, the *administrative* management of problems in society. It tries to provide the conceptual basis for a sociology that is functionalized as a *social technology.* It rests, so Habermas contends, on the equation of "power" and "truth," whereby the meaning of the latter is reduced to functional correctness. This makes power immune against questions from those human subjects who are not yet reduced to sheer instrumental thinking. If this happens, the emancipation of man from repression would be impossible because those in power and those without power would not understand it as a need anymore. This utopia could only become reality were a theory of Luhmann's kind indeed to take leadership in society. Then, however, society and evolution could not be understood anymore, since this theory has lost an adequate sense for the problem of how the need structure of man influences his social reality and its changes. Therefore Habermas hangs on to the concept of reasonable subject as the key concept of sociology.[11]

Habermas nevertheless agrees with Luhmann that there has been a certain overemphasis on subjectivistic orientations in recent sociology (p. 180). This emphasis seems to have emerged as a reaction towards the objectivistic trends that dominated the field in the fifties and sixties. Habermas obviously does not want to be understood as sharing either one of these trends. Human subjects with their interest in successful order and orderly success do not first establish a shared sense and then determine their subject nature in terms of this sense. Instead, it is Habermas's suggestion that establishing sense and the constitution of self take place "uno actu," in one act. The individual constitutes itself as an Ego *not after* having distinguished itself from Alter, but *in* the act of making that distinction; or, while one identifies oneself with others, one retains one's discreteness (p. 127). Further clarification is provided by careful study of the nature of discourse. It is taken up when senseful order, valid so far, is challenged. Individuals and individuals in groups which feel oppressed put forth their subjective questions for the acceptability of their expectations. These expectations are not *first* senseless intentions of the repressed groups which *then* become culturally understood expectations (pp. 190–191). Even though they are met with antagonism, groups or individuals in opposition acknowledge each other as subjects. They understand each other in spite of the fact that their discourse has yet to re-establish an order acceptable to all through its foundation on a new view of the world. As this process of finding new sense in life eventually succeeds, the meaning of human subjects, is of course, redefined. Not out of this sense, however, but *in view* of this sense, i.e., "uno actu" with its emergence, subjects understand themselves anew as social beings in consensus. This is to say that their life now is as little constituted by sense as it was in the preceding crisis. But now human subjects can speak about their existence in new terms which do not justify the repression of previous subjective expectations anymore. Finding new sense is possible because men's being, though not preceding sense, is more than just sense. Together with what Luhmann calls the material substrate, it makes up man as a cognizing subject capable of creating new forms of life. Man understands himself in terms of these forms "uno actu" with their emergence, but they do not constitute him as a subject.

This is certainly not an idealist concept of man. Furthermore, on the basis of his dialectical position, Habermas need not assign second rank to the human subject in the attempt to develop an evolutionary concept of society. This, of course, implies a notion of sense incompatible with Luhmann's. His theory can even allow for the emancipation of man in praxis from this position without having to fear that praxis would suffer. Man's grounding in nature provides him with a secure rail for not venturing off into strange horizons of possible sense alien to that of praxis.

The emergence of change would not remain arbitrary. Habermas would admit that it was modern man who detected that the order of life rests on his own nature and that all systems of thought which try to back a definite organization of life are mere ideologies. But this does not mean that the human subject was an invention of the nineteenth century, as Luhmann says (p. 351). It was always embedded in the intersubjectivities of previous modes of production, in view of which man understood himself. History as the process of emancipation of the subject finally leads to the "death of ideology." The subject knows itself now as the only condition of order; it has no ideologies left (p. 102 Lg).[12]

In view of repression, discourses have to determine whether interests can be universalized. "Universalizability" (not new ideologies!) is the only reasonable criterion left in modernity (pp. 148–149 Lg) on the basis of which an order of social life can be founded. This implies reasoning with those making claims. Without this mediating relation, leadership in society can only predetermine suggestions and hand them out for people's acceptance thereafter. This kind of normative prescription, as it would seem to flow from a sociology à la Luhmann, takes on the nature of an ethic which concretely anticipates "what is to be done." In Habermas's understanding, this would repeat Max Scheler's and Nicolai Hartmann's futile attempts to lay down a foundation for a concretely or materially substantiated value ethic. It would equally be bound to failure (pp. 137–138 Lg). Norms, where necessary, in view of the development of the productive forces in modern society, can only be determined on the grounds of universalizability and become acceptable through reasonable discourse among human subjects.

It is Luhmann's contention that the complexities of the modern world are so great that discursive reasoning about their causalities among all concerned is practically impossible (p. 397). Communicative exercises aiming at that have become futile because those who understand today's problems and their potential solutions can no longer speak to those who are laymen, i.e., men of praxis. Reason in these circumstances has ceased to be a means of communication. The masters' comprehension is exaggerated and that of the servants is lost in specialization (pp. 327–328). Modernity has to live with that. This means to Luhmann that contemporary society has to look for different ways of solving problems and transmitting solutions to the wider social system. A political constitution based on "reason," "truth," "legitimation," "power," etc., does not seem to be capable of handling modern social systems anymore (pp. 382–383).

Science could fulfill its leading function in this situation if it would learn to see its activity as the technical production of sense (pp. 359–360). Luhmann points out that his concept of "sense" in this connection is to be understood differently from its traditional meaning. He thinks that "sense" should go beyond the level where one used to make the old distinction between theoretical and practical reason (in the Kantian sense of the word). It simply should mean increase in selectivity. This angle on the view of "sense" as a strategy for reducing complexity brings out also its intrinsic aim at efficiency. The technicality of sense lies in the formulation of insights in such abstract and general terms that particular understandings can easily be substituted by dissimilar though functionally equivalent ones (p. 349). A science which operates in this fashion has, of course, to be aware of its own contingencies. Therefore it no longer aims at finding *the* truth. Science has to transcend that plane on which one still hopes for such things. It has to content itself with the role of pointing out contingencies (pp. 383–384) and possibilities. Normative imposition of these recommendations is obviously inconceivable in Luhmann's theory. Science as the leading subsystem can only think of motivationless acceptance of its output by the wider society (p. 144, see also footnote 5 there).

If science understands its activity more clearly in these terms, its work and the transmission of its findings can also be better organized (p. 349). For example, themes and contributions of scientific encounters (e.g., meetings, controversies, interpretations, etc.) could be defined more clearly (p. 329). This way the determination whether contributions belong to a program or not could be handled more easily, and also their elimination. Resorting to "perfectionist concepts" like "God," "freedom," "justice," etc., could be banned immediately, as Luhmann believes (p. 325). They have to be excluded, since they close the discussion and thus the search for alternatives. "Dogmatic" recruitment to schools would be out altogether (p. 340).

It should be remembered in this connection that Luhmann does not suggest a theory which eliminates diversity in points of view; in this sense it is a pluralistic theory. Habermas also admits that Luhmann's proposal does not present the familiar appearance of a neo-positivist construction (pp. 145–146). The traditional positivistic closure of dynamic developments, be it in theory or praxis, is completely avoided in Luhmann's thinking. Its analytical opportunism goes beyond even the strategic considerations which underlie neo-positivistic ways of concept formation, in so far as Luhmann's theory contemplates its own contingencies. It aims at creating open systems and open minds.

Granting all this, Habermas nevertheless points out that there are still severe limitations in Luhmann's theory of sense. One form in which they become manifest lies in the theory's inability to analyze crisis situations of social systems and their management adequately. This deficiency could only be overcome if Luhmann's theory were enriched by a more sensible understanding of man's peculiar ways of communication, learning and/or socialization (pp. 204–205, pp. 9–19 *Lg*). Proper reflexion on these human activities, however, would negate the validity of some basic concepts in Luhmann's thought.

The process of human (and humane) socialization cannot be grasped in terms of sense systems' "actions" and "experiences," as Luhmann understands them, since they are not each reflexive as such. Socialization cannot be described by simply assuming "action" on the "teacher's" side and passivity ("experience") on the "student's." Learning, like speech among humans in general, involves the "re-creation" of the meaning of what has been said in the minds of those who learn or listen. This is also to say that the seemingly passive recipients of messages have to be active in the act of understanding. This, however, is not assumed in Luhmann's ideas on communication.

Activity is also required of the wider society when it comes to accepting (and understanding!) the output of the leading societal subsystem. Otherwise this leadership would be impossible. Such activity, however, depends on a motivation on the part of people to engage in it. Therefore motivationless acceptance appears as a contradiction in itself, as long as we wish to speak about human society.

These considerations illustrate how cybernetics, as the insufficiently transcended breeding ground of Luhmann's systems theory of sense, makes itself strongly felt through a burdensome heritage. In Habermas's view (p. 186), it gives Luhmann's notion of sense a strangely monological character. It turns the sense system into a monad. The dynamism in the complexity/contingency relation between sense and environment takes on a lifeless and bloodless nature, since it rests on the reductive ability of that monad. As a cybernetically dynamized monadology (p. 230), Luhmann's systems theory of sense represents to Habermas the highest form of technocracy yet developed (p. 145).

Some of its limitations are also expressed, as was seen above, by its inability to reason about norms, legitimation, etc. However, Habermas concedes that this keeps Luhmann's theory ultimately from becoming normative itself (pp. 189–193 Lg). It lacks adequate self-understanding, particularly of its own concept of communication, when it expects motivationless acceptance of functional proposals. Then, indeed, legitimation in its classical and also critical meaning as reasoning about the validity of world views and their backing of norms and values (pp. 246–247) becomes superfluous. In keeping with its sheer instrumental rationality, Luhmann's theory calls only for rationalistic legality in terms of procedural correctness (pp. 134–137 Lg). In such an environment motivationlessness is functional. It becomes a condition for the leadership of a systems theory of sense in society.

To Habermas, however, it appears to be doubtful also that Luhmann's unreasoned assumption of a general interest in functionality could solve the social problems that would arise with motivational deficiencies. Even if introduced as a remedy, an interest in functionality would at best be explained by an interest in privatized consumption and as such lead to a certain mass loyalty to the social system. Consumerism, however, has shown itself vulnerable to crises in the generation of motivation, even where the societal infrastructure (leisure, access to educational and health services, etc.) secures a high level of satisfaction (pp. 106 ff Lg, particularly pp. 113–117 Lg).

In the final analysis, the debate between Luhmann and Habermas turns upon the question of our "partiality for reason," as Habermas puts it in the final pages of the *Legitimation Crisis*. There, he concedes to Luhmann that it is conceivable that the complexity of modern society makes reasonable discourse about that complexity impossible. This would imply an alternative to a human existence grounded in reason. This alternative would manifest itself, for instance, in an eccentric administration without openings for appeal. It would mean the final abolition of man as being subject to his own destiny.[13] In view of this, Habermas confesses his "partiality for reason." He brings up the question, whether one can reasonably argue that social individuals should not determine their identity through reason (p. 194 *Lg*).

Certainly, the complexity of society may appear, or may be made to appear, opaque. And yet, man cannot resign in view of the difficulties of human enlightenment by resorting to what appears to be today's opposed choices, i.e., either a decisionism à la Luhmann or a Marxist orthodoxism. "Both ways are closed to a praxis, which ties itself to reasonable will" and which "demands theoretical clarity on what we do not know. Even if we do not know much more today than what my argumentation sketch suggests . . . this circumstance . . . would not paralyze the determination to take up the fight against the stabilization of a naturally grown ("naturwüchsig") societal system beyond the heads of its citizens for the prize of a, let it be said, Old European Dignity of Man" (pp. 195–196 *Lg*).

NOTES

1. See J. Habermas and N. Luhmann, *Theorie der Gesellschaft oder Sozialtechnologie* (Frankfurt: Suhrkamp, 1971), pp. 25–26. Quotations from and references to this book are being indicated by adding the number(s) of the page(s) concerned to the particular passage of this text. Translations from this and all other German texts are the sole responsibility of the author.

2. By now there exist three supplementary volumes of essays from various authors (published by Suhrkamp, Frankfurt) under the title of the Habermas-Luhmann book.

3. F. Maciejenski, Vorwort in *Theorie der Gesellschaft oder Sozialtechnologie,* Supplement I (Frankfurt: Suhrkamp, 1975), p. 7

4. H. Hentig, "Komplexitätsreduktion durch Systeme oder Vereinfachung durch Diskurs," in *Theorie der Gesellschaft oder Sozialtechnologie,* Supplement I, 1975, p. 131.

5. See e.g. W.-D. Narr and D. H. Runze, "Zur Kritik der politischen Soziologie" in *Theorie der Gesellschaft oder Sozialtechnologie,* Supplement II (Frankfurt: Suhrkamp, 1974), pp. 7–17.

6. Some seem even to think that the adoption of that idiom makes Habermas a loser in this controversy, see e.g. W.-D. Narr and D. H. Runze, op. cit., p. 79.

7. Regarding this notion, see L. Eley, "Komplexität als Erscheinung" in *Theorie der Gesellschaft oder Sozialtechnologie,* Supplement II, 1974, p. 143.

8. See K. O. Hondrich, "Systemtheorie als Instrument der Gesellschafts analyse," in *Theorie der Gesellschaft oder Sozialtechnologie,* Supplement I, (Frankfurt: Suhrkamp, 1975), p. 111; and also, L. Eley, op. cit., p. 130.

9. See also F. Maciejewski, "Sinn, Reflexion und System," in *Zeitschrift fur Soziologie,* 1972, pp. 139–155.

204   FRIEDRICH W. SIXEL

10. P. Hejl, "Zur Diskrepanz zwischen struktureller Komplexität und traditionalen Darstellungsmitteln der funktional-strukturellen Systemtheorie," in *Theorie der Gesellschaft oder Sozialtechnologie,* Supplement II, 1975, p. 162. For a concise introduction on Marx's thought as a theory of cognition, see A. Schmidt, *Der Begriff der Natur in der Lehre von Marx* (Frankfurt: E.V.A., 1974), pp. 107ff.

11. See also K. Eder, "Komplexität, Evolution und Geschichte," in *Theorie der Gesellschaft oder Sozialtechnologie,* Supplement I, 1975, pp. 33–34.

12. Quotations from Jürgen Habermas, *Legitimations probleme im Späts-Kapitalismus* (Frankfurt: Suhrkamp, 1973) are given in the text by page number followed by the abbreviation *Lg.*

13. For this conclusion see also: K. H. Tjaden, "Bemerkungen zur historisch-materialistischen Konzeption der Struktur gesellschaftlicher Systeme," in *Theorie der Gesellschaft oder Sozialtechnologie,* Supplement I, 1975, p. 81.

SCIENCE, CRITIQUE, AND CRITICISM: THE "OPEN SOCIETY" REVISITED

H. T. WILSON

In what follows, I address myself to a set of issues all too readily bypassed or ignored by advocates of Karl Popper's open society thesis.[1] I am particularly concerned not only with the reformist implications of his thesis, but with the actual structure or form of the argument itself. Popper's condemnation of social theorizing for its alleged historicist and holistic features is well enough known in its general outlines to constitute an explicit taken for granted by his supporters. Indeed it is at least as well known as the logic of scientific discovery on which it is, in a certain sense, based. I want among other things to explore this relationship in later pages, in order to suggest its deterministic and manifestly unscientific aspects. Then I want to focus on the debate between Marcuse and Habermas regarding the need for and possibility of a "new science" as a prelude to analyzing critically Habermas' most recent thoughts on domination, communication, and change. Finally, I shall conclude by noticing some of Popper's latest studies, in order to show how much they diverge from his stated requirements for "theorizing," and will compare them to the direction of Habermas' efforts. Throughout we shall of necessity be preoccupied with the thought of Max Weber, for I believe it is Weber who constitutes a basic point of departure and problematic for *both* Popperians and critical theorists.

That Popper's thesis in *The Poverty of Historicism* and *The Open Society and its Enemies* had become his *cause célèbre* became plainly evident in 1961, when Popper and others were asked to contribute to the deliberations of the German Sociological Association.[2] The well-known "Popper-Adorno Controversy" which emerged from this interaction between Popperians and critical theorists appeared to each side to demonstrate the validity of their respective arguments and claims. Popper's interest in the controversy was obvious: he had been a relentless critic of "total reason" almost since his escape from central Europe in the 1930s. Indeed, his concern was so great that he allowed himself to violate his own "scientific" standards with impunity, particularly in *The Open Society and its Enemies,* with its decidedly anti-German tone in the later pages. Apart from the assumptions which underlie Popper's claim to a *logical* relation between ideas and action, itself a violation of any conceivable notion of "openness," critical theorists objected to the way in which he lumped Plato, Aristotle, Hegel, Marx, Heidegger, the sociology of knowledge, and themselves together as historicists and holists when the *differences* serve to define the basic contours of modern philosophy itself.

Popper, to be sure, always appears to have been uninterested in the perennial debate between the ancient and the modern teaching in philosophy. But the fact that he failed to recognize critical theory's repudiation of both Heidegger and the sociology of knowledge reaffirmed the view of Adorno and others, expressed in 1961, that Popper was fundamentally ignorant of important matters in philosophy and social theory. All one could say of the discussion of modern philosophy and theory in *The Open Society and its Enemies* was that it occasionally managed to make constructive distinctions between Hegelian and Marxian dialectics, though even here Popper's purpose is never in doubt. The overriding theme—that totalitarianism is given substantial aid and comfort by thinkers committed to what Albert called "total reason" in their analysis of social, political, and cultural phenomena—remains, premised as it is on the claim that there is a *logical* relation between theory and practice.[3] In throwing his vaunted scientific standards so completely to the winds when he turned his hand to society and politics, Popper had performed an intellectual operation not dissimilar to the practical requirements of the Nuremburg Trials, where liberalism also made a mockery of itself by turning away from the very standards which it originally had put forward in defense of its superiority over concepts of "natural justice."

Now, fifteen years later, Popper had toned down a good deal of his earlier criticisms in favour of relatively specific procedural complaints. Having been asked to participate as an outsider in a conference on "the logic of the social sciences," Popper had formulated his views in the form of twenty-seven theses, to which he expected a thesis by thesis response from Adorno. Adorno, however, refused to respond in this manner, and chose to present an alternative position instead. Popper claimed that as a consequence none of his theses had been discussed, while Adorno made the very cogent point that to accede to Popper's allegedly "procedural" demands would constitute a *de facto* compromise to the latter's incremental logic. Popper wanted Adorno to respond to *his* points, and generally to follow the organization of *his* presentation as a respondent, but Adorno insisted that he could only respond by reiterating the overall position of critical theory to "positivism" in the social sciences. This, of course, included an attack on Popper's "observer with a problem" approach transposed from the natural to the social sciences.

At the same time, however, Popper and Albert had a point when they criticized Adorno for "loading" the debate by editing and modifying his own contributions and adding yet others, thereby giving the published product an appearance substantially at variance with what had in fact transpired during the conference eight years earlier.[4] Each side, it appeared, had clearly distinct (and conflicting) views of what conferences of this sort were supposed to accomplish, as well as differences about the proper relationship between conference proceedings and subsequent publications. Popper's concern for procedure, including fidelity to the sufficiency of the proceedings themselves, was overridden by Adorno's determination to present a coherent statement of the debate which allowed the critical theorists to "catch up" with the Popperians.

I cite the *Positivismusstreit* here as an illustration of the very difficulty which both Popper and critical theorists claim to be speaking to, namely, the problematic role of knowledge and opinion in its relation to social and political practice. The "rules" Popper believes are essential to informed debate and "positive" results are held up as evidence of distorted or deformed communication by critical theorists, who point to the linear, mechanistic, and manifestly undialectical character of such requirements as proof of their subordination to a technologically biased notion of "progress." Critical theorists see as problematic the refusal of positivists, including Popperians, to acknowledge the existence of social contradictions embedded in the structure of society, and instead to seek to ignore or cover over these contradictions through speech and language eschewing a dialectical in favour of a "scientific" method of analysis. Such a posture begins by abstracting the individual out of a social structure with which he is reflexively involved *as a member* in order to reconstitute him as an observer with a problem. The idea that society itself (in contradistinction to nature) has a problem to which reflexivity is a *response* borders on heresy for Popper, hostaged as he is to the man-nature, mind-body, subject-object, value-fact, and ends-means dichotomies.[5]

Perhaps the most important point which Popper has consistently chosen to ignore bears on critical theory's critique of Marx. Ironically, critical theorists and Popper both agree, albeit for radically different reasons, that Marx's infatuation with an Enlightenment notion of science, particularly the association of science and social progress, is problematic. In contrast to Popper's (and Hayek's) fear of such "scientism," given his stated commitment to safeguarding the heritage of the Enlightenment as it is embodied in the work of Kant, critical theorists challenge the traditional conception of theory which they believe can be discovered in *both* Marx and Popper.[6] Critical theorists construe as "scientism" not their allegedly historicist and holistic efforts, but rather any notion of theorizing which puts science itself forward as a model, however distant the model may be.[7] Critical theorists want to point to the contradictory character of science itself as method and institution in order to contrast its emancipatory promise with its performance to date as a support for domination. They cite as proof of scientism the present cultural value placed upon science, understood as a neutral institution and method concerned with the dispassionate accumulation of knowledge about nature.[8]

When critical theorists include Marx in their critique of traditional theory, they mean to speak to his commitment to "scientific" as against "utopian" socialism as one which constitutes a *limit* to critical reflection. Popper, on the other hand, equates just such a limit with the intellectual responsibility he discovers in science's subordination to "critical rationalism."[9] Marx, critical theorists allege, though conscious of domination, failed to relate the fact of domination to the conditions by which the oppressed might come simultaneously to realize and act upon it. It was precisely Marx's refusal to challenge fundamentally science's view of theory as an instrument or means which, they claim, led him to be unreflexive toward *it* in his haste to give his critique of political economy "scientific" respectability.[10] Standing behind capitalism both logically and chronologically is science as an exemplar of a partial reason whose demands have become irrational because they are presently all but unchallenged. Modern science is so embedded in our construction of the social world that its causilinear, mechanistic, and undialectical vision almost totally conditions our view of social change. It institutionalizes domination in the most subtle conceivable way, since its transformational concerns with the mastery and domination of nature have as their inevitable counterpart a legitimation of the domination of some men by others.[11]

Critical theory thus wants to extend the ambit of reflection so that it includes what *it* calls scientism. Since Marx, as well as Popper, is specifically "on the agenda" in any such undertaking, it is important to be clear on what is meant when critical theory is termed a "Hegelian" Marxism. Extension of dialectical reflection to science serves to radicalize further a concern which, however, remains essentially Marxian rather than Hegelian in its substantive aspects. It is certainly not by this account a "deformed" Marxism, as two widely divergent critics have recently argued.[12] The idea is to reassert the dialectic, but not to alter Marx's determination to turn it directly on society rather than "straining" it through nature as Hegel did. This is clear from the obvious support for Marx's critique of Hegel's position on bureaucracy, civil society, and the end of history in the universal and homogeneous state found among the first generation of critical theorists. While they extend the method (or mode) further than Marx did so that it now subjects science (as well as capitalism) to critique, this leads them to the view that Hegel's vaunted ideal of universal recognition is not, after all, beyond domination. For reasons which should become clear further on, this ideal is also Popper's, if only by default. His argument regarding the relationship between science, technology, the social sciences, and politics depends heavily on the work of Weber, minus, of course, the more dismal aspects which emerge from the concept of rationalization and science's sustaining role in this process. Though Weber dreaded universal recognition, he saw no alternative to it, with the result that he encouraged the social sciences to assist in building a world he could not stand.[13] That Popper has resolved this difficulty in an interesting way can readily be seen from close scrutiny of his major arguments.

I

A good deal of Popper's intellectual edifice rests upon what I shall call the "distant-model" status of science. By this I understand a model of intellectual activity which, while constituting a "paragon" example of human rationality in the world, is not available for emulation by those disciplines concerned with the study of social, political, and cultural phenomena. Popper, along with Hayek, believes that it is precisely the attempt to emulate the *objectives* of research and scholarship in the natural sciences which has been instrumental in generating intellectual supports for totalitarianism.[14] The "myth of total reason" is the key to understanding why proponents of holism (collectivism) and historicism (scientism) are enemies of the open society as Popper conceives of it. And the reason why science *must not* function as a model in the social and political realm is because for Popper there is a *logical* relation obtaining between the structure of scientific theories and their technical applicability, "which also implies a specific relationship between theory and practice, and between scientific discovery and its practical application."[15]

It is at the very least paradoxical that Popper's concern to restrict science, premised on a parallelism between science and politics, ends by underscoring science's superiority by insisting on the exclusivity of its research objectives. There is, after all, a form of collective self-criticism—critical rationalism—operative in science which guarantees that, though individual scientists may fail to be sufficiently rigorous in their commitment to criteria of falsifiability (as opposed to verifiability), the "community" will correct this individual defect.[16] More important than this, however, is the very direction, and ultimate objective, given in scientific research, which not only derives from the self-correcting role of critical rationalism, but needs this process to realize itself in "progress." Science, it turns out, does, and alone can afford to, move in a direction diametrically opposed to both social and political practice and its disciplined observation and study (the social sciences).

Popper made this clear in a recent essay when he pointed out:

Admittedly the growth of applied knowledge is very similar to the growth of tools and other instruments: there are always more and more

different and specialized applications. But pure knowledge (or fundamental research as it is sometimes called) grows in a very different way.
It grows almost in the opposite direction to this increasing specialization
and differentiation. As Herbert Spencer noticed, it is largely dominated
by a tendency towards increasing integration towards unified theories.[17]

Three factors need to be separated out and distinguished in Popper's
reasoning as it relates to the piecemeal approach: method, direction,
and objective. Of the three the objective is most central, for it conditions the method by dictating the direction of its efforts. Popper
accepts that science, the social sciences, and social and political practice all must adopt the piecemeal approach, but it is the problem-
solving or "technological" function of the latter two activities which
ideally determine their movement in the direction of specialization
and differentiation.[18] Only science is authorized to aim at *truth* as its
objective, while both practice and its disciplined observation must
instead seek *success*. A success orientation favouring a problem-solving approach guarantees that piecemeal social engineering will yield
up "responsible" politics and a responsible social science.

Popper condemns what he construes as Marxian "scientism" on
similar grounds, but to entirely different ends from those put forward
by critical theorists. The alleged parallelism of scientific theory and
practice, coupled with the *logical* relation he claims to find between
the structure of scientific theories and their technical utilization, leads
him rigidly to distinguish science from all forms of "technology,"
whether natural or social in character. It is because he believes in the
power of the scientific model harnessed to the objective of truth and
to a general direction favouring integration and unity that he dreads
social and political theories which act irresponsibly in the *absence* of
critical rationalism. After all, if a logical structure ties together scientific theories and their technical utilization, there may well be a similar
interdependence between the study of social, political, and cultural
phenomena and its "effects."[19]

The result of these strictures is that Popper is left with a very
Weberian bifurcation between science and politics, with the social
sciences treated as "technological" problem-solvers and therefore part
of practice rather than science. The implications for what passes for
theory in these "social technologies" must be clear. The social
sciences become handmaidens in the effort to formulate "responsible"
social and political aims, which means that theories in these disciplines function exclusively as instruments whose value lies not in their

search after truth but rather in the degree to which their assessments are correct and their utilization achieves the desired practical results. Popper seems to improve on the quandary Weber finds himself in when the latter realizes that science can play no "positive" role as a model for social and political practice after all. Yet I submit that the improvement on Weber's dilemma is illusory, since it relies on an unwarranted distinction between science and technology which the very development of modern technology disputes.

Popper's rendition of the conflict between the emancipatory and the dominative function of science is no less unsatisfactory than Weber's. Indeed, Popper would likely see the dominative role of science to be purely a function of the effort to realize science's objective (truth) through the construction of social and political theories, which is to say that there is no dominative or control element *inherent* in the method, direction, and objective (structure) of science itself. This may be problematic, even for philosophers of science generally supportive of Popper's main line of argument on these matters. They point out, for example, that contemporary technology can *only* be explained by reference to modern science, with its emphasis on the discovery of laws of nature *in the interests of* the domination of nature.[20] Indeed, Bacon wanted to overcome the limitations of "traditional techniques" at least as much as he wanted to put a stop to what he termed sterile speculation, which "is but a courtesan . . . for pleasure and not for fruit or generation." At the same time, Bacon defended a limited speculative element in science: it was not to be harnessed exclusively to practice. Thus his concern for "experimenta lucifera," idle curiosity as indispensable to the transformational project as "experimenta fructifera" *given* the objective, the experimental method, and the resulting direction the method would take science in.[21]

This leads to other difficulties which it has been the conscious effort of Marx and the critical theorists to try to overcome. Weber's "Mexican Standoff" between science and politics led him to construe the "demonic disorder" he observed in Wilhelmine politics to be something essentially given in the human condition. What looks like an improvement on Weber's dilemma is in fact evidence of incredible naiveté on Popper's part. Failure to acknowledge the present dominative aspect of modern science, and the resulting tendency to confuse this feature with its status as a *means* to emancipation, leads Popper to treat politics in the advanced "liberal" societies as virtually untouched by the impact of science. Keeping the scientific model out of social and political practice, in the main by keeping the study of society and politics responsible to incremental success criteria, is thought to be sufficient to perpetuate a pluralistic society based on bourgeois negative freedom.

What Popper's naive view of science as inherently emancipatory virtually guarantees is precisely the inability to notice its role as a support for domination through both the material and the social technologies he recommends to us. Popper's approach, in other words, cannot account for the structure of advanced capitalist societies whose pre-eminent characteristic is precisely the *absence* of the pluralism and negative individualism he believes constitutes their ultimate vindication. As soon as it becomes possible to point out various features of this structure, in particular the functional articulation between allegedly discrete elements, (e.g., applied science between "pure" science and technical utilization), the present role of science as a model for domination and (along with capitalism) exploitation reveals itself, and, in the process, confirms its origins and "motive force."[22]

The dialectical commitment of critical theory's effort at a partial reflection which abjures both a correspondence view of truth and inwardness for its own sake is irresponsible for Popper because it seeks truth through reflection rather than restricting itself to externally defined success criteria which call for a piecemeal problem-solving or technological approach. Truth can be responsibly pursued only by that activity whose sole concern is with *nature* rather than man, which is to say that implicit in Popper's concept of science as activity, institution, and method (not surprisingly) is the Cartesian dichotomy between man and nature without which science's project of transformation through domination is inconceivable. Proceeding from the man-nature dichotomy are the false distinctions between mind and body, subject and object, ends and means, and values and facts cited earlier which dialectical reflection, in explicit opposition to *either* causilinear *or* functional approaches to explanation, wishes to overcome.

This suggests an alternate model of social change itself, which Popper can only oppose by equating "total reason" with totalitarianism. Popper refuses to acknowledge as problematic the fact that in the advanced societies as a whole no real alternative exists in social and political thought to the "muddling through" mentality given in the piecemeal approach. Popper labels as pre-rational, because pre-scientific, the commitment to dialectical thinking, and to reflexivity as opposed to disciplined observation in the study of social and political phenomena.[23] Again the false distinction between truth and success presents itself here, as a number of Popper's fellow-travellers have recently pointed out. Even where incrementalism can be seen to constitute a basis for *both* policy formulation *and* implementation, we get what economists call "aggregate effects" not discernible in, nor anticipatable prior to, the onset of specific piecemeal efforts.[24] Bateson has referred to this as the "double-bind" phenomenon, but critical theory wants to underscore the emancipatory potential here as well as in science *per se* by not letting such an observation lead to either pessimism and resignation or to still more "piecemeal social engineering."

The question, then, is not simply what functions a social science subordinated to the limited rationality given in unreflexive practice performs in the advanced societies, but concerns instead the larger problem of domination found in modern experimental science, with its reified dichotomies masquerading as empirical reductions of observed "concrete" phenomena in the "real" world. Popper's very refusal to take the reflexive commitment, as distinct from disciplined observation, seriously makes it impossible for him to see that it is the *contradiction* between science's present dominative role and its emancipatory potential which is largely responsible, along with contradictions in systems of production and administration, for the fact that his theory of society and politics cannot account for the structure of the advanced societies today.

To be sure, this difficulty is further compounded by the unique way in which Popper manages to combine a liberal theory of the individual with a conservative conception of society as largely the product of spontaneous developments emerging out of custom and tradition.[25] For Popper Weberian nominalism does not serve to draw the contours of society as an artificial aggregation which is no more than the sum of its parts, but appears to constitute instead a model for *scientific* activity given the ongoing process of daily life as a backdrop. Indeed Popper's cautious attitude, even toward the piecemeal or incremental approach, appears to be motivated by a fear which is best expressed in his condemnation of "Utopian social planning" (which of course he equates with the irresponsible commitment to truth found in dialectics and reflexivity), namely, unplanned planning taking the form of piecemeal improvizations directed to *undoing* the plan itself. Popperian naturalism regarding society, when combined with a liberal and rationalist view of the individual, makes it impossible for Popper to comprehend the very developments which have been brought to light by the sort of intellectual efforts he believes to be irresponsible and dangerous, as well as "pre-scientific."

II

In the next two sections I want to discuss the work of Jürgen Habermas as it relates to his modification of Marcuse's critique of Weberian rationalization, as well as his most recent work addressed to the issue of the consciousness of domination and the dialectical theory of social transformation he believes both to proceed from and embody this consciousness. Here the objective will be to demonstrate some problems given in Habermas' Weberian reconceptualization, as well as to suggest why critical theory's view of Marx as a "traditional" theorist on the matter of consciousness and its relation to the transformation of capitalist society may be mistaken. The issue in the case of Habermas' effort is whether there is sufficient grounds for delineating a *qualitatively* distinct society from the one conceived of by Marx as an extension of the capitalism of his day to justify a new theoretical structure for the critical analysis and transformation of social and political practice.

Marcuse's main objective in "Industrialization and Capitalism in the Work of Max Weber," presented originally at the centenary conference marking Weber's birth, was to indicate the *political* character of Weber's allegedly "formal" concept of Western rationality.[26] Marcuse was particularly concerned about the fated and irresistible character of the so-called rationalization process which, according to Weber, constituted a culmination of the practice of capitalism in a dead (bureaucratic) mechanism, an unwound mainspring emptied of all possibility. Paralleling this development for Weber was another unilinear process emanating more specifically from Protestantism and the derived "spirit" of capitalism, namely, the gradual banishment of mystery from the world. Borrowing from Schiller, Weber referred to this parallel process as the "disenchantment" or "demagicalization" of the modern world.[27]

What is missing in Weber's overarching category of rationalization is not just the presence of an optimism sufficient to justify the possibility of possibility. There is also evident here a failure to discriminate between discrete features of the alleged phenomenon itself, for example the different roles played by science, capitalism, bureaucracy, the rule of law, and the social sciences themselves as distinct elements requiring specific recognition and treatment.[28] Marcuse is anxious to show that Weberian rationalization covers over the reality of irrational domination in order to show that rationality itself is ultimately irrational. Marcuse refuses to accept this assessment, arguing instead that the rationalization process is irrational because it serves to cover over the fact of *domination*. It therefore takes reason's name in vain. Reason is not irrational: what is called reason can *appear* irrational when its *partial* rationality is equated with the whole. Once rationalization is understood to mean "rational(ized) domination," our faith in reason is renewed and we are not required to equate present developments with anything but a *false totality*.

Marcuse takes explicit exception to the materialist view of Ernst Bloch, which argues (following Marx) that the reason of modern science was fundamentally distorted by capitalism. This fact explains on its own the present dehumanized technology we face, one which functions under the guise of reason as a force for domination. Science as a consequence is argued by Bloch to have been initially good; its clear technological disposition is a function of its subordination to capitalism, rather than being inherent in its epistemic structure.[29] Since for Marcuse the fusion of technology and domination is part of a "world project" in which modern science participates directly by dint of its logic and structure, social transformation in the direction of overcoming this domination would require not only a new technology but a new science. If capitalism is not "responsible" for distorting science in order to generate a technological domination which masquerades as rationality, then overcoming capitalism without overcoming science is insufficient and unsatisfactory.[30]

Habermas treats Marcuse's position as a restatement of the concern in Protestant and Jewish mysticism with the "resurrection of fallen nature."[31] Domination and mastery are virtually *built-into* modern science, claims Marcuse, citing "its own method and concepts" as a basis for arguing that such an orientation to nature could not help but generate a similar attitude on the part of some men to others.[32] It is the idea of *rational* domination which is new here, not domination *per se*. From it is derived the view that capitalism received more than simply aid and comfort from science, particularly following nineteenth-century industrialization. If this is indeed the case then Marcuse is in fact suggesting that modern science provided a basic model and *Weltanschaung* which was indispensable to the later construction of social reality under capitalism. Capitalism itself *followed from*, and sought to "capitalize" upon, the model of rational domination already developing in modern science.

If Marcuse is arguing that a "new science" is required in order to render modern technology rational and transform capitalism into a more human collective, then the question arises as to what exactly this means. Is it a lament for the fact we got the science we got instead of something better? Or is it rather the hope that out of the science we got we can *create* something better as a consequence of having had it? If the first, then Marcuse is dangerously close to Weber, since there is no way out of "rational domination" as a synonym for the rationalization process. All we can do is point out that this reality is not proof of the hideousness of reason, but rather indicates the triumph of a partial reason which has forgotten its subordinate status in its determination to constitute itself as the totality. If the second, then the possibility of a new science might be readily conceivable in some of the new concerns scientists are beginning to exhibit, for example, for ecological responsibility and weapons control.

My difficulty with Habermas' critique of Marcuse derives in large part from the fact that I believe that the second meaning is the correct one, and that therefore the possibility of a new relation to nature viewed as a living partner rather than a neutral externality which excludes us is not as ridiculous as it seems to Habermas. Habermas appears to be in essential agreement with Popper on this score: there is a *logic* of science and the overcoming of this logical structure means the overcoming of science *per se*. "The idea of a New Science will not stand up to logical scrutiny any more than that of a New Technology, if indeed science is to retain the meaning of modern science inherently oriented to possible technical control." Habermas goes on to cite Marcuse's book *One-Dimensional Man*, where he allegedly contradicts himself by saying that to revolutionize technological rationality we only need to transform the institutional framework. "The structure of scientific-technical progress would be conserved, and only the governing values would be changed," concludes Habermas.[33]

Habermas fears the tendency in Marcuse to fragment the problem of rationality in such a way that one element becomes of primary concern, while others are viewed as products of an earlier "distortion."[34] What Marcuse is arguing may be contradictory in a sense legitimate for critical theorists, if he knows he is doing it and intends to do it. On the other hand, it seems to me not inconsistent to argue that (1) a new science is needed, and that (2) it can come about if the system of production is transformed, if it is accepted that (3) this new science would be defined in terms of its "works," while its logical structure was maintained intact. Habermas believes that modern science is *inherently* instrumental, that is, technological, thus that its uses are virtually preordained by its formal epistemic structure. Thus his tendency to speak of "scientific-technical progress." By construing the hope for a new science *undialectically* as an *alternative* to what we got rather than a possible development out of it, Habermas has been unduly cavalier with Marcuse's (and others') argument. Habermas has adopted a *causilinear* notion of beginning and ending which abjures the possibility of novelty through evolution altogether.[35]

III

The direction this takes Habermas in is now wellknown. Habermas returns *to Weber* as an antidote to what he considers to be an unsatisfactory formulation by Marcuse (and Marx), namely, Marcuse's emphasis on "the political content of technical reason" that he discovers in Weber's allegedly formal concept of rationalization as a process and a fate. When I say Habermas has "returned" to Weber I mean that he takes Weberian rationalization as his point of departure in reformulating the problem of rationality in the advanced societies. In order to overcome Marcuse's fragmentation, Habermas creates one of his own which is derived directly from the distinction in Weber between rationalization and the disenchantment of the world. For rationalization Habermas substitutes *work,* or "systems of rational-purposive action." For the disenchantment of the world he substitutes *interaction,* or "symbolically-mediated interaction." The first is governed by technical rules, the second by consensual norms.[36]

Habermas argues that it is precisely the threat posed to the autonomy of symbolically mediated interaction by the non-speech of scientific-technical talk which accompanies the increasingly ascendant role of systems of rational purposive action which delineates the contours of the problem of freedom and the possibility of social transformation. The latter he refers to as "emancipation." Habermas is clearly Weberian in his assessment of the contemporary situation in the advanced societies, for he sees rationalization and its non-speech as phenomena which have burst their proper bounds. Whereas prior to the last fifty or seventy-five years systems of rational purposive action (work), and the partial (because technical) rationality which is their hallmark, were *embedded* in an institutional framework that favoured interaction, and accompanying socio-cultural values different from (and probably in opposition to) those of work, rationalization in the form of the domination of systems of rational purposive action appears to be creating *its own* institutions (e.g., "rational domination") and annihilating those which formerly prevailed.[37]

Reliance on such an ecological metaphor is problematic to the extent that it allows the theorist to fall into a causilinear and mechanistic cast of mind which first construes ensuing developments unilinearly (and pessimistically), then seeks to generate an option based upon a similar logic devoted to "overcoming" these trends through action. In this case the action derived is paradoxical because it simultaneously aims at heightening the consciousness of domination while it relies on this very heightened consciousness to effect emancipatory changes. It was Habermas' view in "Technology and Science as Ideology" that capitalism had largely (if temporarily) *succeeded* in legitimating its domination through the permanent expansion of systems of rational-purposive action, and their concurrent "rationalization," and this worried him. Legitimation is primary, which is to say that Weber's way of conceptualizing the relation between rationalization and disenchantment is incomplete because it fails to account for the prior consciousness which makes "rationalization from below" both possible and uniquely modern.

This leads in turn to the view that, for the first time, such pressure from below *calls forth* "rationalization from above," that is, from those supporters of the bourgeoisie who are experts in reshaping and modifying existing value systems or in generating new ones. If we define as "ideology" any systematic attempt to challenge the credibility of traditional values and belief systems, then there are no "pre-bourgeois" ideologies, and modern science emerges as the pre-eminent institutional basis for the bourgeois critique. But Habermas is here making Marcuse's case since for him rationalization from below is chronologically prior and constitutes the basis for the later-to-develop articulation between science and technology. It is only *after* an interdependence between science and technology develops in the nineteenth century that science begins to contribute to rationalization from below. To say that science contributed *earlier* through its very form, and not just through the intentions of individual scientists, to legitimating capitalist industrialization, or even to the legitimation of limited systems of rational purposive action prior to industrialization, is to assume that such a claim, even if true, establishes its *inherently* technological and instrumental character. It does not.

But even if we acknowledge such a claim, this in no way reaches the earlier point regarding my interpretation of Marcuse's notion of a "new science." Habermas can only speak to this by arguing that Marx's critique of political economy is no longer sufficient because it assumed that political economy constituted the prevailing legitimizing ideology, which in turn presupposed that society and the state were in a particular relation to one another as substructure and superstructure. Habermas thinks that by pointing to state intervention he can show the inadequacy of Marx's critique, given changed conditions, when those very changed conditions were anticipated in Marx's critique itself as ones which would generate contradictions and challenge the existing system of legitimations.[38] Habermas wants to underscore capitalism's uniqueness, not as a system (like any other) where productive forces lead to "structural modification of the institutional framework," but rather as one which for the first time in history establishes the legitimacy of its domination not "from the lofty heights of cultural tradition" but instead "from the base of social labour." Being uniquely dependent for its legitimation on its *productive capacity,* its strength as a system, secure in the short-term, is clearly endangered in the long run if Marx's thesis regarding the decreasing capital-forming capacity of technological improvements is correct.

Habermas' Weberian reformulation of the Marxian distinction between production (work) and politics and culture (interaction) bifurcates industrial society, then, on the basis of the source and character of legitimation. Not just the source (from below) but the character: it is self-sustaining so long as the "logic" of capitalist industrialization holds sway. This logic presumes a continuing direct relationship between increases in technological efficiency, and technical advance generally, and profit maximization, however short or long-term it may be. It is the resulting process whereby the political system and the culture are "adapted" to the new requisites of economic-technological (instrumental) rationality which, Habermas argues, Weber has in mind when he speaks of "rationalization." Presumably it is Weber's failure to specify more clearly than he did the distinction, and the processual relation, between rationalization from below and rationalization from above which is problematic, since it might be argued that this in particular is responsible for Weber's failure to see a way out of what he believed to be an inexorable and irreversible process. Habermas, in reducing the key theoretical concept of the master reductionist himself, has drawn attention, he believes, to the dependence of Weber's pessimism on precisely the *refusal* to reduce "rationalization" so that a possibility of social transformation might show through.

Again, it is the role of modern science (and technology) as an agent legitimating the ("rational") *domination* characteristic not only of the advanced societies but of their pre-industrial capitalist predecessors, and not just its role as a *productive force* generating the exponential growth of modern technology, which Habermas puts forward as evidence of the need for a crucial reformulation of the system of legitimation which prevailed when Marx wrote. The issue here is whether we are authorized to distend these two functions—the ideological and the economic-technological—or rather see in science's capacity to lend support to the claim of rational domination the realization by those so convinced that, at least in a general sense, it *really does* constitute a central productive force. Habermas would likely not disagree; indeed he makes this very point a number of times in his writings. The problem would then appear to lie *not* with the status of this observation, but in the fact that its correctness establishes the presence of an institutional support (or legitimation) for a system of allegedly rational domination based on production which is really not rational at all. That Weber could see no way out, having made precisely this claim, is a major point of departure for Habermas in his critique of Marcuse.

Our point, however, is that there is a substantial difference between the claim that science is *now* a legitimating force as a consequence of its contribution to production, and what Habermas really needs to establish, namely, science's *inherently* technological character. The first claim may well require that certain observations of Marx's critique be updated, addressed as it was to political economy, while the second, intended to replace the Marxian analytic altogether, demands that Habermas show that science constituted a central legitimating force *prior to* its emergence as a central productive force, and this he fails to do. He thinks that the central role of science in production and technology disputes Marx when its long-term effects will likely assist in making Marx's case. It is modern science which is allegedly "responsible" for the collapse of legitimating systems *independent of* production, as the following statement by Habermas makes clear:

> As long as the productive forces were visibly linked to the rational decisions and instrumental action of men engaged in social production, they could be understood as the potential for a growing power of technical control and not be confused with the institutional framework in which they are embedded. However, with the institutionalization of scientific-technical progress, the potential of the productive forces has assumed a form owing to which men lose consciousness of the dualism of work and interaction.[39]

Habermas' insistence in speaking of "scientific-technical progress" here presumes the very claim we dispute, namely, that science is, and was, *inherently* technological even prior to its emergence as a central productive force harnessed to modern economic and military technology by industrial (corporate and state) capitalism. Habermas' assumption is premised on critical theory's view that knowledge is *never neutral,* and that therefore the critique of reflection realized by science constitutes proof of its *opposite* orientation. This, in turn, depends upon a particular view of "inherent" in the claim that science is inherently technological. Inherent here refers to formal epistemic structure, and effectively defends a logical relation between theory and practice not unlike Popper's claim, but of central significance to a proper understanding of Habermas in particular. This point is given detailed discussion in the next section. Habermas' concern with the fact that science has become a legitimizing ideology, "detaching society's self-understanding from the frame of reference of communicative action and from the concepts of symbolic interaction," thus substitutes criticism of science's present role premised on its alleged *former* function as a legitimating agent for an analysis of the problems which arise out of its *actual function* as a central productive force. Thus the point made earlier regarding Habermas' interpretation of Marcuse's interest in a "new science."[40]

Habermas' intellectual support for these claims includes Arnold Gehlen, a thinker whose picture of the advanced societies is hardly less reversible than that of Weber, Arendt, or Ellul. Habermas himself, however, sees in the *empirical* irrelevance of some of Marx's observations about class and class conflict (which he confuses with the alleged irrelevance of the Marxian analytic itself) a sort of Marcusian one-dimensionality. Though class antagonisms have not been abolished but remain latent, the idea that the underprivileged might overturn the system by revolution becomes incomprehensible. While effectively disfranchised, they are not, however, exploited, "because the system does not live off their labour." It is precisely the *internalization* of the work-oriented non-speech beholden to scientific-technical progress which annihilates the possibility of "seeing beyond" the presently prevailing industrial system of one-dimensional society for the large majority. Thus the new form of legitimation, having "cast off the old shape of ideology" as an external rationalization of one class's power over another, can only be overcome by first comprehending a *general emancipatory interest* on the part of the entire human race rather than the liberation of one class.

It seems to me that here Habermas once again accedes to an *empirical* notion of concreteness which reconstructs Marx as a social scientist, and thereafter formulates his concepts of labour *economically,* and of class and class conflict demographically. In the first place it is clear that Marx saw proletarian emancipation as the basis for the liberation of *all* men, and not just the working class. Second, however, is a difficulty in handling Marx as a theorist which strikes me as really problematic for Habermas, and for those who concur in his revised analysis of the situation. In reformulating key Marxian notions like labour, class, and mode of production empirically, Habermas wants to distend collective cultural and linguistic aspects from these allegedly "substructural" characteristics in order to show that it is "symbolically mediated interaction" which stands behind the substructure-superstructure dichotomy and constitutes an analytic with clearly remedial and transformational possibilities.[41] Note, however, that in order to accomplish this, it becomes necessary for Habermas to *reformulate* these Marxian notions by reducing them to the empirical phenomena in which their meaning is alleged to be exhausted. Thus, Marx's claim in *The German Ideology* and elsewhere which establishes the theoretic intention given in the use of terms like labour, class, and mode of production is lost, or rather ignored in favour of a functionalist conception of meaning in line with reduction and empirical concreteness.

IV

Earlier we stated the importance to Habermas of Popper's claim of a *logical* relation between theory and practice, and now we must expand on this point. It is important to see in Habermas' endorsement of a critical social science reconciling reformism with structural critique an *extension* of Popper's claim. Habermas effectively accepts the claim, but then employs it against *both science and historicism,* since in the first case he wants to show science's alleged inherently technological and instrumental character, thus its limit as a model for self-reflection. To depend on a claim to "inherency," as Habermas does in the case of science in its relation to technology and associated instrumental rationality norms, is to rest that claim on the assumption of a logical relation between a science which cannot be neutral and its alleged inevitable product—political domination underwritten by norms of technological rationality. In the process Habermas seeks to make a case for an alternative logically related combination—theory and practice. Only by reformulating science *as* technology can he make his case, given the distinction he enforces between *techne* and *praxis,* the first instrumentally rational and the second premised on collective self-reflection.

As for our claim that Habermas allows the postulation of a logical relation between knowledge and practice to be turned against historicism, we could cite his substantial differences with Marcuse, indeed the entire first generation of critical theorists as well as Marx himself, in support of it. Marcuse, for example, is alleged to have been unable to break free of Marx's critique of ideology which limited itself to critique within the existing conceptual and institutional structure. Concerned in the main with grounding Marx's theory ontologically, Marcuse ignored the need for an epistemological grounding because he refused to challenge reliance on "objective conditions" allegedly present in Marx. He therefore is guilty of "short-circuiting" the problem of reflection. It is precisely the compatibility of bourgeois ideology with the status quo in one-dimensional society which demands that critical theory escape Marx's dependence on the very institutions he is criticizing.[42] Habermas believes that Marx's critique of ideology is no longer revolutionary but in fact has been absorbed into the status quo, thus that critical theory must reconstruct its foundations if it is to remain relevant.

We have attempted to take issue with Habermas in order to suggest the instrumental and interventionist implications of his effort to overcome the tension between concept and object, given his attempt to generalize a Socratic vision of social change through reflection, which depends on the assumption of universal intelligibility. In his critical social science, theory's role is necessarily diminished: it becomes an instrument or agent whose value lies in what it suggests we seek to grasp by reformulating it in the form of testable, falsifiable, hypotheses. Even more to the point is the propriety of the unreflective *success* orientation ordained for the so-called social technologies by Popper. Habermas' attempt to weave a middle path between the Scylla of piecemeal social engineering and the Charybdis of historicism must ultimately fail and probably in favour of the former, if only because Habermas has become an uncompromising opponent of historicism who appears to accept Popper's claim to a logical relation when applied to the student protest movements of the late 1960s in Germany.[43]

In effect, what Habermas is anxious to realize is a revised version of Popper's open society thesis which takes account of the need to extend critical reflection to science itself. It is in doing this that he seeks to show the limited validity of science's (distant) model status, given the fact that it is both inherently technological and a *social and intellectual* force legitimating ("rational") domination. Thus an emphasis on the assertion of a logical relation between knowledge and its utilization, turned against a science whose claim to neutrality is now revealed as sheer ideology, demands an alternative model for the truly rational society. What Habermas is saying to Popper is that *science as well as historicism* is an enemy of the open society. Since it is alleged to be inherently technological, it must not be allowed to masquerade as the paragon of reflection. Critical rationalism, in other words, is insufficiently reflexive about its own auspices, which "really" favour success rather than truth, after all is said and done. Science, being instrumental *(techne)* must subordinate itself to *praxis*. With this, Popper's vaunted distinction between science and technology itself collapses.[44]

In his latest work, *Legitimation Crisis,* Habermas has made his intentions even more explicit. Complementing his subordination to

Weber and Popper is the almost Parsonian character of a non-analytical scheme for formally (synthetically) conceptualizing the crisis he now needs to find evidence for outside himself. Habermas would probably be the first to agree that these recent developments in his thinking clearly portend the end of critical theory. This to the extent that we understand the tension between concept and object, the partial reflexivity of a *"negative* dialectics," to be the essence of critical, as opposed to traditional, theory in the work of Horkheimer, Adorno, and Marcuse.[45] Given in the notion of the critical theory is also the priority of theorizing itself, in contrast to the Popperian notion which views theory as valuable only when it is structurally decomposed into testable, falsifiable hypotheses oriented to resolving the curiosities of a neutral observer eschewing reflexivity. Habermas, we submit, seeks a middle way between these polar alternatives; thus his critique of both Popper and the historicism of critical theory in behalf of a critical social science committed to "radical reformism" through critique.

What is of enduring significance about Habermas' reformulation, however, is the degree to which he accedes to the basic requirements of a positivism he once abjured in search of a reconciliation of concept and object, theory and practice, analytic and remedial. Most prominent, of course, is the subordination to reductionism which serves to establish the priority of an empirical notion of the concrete and the abstract in his thinking. In addition there is the conviction that theory must itself *endorse* incrementalism *positively,* which indicates a clear shift toward social science interventionism and the view of knowledge as a grasp rather than a glimpse. Finally there is the reliance upon Weber's view of rationalization as an abstract totality which simultaneously indicts science *as* technology while it seeks to *use* this as leverage for endorsing a focus on symbolically mediated interaction and "communicative competence" as a "getting behind" the negatively dialectical tension between analytic and remedial in both Marx and the first generation of critical theorists, particularly Marcuse.

Habermas' commitment to reason, as noted, presumes universal intelligibility while it seeks to overcome the defects of "Utopian social planning" pointed out by Popper.[46] In attempting to demonstrate the validity of an effort to generalize the Socratic ideal, he hopes to overcome the dangerous excesses of historicism which he believes he observed in the student protest movements of the late 1960s. Extending Popper's critique, and modifying it so that it fits modern science, allows him to see in an empirically reduced notion of rationalization a possibility for transformation which Weber, tempted to see reason itself as ultimately irrational, could not see. The Weberian analytic is thus maintained in a way that Popper will be little more willing to accept than he did the original Weberian formulation, unreservedly critical of science as it was. While Popper may well appreciate Habermas' clear preference for Socrates over Plato for reasons not unlike his own,[47] he is not likely to accept his critique of science as inherently dominative and technological, thus subject to the same claims regarding an alleged logical relation between knowledge and its utilization that Popper puts forward in condemnation of historicism.

And then there is Marx, and his relation to the allegedly Hegelian Marxism of the first generation of critical theorists. We have taken specific issue with Habermas and his supporters on the question both of their interpretation of Marx as a theorist and their claim to have overcome the tension between the analytic and remedial in a way which allows them to "stand behind" the Marxian focus when they in fact depend on the failure of the economic system to give them their chance. Marx was only too well aware of the unpredictability of political life; and this is something Habermas has sought to correct by showing that it need not be the case and ought not to be the case. The real question for Habermas must remain whether, in achieving a *theoretical* reconciliation between theory and practice, he has not so radically transfigured theorizing that it has no choice but to accede to the "facts." The loss of that tension between concept and object given in the critical theory as a negative dialectics would then signify the triumph of Hegel, but the unreflexive Hegel who endorsed civil society rather than the author of the modern teaching whose method Marx sought to recover and whose vision he sought to redirect.

NOTES

1. Relevant works include: *The Logic of Scientific Discovery* [(New York: John Wiley, 1958); originally published in 1934–35]; *The Poverty of Historicism* [(London: Routledge and Kegan Paul, 1957); originally written in 1935–36]; *The Open Society and its Enemies* (London: Routledge and Kegan Paul, 1945); *Conjectures and Refutations* (London: Routledge and Kegan Paul, 1963); *Objective Knowledge* (London: Oxford University Press, 1972); and "Normal Science and its Dangers," in *Criticism and the Growth of Knowledge,* edited by Imre Lakatos and Alan Musgrave (London: Cambridge University Press, 1970), pp. 51–58.

2. Published, in considerably modified form, as *Der Positivismusstreit in der Deutschen Sociologie* (Neuweid/Berlin, 1969) and in English as *The Positivist Dispute in German Sociology* (London: Heinemann, 1976 forthcoming), translated by Glyn Adey and David Frisby. Also see *Positivism and Sociology*, edited by Anthony Giddens (London: Heinemann, 1974) and David Frisby, "The Popper-Adorno Controversy: the Methodological Dispute in German Sociology," *Philosophy of the Social Sciences*, Vol. 2, No. 2 (June 1972), pp. 105–119.

3. Hans Albert, "The Myth of Total Reason," in *The Positivist Dispute in German Sociology*, pp. 163–197, and in *Positivism and Sociology*, pp. 157–194.

4. The conference itself had taken place in 1961. See the comments of David Frisby in "Introduction to the English Translation," *The Positivist Dispute in German Sociology*, ix–xxxxiv.

5. See Theodor Adorno, "Sociology and Empirical Research," in *The Positivist Dispute in German Sociology*, pp. 868–86; and David Frisby, "The Popper-Adorno Controversy," *op. cit.*

6. Max Horkheimer, "Traditional and Critical Theory," in Horkheimer, *Critical Theory* (New York: Seabury Press, 1974), pp. 188–243, and postscript, pp. 244–252; Horkheimer, *The Eclipse of Reason* (New York: Seabury Press, 1974). Also see Albrecht Wellmer, *"Critique of Instrumental Reason* and *Critical Theory,"* in Wellmer, *Critical Theory of Society* (New York: Herder and Herder, 1970).

7. Trent Shroyer, "Toward a Critical Theory for Advanced Industrial Society," in *Recent Sociology, Number 2*, edited by H. P. Dreitzel (New York: Macmillan, 1970), pp. 210–234; H. T. Wilson, "Capitalism, Science and the Possibility of Political Economy," (unpublished paper).

8. John O'Neill, "Scientism, Historicism, and the Problem of Rationality," in *Modes of Individualism and Collectivism*, edited by John O'Neill (London: Heinemann, 1973), pp. 3–26, especially p. 3, note 5; O'Neill, "The Responsibility of Reason and the Critique of Political Economy," in *Phenomenology and the Social Sciences*, edited by Maurice Natanson (Evanston, Illinois: Northwestern University Press, 1973), pp. 279–309.

9. See Popper, *Conjectures and Refutations*, pp. 33–65, 215–250; and Popper, *Objective Knowledge*, pp. 32–105; Popper, *The Logic of Scientific Discovery*, pp. 15–23 (preface to the English edition, 1958).

10. Albrecht Wellmer, "Latent Positivism in Marx's Philosophy of History," in Wellmer, *op. cit.*, pp. 67–119.

11. William Leiss, *The Domination of Nature* (Boston: Beacon Press, 1974).

12. See Alasdair MacIntyre, *Marcuse* (London: Collins, 1970), especially chapter 2; Goran Therborn, "The Frankfurt School," *New Left Review*, No. 63 (1970), pp. 65–96; and Therborn, "Jürgen Habermas," *New Left Review*, No. 67 (May–June 1971).

13. Max Weber, "Science as a Vocation," in *From Max Weber*, edited by Hans Gerth and C. Wright Mills (New York: Oxford University Press, 1946), pp. 129–156, at pp. 137–141. Also H. T. Wilson, "Reading Max Weber: The Limits of Sociology," *Sociology* Vol. 10, No. 2, May 1976, pp. 297–315.

14. Popper, *The Poverty of Historicism;* Frederick Hayek, *The Counterrevolution of Science* (New York: Free Press, 1955).

15. Albrecht Wellmer, "Empirico-Analytical and Critical Social Science," in Wellmer, *op.cit.*, pp. 9–65 at p. 20. Also Popper, *The Poverty of Historicism*, pp. 49–52. An excellent critique of Popper's claims is Laird Addis, "The Individual and the Marxist Philosophy of History," in *Readings in the Philosophy of the Social Sciences*, edited by May Brodbeck (New York: Macmillan, 1968), pp. 317–335.

16. As discussed by Popper in *The Logic of Scientific Discovery*, pp. 27–111 at pp.

86–92, and attacked by Thomas Kuhn in *The Structure of Scientific Revolutions* (Chicago: University of Chicago Press, 1962). See especially the enlarged 1970 edition, which includes the 1969 postscript. Also see generally *Criticism and the Growth of Knowledge*.

17. *Objective Knowledge*, p. 262.

18. See *The Poverty of Historicism*, pp. 130–143.

19. See *The Open Society and its Enemies*, introduction and chapter one.

20. On the relation between science and technology, see Mario Bunge, "Technology as Applied Science," *Technology and Culture*, Volume 7 (1966), pp. 329–347. Compare to Hans Jonas, "The Practical Uses of Theory," in *Philosophy of the Social Sciences*, edited by Maurice Natanson (New York: Random House, 1963), pp. 119–142.

21. See René Dubos, *The Dreams of Reason* (New York: Columbia University Press, 1961), pp. 12–29; and Moody Prior, "Bacon's Man of Science," in *The Rise of Science in Relation to Society*, edited by Leonard M. Marsak (New York: Macmillan, 1964), pp. 41–54.

22. See Weber, *op.cit.*, for this tension between science's dominative and emancipatory aspects, which, however, is resolved in favour of science given Weber's refusal to leave his sociological post and theorize. For a critical analysis, Wilson, "Reading Max Weber," *op. cit.*

23. In *Conjectures and Refutations*, pp. 312–335, and more generally in his discussion of Hegel and Marx in *The Open Society and its Enemies*.

24. A recent spate of materials from disillusioned incrementalists bears this out. See especially Thomas Schelling, "On the Ecology of Micromotives," *The Public Interest* (Fall, 1971), pp. 59–98; Kenneth Boulding, "The Economics of the Coming Spaceship Earth," in *Population, Evolution and Birth Control*, edited by Garrett Hardin (San Francisco: W. H. Freeman, 1969); A. E. Keir Nash, "Pollution, Population and the Cowboy Economy," (review essay), *Journal of Comparative Administration* (May 1970), pp. 109–128; and Alastair Taylor, "The Computer and the Liberal: Our Ecological Dilemma," *Queens Quarterly* (Autumn 1972), pp. 289–300. Critical theorists anticipated the ecological dilemma these materials take up some thirty-five to forty years ago.

25. See *The Poverty of Historicism*, pp. 64–70, 130–143; *Conjectures and Refutations*, pp. 120–136, and especially Frederick Hayek, *The Counterrevolution of Science*, pp. 80–102.

26. In *Max Weber and Sociology Today*, edited by Otto Stammer (New York: Harper and Row, 1971), pp. 133–151 and, in somewhat revised form, in Herbert Marcuse, *Negations* (Boston: Beacon Press, 1968), pp. 201–226.

27. Weber, *op. cit.*, pp. 137–141, and editorial commentary pp. 51–52, 73–74.

28. See Karl Löwith, "Max Weber's Interpretation of the Bourgeois-Capitalistic World in terms of the Guiding Principle of Rationalization," in *Max Weber*, edited by Dennis Wrong (Englewood Cliffs, N.J.: Prentice Hall, 1970), pp. 101–122. Also my forthcoming *The American Ideology* (London: Routledge and Kegan Paul, 1976) for analysis of the role of these institutions in framing the "problem of rationality" in its relation to domination in the West.

29. Here it is important to distinguish between *three* possible "orientations" on the part of science, not two: (1) its *inherently* technological character; (2) its inherent goodness (Bloch); and (3) its *neutrality*. Habermas adopts the first position, while we argue for a position closer to (3). This in spite of critical theory's claim that knowledge can *never* be neutral.

30. Compare to Weber, *op. cit.* on the relation between science and technology. Also see Max Weber, *Theory of Social and Economic Organization*, edited and translated by

Talcott Parsons (New York: Free Press, 1947), pp. 158–164, where Weber deals with the *economic* factor in its influence on the scope and direction of modern technology.

31. Jürgen Habermas, "Technology and Science as Ideology," in Habermas, *Toward a Rational Society* (London: Heinemann, 1971), pp. 81–122 at pp. 85–86.

32. In Herbert Marcuse, *One-Dimensional Man* (Boston: Beacon Press, 1964), pp. 166–167. Also see Leiss, *op. cit.*

33. Habermas, *Toward a Rational Society,* pp. 88–89. See Marcuse, *One-Dimensional Man,* pp. 234–239.

34. See Habermas' earlier essay, prepared originally for the 1961 German Sociological Association meetings, "A Positivistically Bisected Rationalism," in *The Positivist Dispute in German Sociology* (in press), pp. 198–225, reprinted in *Positivism and Sociology,* pp. 195–223, as "Rationalism Divided in Two."

35. See Kurt Wolff, "Beginning: In Hegel and Today," in *The Critical Spirit,* edited by Kurt Wolff and Barrington Moore (Boston: Beacon Press, 1967), pp. 72–105.

36. Habermas, "Technology and Science as Ideology," *op.cit.,* pp. 91–94. As we shall see, Habermas' bifurcation itself sunders a totality he once defended against Albert, *op.cit.,* in order to reduce, then *formally* reconstruct, with results similar to those he once criticized in others.

37. *Ibid.,* pp. 96–99.

38. For a general critique of the "one-dimensional" argument which Marcuse and Habermas share, see Paul Mattick, "The Limits of Integration," in *The Critical Spirit,* pp. 374–400, an attempt to demonstrate the continuing relevance of Marx's *economic* argument to the advanced societies. Compare Mattick's analysis to that of Trent Shroyer, a disciple of Habermas, in *The Critique of Domination* (New York: George Braziller, 1973).

39. Habermas, "Technology and Science as Ideology," *op. cit.,* p. 105.

40. *Ibid.,* pp. 105–106. Imposing the reconstructed bifurcation between work and interaction on feudal society seems especially problematic, given the usual reference to medieval collectives as totalities. In this analysis (Marx's), the separation itself is a unique feature of *bourgeois* society.

41. On Marx as theorist, see Alan Blum, "Reading Marx," *Sociological Inquiry,* Volume 43, No. 1, pp. 23–34; and especially *Theorizing* (London: Heinemann, 1974), pp. 247–265.

42. Jeremy Shapiro, "From Marcuse to Habermas," *Continuum,* Vol. 8, Nos. 1 and 2 (Spring–Summer, 1970), p. 71.

43. See Habermas, *Toward a Rational Society,* pp. 1–49. On the complementarity between Popperian social science and Habermas' critical social science, see Gerard Radnitsky, *Contemporary Schools of Meta-Science,* (Göteborg, 1970).

44. See Popper, *Objective Knowledge,* p. 262, for this argument, discussed in Sections I and II, this essay. Also *The Poverty of Historicism,* pp. 56–62.

45. Especially Horkheimer, "Traditional and Critical Theory," and "Postscripts," op. cit.; and Adorno, *Negative Dialectics.*

46. Popper, *The Poverty of Historicism,* pp. 64–76.

47. As stated in *The Open Society and Its Enemies,* pp. 227–228.

COMMUNICATIONS AND EMANCIPATION: REFLECTIONS ON THE LINGUISTIC TURN IN CRITICAL THEORY

ALBRECHT WELLMER

In the last section of the *Economic-Philosophical Manuscripts,* entitled "A Critique of Hegel's Dialectic and General Philosophy," Marx formulates the principle for a materialist critique and re-interpretation of Hegel's *Phenomenology* when he states: "The outstanding achievement of Hegel's Phenomenology—the dialectic of negativity as the moving and creating principle—is, first, that Hegel grasps the self-creation of man as a process, objectification as loss of the object, as alienation and transcendence of this alienation, and that he, therefore, grasps the nature of labour, and conceives objective man (true, because real man) as the result of his own labour."[1] According to Marx, a demystification of Hegel's philosophy of spirit provides us with the clues for a materialist interpretation of world history as the self-creation of man through labour. Marx calls his philosophy of labour "naturalism" or "humanism" and he opposes it to both idealism and the older forms of materialism (i.e., in particular the "physicalist" materialism of the eighteenth century). "We see here," Marx states, "how consistent naturalism or humanism is distinguished from both idealism and materialism, and at the same time constitutes their unifying truth. We also see that only naturalism is able to comprehend

231

the process of world history."[2] In the first of his theses on Feuerbach Marx summarizes concisely what he means by this dialectical overcoming of both idealism and materialism: "The chief defect of all hitherto existing materialism—that of Feuerbach included—is that the thing, reality, sensuousness, is conceived only in the form of the object or of contemplation, but not as human sensuous activity, practice, not subjectively. Hence it happened that the active side, in contradistinction to materialism, was developed by idealism—but only abstractly, since, of course, idealism does not know real, sensuous activity as such."[3]

Now it happened in the context of an epistemological critique of empiricism, that the "active side," as Marx calls it, was "abstractly developed" by idealism. If therefore Marx opposes "real, sensuous activity" to the abstract conception of activity as developed by idealism, it follows that "sensuous activity" for him assumes the peculiar status of a category which is fundamental both as an *anthropological* and as an *epistemological* category. Marx himself unmistakably points to the epistemological significance of this category in his second thesis on Feuerbach, where he states: "The question whether objective *(gegenständliche)* truth can be attributed to human thinking is not a question of theory, but is a *practical* question. In practice man must prove the truth, that is, the reality and power, the this-sidedness *(diesseitigkeit)* of his thinking. The dispute over the reality or nonreality of thinking which is isolated from practice is a purely *scholastic* question."[4] In formulations like this one, Marx anticipates later pragmatist conceptions of knowledge and truth.

Interestingly enough, in his *Theses on Feuerbach,* Marx, as far as he specifies what he means by "sensuous activity" or "practice," does not speak of *labour,* as he does in the *Economic-Philosophical Manuscripts.* He rather speaks of "practical-critical activity," or of "revolutionary practice." A closer reading of the *Manuscripts,* however, would reveal that this difference is rather one of emphasis. For the concept of labour as Marx develops it in the *Manuscripts* is not yet the economic category as it is developed in the first volume of *Capital*; it rather still embraces all "objectifications" and "externalizations" of the "essential powers" of man in his conscious and sensuous activity —i.e., the philosophy of labour is a philosophy of praxis, "praxis" here understood as the world-constitutive and self-generative species life of man.

And yet, it is of course not by accident that in the *Economic-Philosophical Manuscripts* the philosophy of praxis is developed by Marx *as* a philosophy of labour. Due to the internal logic of his materialist re-interpretation of Hegel it is rather labour qua *material production* which for Marx provides the basic paradigm in terms of which he analyses practice as an externalization of the essential powers of man. I cannot here attempt to reconstruct the internal connection between Hegel's philosophy of identity, Marx's critique of Hegel, and the paradigmatic role of "productive labour" in his philosophy of practice.[5] I rather want to point out briefly the epistemological and (possibly) political significance of the corresponding, implicitly reductionist tendency in Marx's conception of sensuous practice. It is this reductionist tendency which, I believe, militates against his own program of a naturalism which would be the unifying truth of both materialism and idealism.

In his theory of historical materialism as well as in his concrete historical and political analyses Marx draws an analytic distinction between two different, although dialectically related, "dimensions" of the reproduction process of societies: the technological dimension *(productive forces)* on the one hand, and the institutional dimension *(relations of production)* on the other. The latter comprises the symbolically mediated forms of social interaction, i.e., forms of social integration (domination) as well as forms of social conflict (class struggle). On the level of anthropological analysis the above distinction made by Marx would require a corresponding conception of man as a tool-making *and* a "symbolizing" animal, with neither determination being reducible to the other. In contrast, in his *anthropological* and meta-theoretical considerations, Marx tries to incorporate the symbolic function into the productive one in order to save the anthropological *primacy* of the category of "material production." Man, *primarily,* is conceived as a tool-making animal. While this means, on the one hand, that Marx's concept of labour inherently comprises the dimensions of social interaction, it means on the other hand that the instrumental "interaction" of man with his physical environment becomes *the* paradigm of interaction, of "sensuous activity" in general. Consequently "productive labour" also provides the basic meaning of "sensuous activity" as an *epistemological* category. If, however, the explication of the epistemological significance of human practice is to be based on the model of instrumental action, then the second thesis on Feuerbach assumes a purely instrumentalist meaning; natural science becomes the basic paradigm for what theoretical knowledge can be, and the relation between science and industry provides the normative model for the relation between theory and practice and their possible unity.[6]

Obviously Marx's own theory of capitalism, i.e., his critique of political economy, does not correspond to this epistemological standard. His theory is essentially a "critical" one: as an analysis of the crisis-mechanism of capitalist society it is at the same time a critique of ideology; as a theory analysing the conditions and the genesis of the exploitation of one class by the other it is at the same time a theory of the revolutionary abolition of this state of exploitation and alienation, and as such it conceives itself as the critical consciousness of the revolutionary process. Marx's program of a naturalism or humanism, as distinct from both materialism and idealism and as their unifying truth, is realized in the critique of political economy as a theory which is neither "scientific" nor "philosophical," or rather, which is scientific and philosophical at the same time. Like scientific theories, it is concerned with the analysis and explanation of empirical phenomena and is internally related to practice as its ultimate test; like philosophical theories, it is concerned with the critique of the misconceptions which a society has of itself, such as institutionalized self-delusions and the ideological abuse of language, and it can become practical only by initiating a process of self-reflection—that is, by awakening class-consciousness. The practice, however, at which this theory aims and which would be its ultimate test is not that of a technical application of nomological knowledge but the historically unique, irreversible, and emancipatory practice of a revolutionary class.

From what I have said so far, it follows that Marx's theory contains an internal, unresolved tension between the dialectical character of the theory of historical materialism and the critique of political economy, on the one hand, and the quasi-reductionist character of his basic anthropological and epistemological assumptions on the other. To recognize this internal tension between different "layers" of Marx's own theory provides us, I believe, with a key for an understanding of certain ambiguities in Marx's own theory;[7] a key also for an evaluation (although not for an historical explanation) of the degeneration of "official" Marxism since the time of the Second International, and for a reconstruction of the basic intentions of various forms of Neo-Marxism which have been developed in opposition to the official, "petrified" forms of Marxism since the early twenties. In this essay I want to show, first, how at some crucial points in the development of Marxist thought the problems contained in Marx's conception of labour come to the fore and, second, how they are related to the recent "linguistic" reformulation of the basic assumptions of historical materialism by Jürgen Habermas.

I

I want to start with a few comments on Friedrich Engels' version of "dialectical materialism." In Engels' theory, the tendency to interpret historical materialism and the critique of political economy according to the methodological model of the natural sciences becomes quite explicit. For Engels, the basic paradigm of revolution was not the French Revolution, as it had been for Marx, but the Industrial Revolution.[8] Correspondingly, he interprets the transition of socialism from utopia toward science literally. He clearly expresses the view that scientific socialism would provide a general knowledge of the laws governing historical and social processes—knowledge which would make scientific control of social processes possible in the same sense in which the knowledge acquired by the natural sciences makes the control and manipulation of natural processes possible.

This "naturalization" of history is also, as has often been pointed out by Engels' critics, the real essence of his "dialecticization"—i.e., "historicization"—of nature. In contradistinction to Marx's historical materialism, Engels' dialectic materialism is literally a "reversal" of Hegelian dialectics. As in Hegel, dialectics for Engels is the moving principle and the principle of movement for a "substance" which guarantees the unity of the world and in particular the unity of nature and history. For Engels, however, this "substance"—as the principle of unity—is "matter" rather than "spirit."[9] As a consequence, "dialectics"—as Engels himself puts it—now becomes a "science" concerned with the general laws of motion and development in nature, history, and thought.[10] This ontological interpretation of dialectics, however, can under materialist presuppositions only lead to a naturalization of history instead of a historicization of nature. Dialectic materialism degenerates into a naturalist metaphysics. Moreover, this materialist "dialectics" leads back to a naive-realistic, i.e., pre-dialectical, epistemology—an epistemology which later on is elaborated by

Lenin in his *Materialism and Empricocriticism* as a picture-theory of knowledge.

The uncritical, ontological conception of dialectics in Engels' theory no longer supports a critical concept of "ideology." "Ideology" is bound to degenerate into a notion designating contents of consciousness in general. As Habermas puts it, "the dependence of consciousness on social being becomes a special case of a general ontological law according to which the higher is dependent on the lower and ultimately everything is dependent on its material 'substratum.' "[11] Consequently the concept of ideology loses the unique strategic significance which it had in Marx's theory, namely, that of a concept signifying a *false* consciousness which *in its falseness adequately expresses* and reflects a "false" social reality. That is a concept of ideology which, rather than signifying a general relationship between matter and spirit, signifies the particular relationship between critique and revolution.[12]

Engels' dialectic materialism, although being a "reversal" of Hegelian idealism, evidently no longer represents a *critical* appropriation of Hegelian dialectics; it is rather a regression to a pre-Kantian form of ontology. In contrast, for Marx dialectics is essentially a historical concept; that is to say, dialectical materialism *is* historical materialism. For Marx, the concept of dialectics would not be applicable to nature-in-itself but only to nature-in-relation-to-man, i.e., to the intercourse between man and nature which is history. While Marx's historical materialism represents a demystification of dialectics, Engels' dialectic materialism represents a re-mystification of materialism: materialism has become metaphysical again.

And yet this is not the whole story. Engels' materialist metaphysics ultimately rests on a hypostatization of the methods of the natural sciences. In an "ontological disguise," therefore, his theory *also* expresses the epistemological consequences which follow if the anthropological primacy of the concept of labour in Marx's own theory is taken seriously. In other words, there exists a subliminal relationship between the epistemological reductionism implicit in Marx's conception of labour and Engels' materialist ontology. The obvious correlates of this materialist ontology, however, are "objectivist" and "determinist" interpretations of historical materialism and the critique of political economy—objectivist and determinist interpretations which actually became current among socialists during the period of the Second International.

Such objectivist misinterpretations of Marx's theory, where they really became dominant, have almost invariably been indicative of a degeneration of socialist *practice*. As a rule they indicate that the connection between theory and practice has been cut off, and that the theory itself has assumed the ideological function of legitimating the bad politics pursued by a party and its leadership respectively. Ironically enough, objectivist misinterpretations of Marxian theory can be used to legitimate two radically opposed, although equally degenerate, forms of "socialist" practice. For the interpretation of this theory as a "scientific" theory exhibiting the "iron laws" of development of history in general, and of capitalism in particular, is inherently ambiguous. It can either mean that revolutionary politics is *unnecessary* (because the breakdown of capitalism is unavoidable), or it can mean that a technocratic revolution-management by an elitist political "vanguard" is *possible* (for the realm of freedom will be established once the capitalist form of property is abolished and the forces of production are developed far enough). In other words, scientistic misinterpretations of Marx's theory can be used to legitimate opportunism and quietism as well as technocratic activism and Stalinism. Of course, objectivist misinterpretations of Marx's theory cannot be held responsible for a degeneration of socialist practice. However, as far as they serve to legitimate a degenerate socialist practice, their criticism becomes an important part of a political critique of socialist practice. For this reason alone, a clarification of the epistemological foundations of historical materialism would be necessary. However, there are also different, more substantive reasons to elaborate the epistemology of historical materialism which I shall indicate in the following sections.

II

Marx assumed that the development of capitalism would not only create the objective conditions of a classless society (viz., the progressive function of capitalism with respect to the development of the forces of production and the increase in the productivity of labour which would make the abolition of scarcity objectively possible), but that it would also by its internal logic create the essential "subjective" preconditions for the self-emancipation of the proletariat. Marx expected that the free and impoverished wage labourer, by the internal logic of the process of mechanization and rationalization of labour and by the internal logic of his self-organization against his capitalist exploiters, would become the self-conscious subject of a proletarian revolution. In fact, however, the self-organization of the proletariat has in many instances only led to a stabilization of the capitalist economy, while successful revolutions have only occurred in more or less "underdeveloped" countries where an impoverished peasantry rather than a highly developed industrial proletariat provided the mass basis for a revolutionary party. While capitalist industrialization so far has not led to socialism, socialism has come into existence only as another road to industrialization. While the established forms of (capitalist) democracy have successfully counteracted the rise of *socialist democracy,* the established forms of (bureaucratic) socialism have successfully counteracted the rise of *democratic* socialism.

I do not believe that the world-historical constellation of political forces to which I am referring is a refutation of Marx's analysis of capitalism. Nor do I believe that it signifies the ultimate defeat of democratic socialism. I do, however, believe that it points to an internal limit of Marx's theory in one important respect. Marx's historical materialism does not provide categories sufficiently clear and distinct to grasp the peculiar rigidity of modern industrial societies with respect to the development of an historical alternative based on the principles of self-determination and democracy. With regard to the conceptualization of the different forms of "rationality" which, according to Marx, are characteristic of capitalist and socialist forms of production respectively, his theory shows a systematic ambiguity. It seems, however, that the attempt to resolve this ambiguity must either lead to a revision of the categorial framework of historical materialism —a revision which would restore the distinction between technical and practical reason—or to the following interpretation (which certainly is not an authentic one given the broader theoretical context of Marx's work). According to this "inauthentic" interpretation, the revolutionary establishment of a classless society would have to be seen as a continuation of that process of "rationalization" which takes place under conditions of capitalist production. This process of rationalization would come to an internal limit under the conditions of private ownership of the means of production. Therefore the expropriation of the exproprieateurs and the dictatorship of the proletariat would be the precondition for the continuation of this process of rationalization—centralization of planning, increase in the productivity of labour, and the administration of things replacing the ruling of people. In other words, according to this latent version of Marxian theory, the transition from capitalism to socialism would mean an extension of the process of rationalization and bureaucratization from the sphere of production to that of the whole of society—corresponding to Engels' vision of a scientific administration of the social process.

I emphasised before, that this is not an authentic interpretation of Marx. It seems, however, that the *categorial* framework underlying his theory of historical materialism does not support those necessary distinctions which would *unambiguously* exclude such a "technocratic" conception of the transition from capitalism to socialism[13]— e.g., the distinction between "reflective" and "productive" knowledge, or between technological rationalization and rationalization qua democratization and emancipation. With "productive labour" as its basic anthropological and epistemological category this theory, moreover, seems to be insufficient even to provide the basis for an adequate *conceptualization* of some of those problems which have been created by the deceptive victories of socialism and the destructive successes of capitalism in our century. In particular, it does not provide a basis for an analysis of the ideological role which science and technology have come to play in the reproduction process of industrial societies.

Max Weber, as is well known, predicted that a socialist revolution could only lead to a new triumph of bureaucratic rationality and therefore to a fortification of that "shell of bondage" in which, according to him, modern man is doomed to live. Weber's prediction is remarkable not because it truly expresses the irresistible force of historical necessity, but because it formulates an antithesis to Marx's conception of socialism and yet, at the same time, is not unambiguously identifiable *as* an antithesis. In his analysis of the process of rationalization and bureaucratization in modern European history, of its internal logic of progress, and its dialectical interdependence with the process of democratization, Weber articulates a problem which for Marx was not yet clearly visible, a problem which, in one form or another, was to become a focus of attention for Neo-Marxist thinking since the early twenties. What first appeared as merely a return to the "true" Hegelian Marx, ultimately led to new conceptions regarding the interrelation between the critique of idealism and the critique of materialism—conceptions in which the critique of instrumental reason as an ideology began to play a predominant role.

III

For Marx the emancipation from philosophy was the precondition for the development of a critical theory of society. Natural science, in contrast, he regarded as the paradigm for a thinking which constantly proves its "truth, i.e., its reality and power, its this-sidedness in practice." Many of the Neo-Marxists since the early twenties hold almost the opposite view, namely, a return to Hegelian or, later on, an adoption of Husserlian or Heideggerian philosophy combined with a critique of scientism. The emancipation from scientism as an ideology for them became the precondition of a restoration of Marxist theory as critique. This was, for example, expressly stated by Karl Korsch. Correspondingly, positivist materialism became a more important target of critique than idealism. This shift of emphasis indicates that with the development of capitalism itself as well as that of the socialist movements, an aspect of "alienation" had moved into the center of attention which for Marx did not yet have a basic significance at all. Lukács' analysis of the reification of consciousness in capitalist society is important not so much because it is an ingenious rediscovery of the early Marx of the *Manuscripts* in the economic writings of the later Marx, but rather because it is the beginning of a critical assimilation of Max Weber's analysis of the historical process of "rationalization" into the corpus of Marxian theory. To be sure, Weber's theory was reinterpreted by Lukács in terms of a critique of political economy. However, this reinterpretation affected both theories, Weber's and Marx's. With Lukács the critique of "technology and science as ideology" (Habermas) begins to replace the critique of the ideology of the exchange of equivalents which had gradually lost its function as an ideological legitimation of capitalism. Correspondingly, the critique of political economy is now being integrated into a critique of instrumental reason.

Lukács, as I said, adopted the concept of "rationalization" from Max Weber and tried to reinterpret it in terms of the critique of political economy. "Rationalization" for him becomes "reification," and "reification" for him is, in the ultimate instance, an expression and a consequence of what Marx analysed as the "fetishism of commodities" in the first volume of *Capital*. The internal dynamics of the capital-labour relationship which has its origin in the "commodification" of labour and which leads to a universalization of commodity relations therefore becomes the "secret essence" and the vehicle of the process of rationalization. Once a society has learned to satisfy all its needs "in terms of commodity exchange," says Lukács, "the principle of rational mechanization and calculability must embrace every aspect of life."[14] Correspondingly the reification of *consciousness* becomes an essential element in the reproduction process of capitalist society. Lukács is the first to criticize the universalization of "formal" rationality not only as grounded in an ultimate irrationality of the system as a whole, but also as a form of ideology which veils as well as legitimates the power-relation underlying the relation between capital and wage labour.

In fact, however, Lukács' brilliant attempt to integrate Weber's analysis of the process of rationalization and bureaucratization into the critique of political economy remains ambiguous. On the one hand he criticizes, like Marcuse and—from a conservative point of view— Leo Strauss after him, the specific restrictions to which the concept of rationality is subjected in Weber's theory—restrictions by which questions concerning ultimate "values" are in principle excluded from possible "rationalization" or from rational discourse. From this perspective Weber's concept of rationalization can only in an ironical sense be directly related to that of "reification." The concept itself expresses the ideology underlying the process of reification. On the other hand, for Lukács the limitations of that peculiar rationality which, by the process of rationalization, becomes a universal form of life, manifest themselves, i.e., "make themselves felt," primarily through the incoherence of the system as a whole, that is, by the lack of integration of the rationalized subsystems into a coherent whole. Lukács still expects that ultimately an economic crisis will reveal the incoherence and irrationality of the capitalist system for everybody and will thereby create the objective possibility of overcoming the reification of consciousness as well as the capitalist form of domination. Like Marx, however, Lukács at this point remains unclear about how *"substantive"* rationalization could be distinguished from the extension of *formal* rationalization to the whole of society. Integrating Weber's analysis simply into the critique of political economy does not provide Lukács with compelling counter-arguments against Weber's pessimist conclusion which he drew from his analysis of the dialectical relationship between "democratization" and "bureaucratization," viz., that socialist democracy would be the ultimate triumph of bureaucracy.

Lukács' attempt to go beyond Weber's abstract concept of "rationalization" and to make the specific political content of the historical process of rationalization visible was part of his larger project to restore the "philosophical" dimension of Marxism. That his attempt ultimately failed is, I believe, in an ironical way related to the fact that his philosophical restoration of Marxism was in some important respects a return to objective idealism. For as far as Marx's historical materialism *is* objective idealism "put on its feet," the problems created by the latent reductionism of Marx's basic anthropological and epistemological assumptions cannot be resolved by a return to objective idealism. It rather seems that the former reflects a structural deficiency of the latter. This would mean that the positivist elements in the Marxist tradition are closely related to an idealist heritage which has not been completely overcome. At this point I would like to focus upon a different although related reason for the ultimate deficiency of Lukács' analysis. According to Lukács the progressive reification of consciousness reflects the universalization of the commodity form in capitalist society. This universalization of the commodity form, however, corresponds to the internal logic of the capital-labour relationship. Now it seems that at the time at which Lukács wrote *History and Class Consciousness* the conception of the autonomously developing economic "base" had already, strictly speaking, become obsolete. Because of the increase in state intervention and the growing interdependence of scientific research and technology, the particular constellation of economics and politics that had been characteristic for liberal capitalism had changed. No longer could the relationship between the economic and the political system be simply regarded as that between "base" and "superstructure." Weber's analysis already referred to a situation in which this mutual penetration of economic, political, and "scientific" subsystems had become clearly visible. With this new constellation of "base" and "superstructure" the presuppositions of the critique of political economy, strictly speaking, ceased to be valid. The new increase of "formal" rationality which resulted from this new constellation, and the threat it contained with regard to the chances of socialist movements, could therefore hardly be adequately analysed on the basis of those presuppositions. In particular, Lukács' attempt to relate the process of reification directly to the universalization of the commodity form prevents him from grasping fully the peculiar novelty of the technocratic ideology which he is criticizing, and its peculiar function in a *post-liberal* phase of capitalism. This ideology is, as Habermas has pointed out, *new* compared with older forms of legitimation—including the bourgeois ideology of just exchange—in that it "severs the criteria for justifying the organization of social life from any normative regulation of interaction, thus depoliticizing them."[15] Technocratic consciousness does not, like traditional forms of legitimation, reflect "the sundering of an ethical situation." It rather reflects "the repression of ethics as such as a category of life."[16]

The ideological nucleus of this technocratic consciousness is, according to Habermas, the elimination of the distinction between the "technical" and the "practical." It therefore can no longer simply be understood as justifying a particular class's interest in domination and as repressing another class's interest in emancipation. It rather affects, as Habermas says, the "human race's emancipatory interest as such." Correspondingly, the critique of this ideology can no longer simply aim at revealing its particular class content. It rather has to restore first of all the very dimension of the "practical" which all former ideologies still presupposed.

> The new ideology consequently violates an interest grounded in one of two fundamental conditions of our cultural existence: in language, or more precisely, in the form of socialization and individuation determined by communication in ordinary language. This interest extends to the maintenance of intersubjectivity of mutual understanding as well as to the creation of communication without domination. Technocratic consciousness makes this practical interest disappear behind the interest in the expansion of our power of technical control. Thus the reflection that the new ideology calls for must penetrate beyond the level of particular historical class interests to disclose the fundamental interests of mankind as such, engaged in the process of self-constitution.[17]

IV

The thesis that the new technocratic ideology is different from any previous ideologies in that it not only suppresses the emancipatory interest of a specific class but threatens the emancipatory interest of the human species as such had already in various forms been developed by T. W. Adorno, M. Horkheimer, and H. Marcuse. Unlike Lukács, these philosophers were aware that the transformation of the critique of political economy into a critique of instrumental reason reflects the historical transformation of liberal capitalism into organized capitalism. What they held in common was the view that with the emergence of organized capitalism a closed universe of "instrumental reason" or "one-dimensional rationality" was being created which not only threatens the chances of emancipatory political movements but also threatens the emancipatory impulses of the suppressed masses as such. Let us make the difference with Lukács a little clearer. If the universal "reification of consciousness" (the progressive instrumentalization of reason) is not only the expression of an economic crisis-mechanism which, while it is approaching its catastrophic end, subjects all spheres of social life to the commodity form, *but* if it is *also* the expression of a political reorganization of capitalist economy which successfully counteracts its self-destructive tendencies, then the threat against emancipatory movements, against the emergence of "class-consciousness" (which is contained in this process of reification), will be much more severe than Lukács was ready to admit. For then it would seem that the political emancipation of the masses, rather than being the "logical" consequence of the unfolding contradictions of capitalism, would have to be achieved *against* the internal logic of the development of capitalism.

I do not believe that this alternative, which seems to emerge in a confrontation of the early Lukács with the philosophers of the Frankfurt School, is a correct one. In part, it of course simply reflects differences of the historical situations in which Lukács on the one hand, Adorno, Horkheimer, and Marcuse on the other, were writing about the reification of consciousness. In part, however, the emergence of this alternative also seems to point to an unresolved problem which the above-mentioned theories seem to share with those of Lukács *and* Marx. I can argue this point here only in an indirect way. It is certainly rather puzzling to compare what Marx said about "instrumental reason" (namely about natural science) and what the philosophers of the Frankfurt School said about it. While for Marx "instrumental reason" (i.e., natural science) is the paradigm of true, non-perverted reason, for the philosophers of the Frankfurt School instrumental reason becomes the paradigm of perverted reason. While for Marx the internal logic of the process of industrialization points toward emancipation, for the philosophers of the Frankfurt School it points toward a new form of servitude: technocratic barbarism. It seems to me that this somewhat puzzling opposition between Marx and his followers not only reflects the historical changes from liberal capitalism to organized capitalism, but that it is also due to the fact that the latent reductionism of Marx's philosophy of history has survived in the philosophy of the Frankfurt School, although, as it were, with inverted signs. This comes to the fore, I believe, in Adorno's and Horkheimer's *Dialectic of Enlightenment.*[18] For here "instrumental reason" becomes the category by which both dimensions of the world-historical process of civilization are conceived, namely, the transformation of external nature (technology, industry, domination of nature) as well as the transformation of internal nature (individuation, repression, forms of social domination). Given this anthropological and epistemological "monism," the philosophers of the Frankfurt School seem to be more consequent and more radical than Marx. For even if the transformation of external nature creates the *objective* possibility of a liberated society, the simultaneous transformation of internal nature is likely to destroy the *subjective* possibilities of emancipatory practice. The "reification of consciousness," which is the price paid for the subjugation of external nature, threatens to destroy in the end the subjectivity of the very subjects who by the transformation of nature had intended their own emancipation.[19]

In an ironical way the latent reductionism of Marx's philosophy of history is here brought to its ultimate consequences. Liberation, however, can now only be conceived as a radical break through the continuum of instrumental reason. As the negation of instrumental reason it would be the resurrection of external and internal nature as well as the beginning of a new history of man. While in Marx's theory there is a tendency to blur the historical *discontinuity* which would separate a liberated society from the universe of instrumental reason, the philosophy of the Frankfurt School is in danger of losing the historical *continuity* which alone could make socialism an *historical* project: liberation becomes an eschatological category.

It seems to me that Habermas' reformulation of the basic assumptions of historical materialism shows a way out of the ambiguities and antinomies of Marxist thought which I have pointed to so far.

Habermas explicitly introduces a categorial distinction into the theory of historical materialism which Marx, in his material analyses, had always implicitly presupposed. Marx distinguishes between two different dimensions in which the self-formation of the human species takes place: that of a cumulative process of technological development (*forces of production,* labour-processes), and that of an emancipatory process of critique and class-struggle *(relations of production)*. What Habermas shows is that this categorical distinction can be developed consistently and with all its epistemological implications only if it is reformulated on a higher level of abstraction as that between *"instrumental"* or "purposive-rational" action on the one hand, and *"communicative"* action on the other. To introduce this distinction means to split, as it were, Marx's concept of "sensuous activity" into two components which are *not* reducible to each other—man as a tool-making animal *and* man as a speaking animal. Only if we make this distinction is it possible, according to Habermas, to reconstruct the interdependent historical processes of technological and institutional development in a way which would not blur the differences between technical progress and political emancipation as well as those between science and critique. Only then can we adequately grasp the peculiar "dialectic of Enlightenment" (Adorno, Horkheimer) by which scientific rationality, which in its historical origins was a vehicle of critique and of emancipation from dogmatically frozen structures of domination, ultimately has become a threat to practical reason as such. To put it in different terms, Marx's distinction between the forces of production and the relations of production has to be restored in a way which makes the epistemological meaning of his concept of "sensuous activity" clear by avoiding the implicit reductionism of Marx's conception of labour. Only then will it be possible to determine the ideological content of Max Weber's concept of "rationalization." Corresponding to Habermas' distinction between instrumental and communicative action we would have to distinguish between *two* historically interdependent yet categorically distinct processes of "rationalization." In the dimension of instrumental action "rationalization" would mean growth of the productive forces and extension of the power of technical control. In the dimension of communicative action "rationalization" would signify processes of emancipation and individuation as well as the extension of communication free of domination.

> While instrumental action corresponds to the constraints of external nature and the level of the forces of production determines the extent of technical control over natural forces, communicative action stands in correspondence to the suppression of man's own nature. The institutional framework determines the extent of repression by the unreflected

"natural" force of social dependence and political power, which is rooted in prior history and tradition. A society owes emancipation from the external forces of nature to labour processes, that is to the production of technically exploitable knowledge (including "the transformation of the natural sciences into machinery"). Emancipation from the compulsion of internal nature succeeds to the degree that institutions based on force are replaced by an organization of social relations that is bound to communication free from domination. This does not directly occur through productive activity, but rather through the revolutionary activity of struggling classes (including the critical activity of reflective sciences). Taken together, both categories of social practice make possible what Marx, interpreting Hegel, calls the self-generative act of the species.[20]

V

I have so far presented Habermas' distinction between "instrumental" and "communicative" action as part of an attempt to clarify the meaning and the epistemological foundations of historical materialism. This attempt has become necessary as a response to a new historical constellation in which not only science has become a primary productive force but in which science and technology themselves have assumed the opaque character of an all-pervasive ideology. The categorial distinction between "instrumental" and "communicative" action is meant to restore within the theory of historical materialism the distinction between "techne" and "praxis," between "instrumental" and "practical" reason, between "productive" and "reflective" knowledge, and finally between two different meanings of "rationalization" and "emancipation." The upshot of the previous discussion is that historical materialism is impossible without an adequate theory of language.[21]

Before I go on to discuss some of the epistemological implications which follow from Habermas' reformulation of the theoretical "program" of historical materialism, let me indicate in a general way how this approach is related to the Marxian program of a simultaneous critique of idealism and materialism. So far I have only indicated that a "linguistic" reformulation of historical materialism is intimately related to a critique of (positivist) materialism, i.e., scientism. It still has to be shown that this reformulation is one of historical *materialism,* i.e., that it implies a critique of idealism as well. Actually this critique of idealism takes place in two steps: the first step has already been done once the problematic of a philosophy of consciousness has been transformed into that of a philosophy of language. This transformation, however, is not an achievement of historical materialism. It is rather an achievement of twentieth-century philosophy—its most significant achievement perhaps. The second step has to be done from within a theory of language as a critique of the various forms of linguistic and hermeneutic idealism. By these brief remarks I not only want to set up a frame of reference for my subsequent considerations, but I also want to point to a second theoretical tradition to which Habermas' theory is critically related: that of a post-Hegelian critique of historical reason. This tradition goes back to some of the Neo-Kantian philosophers at the end of the last century and was continued by hermeneutic, phenomenological, and linguistic philosophers in our century. What these philosophers held in common was the conviction that the natural and "cultural" sciences rest on different methodological and epistemological foundations. Habermas' dualistic interpretation of Marx's conception of "sensuous activity" directly reflects this epistemological dualism. But it does not merely reflect this dualism, it also transcends it in an important sense, as I will try to show.

VI

According to Habermas the distinction between instrumental and communicative action signifies two different, quasi-transcendental frames of reference in which reality is "constituted" and knowledge accumulated.[22] Instrumental action, considered as an epistemological category, represents the cognitive interest in nomological knowledge. In the framework of instrumental action reality is objectified—"constituted"—as nature in the Kantian sense, i.e., as the being *(Dasein)* of things according to general laws. Communicative action, in contrast, represents the cognitive interest in mutual understanding and the practical interest in the securing of an always precarious intersubjectivity. In the framework of communicative action reality is constituted as a community of actors and speakers. While instrumental action corresponds to the *polarity* of subject and object, communicative action corresponds to the *reciprocity* of Ego and alter Ego. As epistemological categories, consequently, "instrumental" and "communicative" action represent the distinction between nomological and instrumental knowledge, on the one hand, and hermeneutic and reflective knowledge on the other. Correspondingly, they also reflect the methodological distinction between the "natural sciences" and "Geis-teswissenschaften." This methodological distinction had first been elaborated by W. Dilthey and some of the Neo-Kantian philosophers at the end of the last century. As is well known, it has ever since remained a highly controversial topic, particularly among philosophers of the social sciences. I shall try to indicate how it has been taken up, modified, and criticized by Habermas.[23]

In various ways Dilthey and the Neo-Kantian philosophers tried to achieve for the historical sciences what Kant had achieved for the natural sciences. They tried to develop a "Critique of Historical Reason" which would delineate the conditions of the possibility of a science of history. These attempts, although none of them was quite conclusive, had one interesting result. They made it clear that a critique of historical reason cannot succeed from within the framework of a philosophy of consciousness. Thus Dilthey, the most important of these philosophers, in his later writings moved from a psychological toward a hermeneutic theory of the "Geisteswissenschaften." The Neo-Kantians, in contrast, particularly H. Rickert, tried to retain the standpoint of transcendental philosophy and to "extend" Kant's critique of knowledge to the field of historical knowledge. This attempt made clear, however, that an extension of Kant's method of critique to the field of historical knowledge is impossible, even if we assume that Kant provided an adequate solution with respect to the natural sciences. The object of the historical sciences cannot be conceived of as being constituted in a sense analogous to that in which for Kant the object of the natural sciences is constituted by a transcendental subject. For in history, as Hegel already knew, the "transcendental" subject confronts its own genesis; the dimension of historical facts, the "constitution" of which is to be explained, is the very dimension in which the transcendental subject of this constitution itself is "constituted" empirically. That this, from the standpoint of a transcendental critique of knowledge, is a paradoxical statement, is certainly not a decisive counter-argument: it merely shows the limits of transcendental philosophy. Rickert's attempt to go beyond Kant and yet retain the standpoint of a transcendental critique of knowledge was bound to fail for similar reasons as Husserl's later attempt to reconstruct the transcendental constitution of the alter Ego and of the human "life-world." Both attempts ultimately took for granted what Hegel in his critique of Kant had already rejected as an inadmissible and uncritical presupposition of epistemology, namely, that a solipsistic transcendental consciousness and its acts can provide the ultimate ground for a critique of knowledge. A critique of historical reason cannot be based on Kant's distinction between the "transcendental" and the "empirical," since in the dimension of historical facts the "empirical" itself assumes a transcendental meaning and the "transcendental" assumes an empirical meaning: the transcendental subject is revealed as a moment rather than the ground of empirical intersubjectivity.

From the point of view of a transcendental critique of knowledge we have here an irresolvable dilemma. Two ways out of this dilemma have become particularly prominent in the history of philosophy: the Hegelian and the empiricist one. Hegel saves the Kantian intention of a transcendental critique of knowledge by *surpassing* transcendental philosophy: "absolute consciousness" becomes the ground of Kantian "nature" as well as of empirical intersubjectivity, i.e., of history. The Empiricists save the moment of historical contingency which is inseparable from human subjectivity: they reintegrate the transcendental subject into Kantian "nature." While Hegel sacrifices the *contingency* of history, the Empiricists sacrifice *history;* while Hegel saves the critique of knowledge by sacrificing the "otherness" in the object of knowledge (including the subject himself), the Empiricists save this "otherness" of knowledge's object by sacrificing the critique of knowledge and the subject *qua* subject with it.

So far I have not mentioned the solution which historical materialism has offered to this problem. However it should be clear by now that this solution offered by historical materialism is precisely the *problem* with which I am dealing in this essay. Although I believe that historical materialism implicitly *does* contain a solution—implicitly, i.e., to speak with Althusser, a solution which is exhibited by the "theoretical practice" of Marx, although not "known" and not adequately expressed by Marx himself—I do not think that this solution has so far been elaborated explicitly in an adequate way. It is precisely the aim of this essay to show that Habermas offers a promising approach toward a theoretical elaboration of this solution—an approach which, I believe, gains its peculiar strength from the fact that it is based on a critique of post-Marxian "idealist" philosophy as well as of contemporary analytic and linguistic philosophy.

Let me come back to our problem. I have pointed to the impasse to which the project of a transcendental "Critique of Historical Reason" necessarily must lead. I have also presented it in a way which shows that Marx's idea of a "naturalism" which critically surpasses idealism and materialism (and which would be "their unifying truth"), again indicates the direction in which a solution has to be found. The first step in this direction is already taken once we make the transition from a philosophy of consciousness toward a philosophy of language: the peculiar relationship between subjectivity and intersubjectivity, between the "transcendental" and the "empirical," which for transcendental idealism remains an insurmountable obstacle, becomes comprehensible once we recognize in it the unique structure of communication in ordinary language. The critique of historical reason consequently has to be developed in terms of a theory of ordinary language.

The development of Dilthey's thinking—from a psychological toward a hermeneutic theory of the *"Geisteswissenschaften"*—as well as that of Neo-Kantian philosophy (Cassirer) and phenomenology (Heidegger) clearly demonstrates, I think, that for any post-Hegelian philosophy of consciousness this transition toward a philosophy of language has proved itself to be an internal necessity, once the problems of history and/or of historical knowledge had moved into the center of attention. On the other side it is equally remarkable that from within the tradition of analytic philosophy a "Critique of Historical Reason" could only be developed (e.g., by P. Winch),[24] after the empiricist and "constructivist" conceptions of language had been subjected to severe criticism and a philosophy of ordinary language had emerged (Wittgenstein).

VII

Let me pause for a moment. I said before that in Habermas' theory the categories of "instrumental" and "communicative action" signify two quasi-transcendental frames of reference in which reality is "constituted" and knowledge accumulated. After having questioned the possibility of a transcendental critique of historical reason, this remark apparently needs some qualification. With regard to the category of "instrumental action," a "transcendental" interpretation seems to have a fairly clear meaning, a meaning which Marx hinted at in a few scattered remarks, particularly in his *Theses on Feuerbach,* and which has been systematically developed by Charles S. Peirce in his pragmatist reinterpretation of Kantian philosophy. If this is granted, however, it becomes clear that the relation between "instrumental" and "communicative action"—considered as epistemological categories—must be an asymmetrical one. For while the category of "instrumental action" has a transcendental significance in the Kantian sense, this cannot be equally true for the category of "communicative action." Although the "constitution" of a world in the behavioural system of instrumental action is essentially mediated by a process of material production, the (transcendental) constitution of "nature" is not at the same time the *production* of nature. Communicative action, in contrast, i.e., symbolically mediated interaction, not only signifies a "transcendental" frame of reference in which historical reality is constituted as an object of knowledge; it signifies at the same time the empirical process by which this historical reality is literally generated—"constituted" in the ontic sense—*as* historical reality. To be more precise: "instrumental action" and "communicative action" signify two different dimensions in which the evolution of the human species takes place. The constitution of society and of nature as objects of knowledge is at the same time the *creation* of a world: the world of historical reality. That means—against Kant— that the (epistemological) constitution of a world is *one moment* of a historical process; and it means—against the empiricists—that it is not only an empirical aspect but an essential *structural* feature of human societies that they have a conception of the world, of themselves, and of their praxis.

VIII

I hope it has become clear by now that Habermas' "transcendentalism" has to be clearly distinguished from the transcendentalism of a Neo-Kantian or phenomenological philosophy of consciousness. So far, however, I have not shown why this "transcendentalism" or "quasi-transcendentalism" should be considered as an epistemological explication of *historical materialism*. Although I have indicated that it presupposes the transition from a transcendental-idealist toward a hermeneutic or linguistic critique of historical reason, the second step in the critique of idealism has still to be taken, namely, the critique of hermeneutic and linguistic idealism.

Although this critique of idealism plays a decisive part in Habermas' theory and has been developed by him in numerous writings, I can only present a brief sketch of the argument here. Let me first try to make the problem a little clearer. Hermeneutic and linguistic philosophers have denied the (epistemological) possibility of developing a theory which would allow us to reconstruct historical developments and social changes by systematically transcending the self-interpretation of a society and of its individuals. They have denied, i.e., the possibility of reconstructing historical processes as processes taking place "in the back" of individual agents who systematically deceive themselves about their mutual social relations and about the meaning of their own actions. In short, they have questioned the legitimacy of the notions of "ideology" and of "false consciousness," which in fact are basic notions of historical materialism. Their basic argument would run roughly as follows: since social and historical reality is essentially a "symbolically mediated," i.e., a linguistically organized reality, the objects and data of social and historical analysis are meaningful in themselves, and they are given *as* objects and data only insofar as they are meaningful. It is precisely their intrinsic meaningfulness which constitutes them as possible objects and data of analysis. This pregiven, intrinsic meaning of the objects and data of social analysis, however, is determined by the symbolic totality of which they are a part, i.e., it is determined by their place in a specific "language game." Therefore—ultimately—the only adequate method of analysis is that of "hermeneutic understanding" and of linguistic analysis respectively. The ultimate frame of reference for such an analysis is the "language game" itself which is under investigation. With regard to the understanding of social reality there is, therefore, for an *empirical* analysis, no court of appeal beyond what the individuals concerned at least *could* say about themselves.

The position which I have presented here is an idealized one. W. Dilthey, among hermeneutic philosophers, and P. Winch, among linguistic philosophers, come closest to it; while, for example, the (post-Heideggerian) hermeneutic philosophy of H.G. Gadamer has certainly left behind the hermeneutic "positivism" which I tried to describe and which seems to be particularly characteristic of the early phases of hermeneutic and linguistic philosophies. I have nevertheless chosen this idealized position, since it contains the clearest and most radical presentation of our problem. For the sake of simplicity let me call this position the "hermeneutic" position.

It is certainly striking to think that this hermeneutic position represents a radical *empiricism.* It will be all the more paradoxical then, if hermeneutic empiricism is criticized as a form of *idealism.* However, this is precisely what Habermas does. According to Habermas, the idealism of the hermeneutic position consists in the fact that it itself is the expression of an inadmissible *idealization,* namely, the idealization that the linguistic organization of social relations and of the motivational base of social interaction has attained a state of "perfection." The assumption that Habermas introduces here is that, with the linguistic organization of social interaction, an ideal norm is inherently given from which the actual structure of social relations, or using this term—of communicative interaction—has deviated more or less in any known historical period. Paraphrasing Marx's dictum that all previous history has been a history of class struggles we could say that all previous history has been a history of "distorted" communication. Obviously such a claim as well as the corresponding critique of hermeneutic philosophy could ultimately only be justified through a general theory of language, a theory of language which would have to be a theory of "undistorted" as well as of "distorted" communication. Habermas has developed such a theory in outline in recent years.[25] In this essay I do not want to discuss this general theory of communication because it is still in a state of development. I rather want to choose a more indirect strategy to substantiate Habermas' critique of hermeneutic idealism and to indicate how he uses this critique to transcend the traditional methodological dualism of "natural science" and *"Geisteswissenschaft"* and integrate hermeneutic philosophy into historical materialism.

Let me first point to an obvious fact. The "theoretical practice" of the social sciences has never been in accordance with either the methodological model of the natural sciences or with that of a pure "hermeneutic" science. Correspondingly, philosophically minded social scientists as well as philosophers of social science have with good reasons rejected the *alternative* which they were offered by radical empiricists on the one hand and radical "hermeneutic" philosophers on the other. In the following pages I want to discuss what the rejection of this alternative by the existing practice of the social sciences means with respect to the competing claims of hermeneutic and empiricist philosophy. Furthermore, I want to indicate how this rejection, once it is *understood,* could affect the practice of the social sciences themselves.

According to Habermas, the hermeneutic position rests on a mistaken idealization concerning the linguistic organization of social relationships. This idealization, it seems, has three different, although interrelated aspects. It is (1) an idealization concerning the *consistency* and comprehensibility of communication; it is (2) an idealization concerning the *potentialities* of communication; and it is finally (3) an idealization concerning the character of the fundamental *agreements* operative in communication. These three idealizations, taken together, elevate the existing self-interpretation of groups and individuals to a position where they cannot be questioned, and what is more, prevent questions concerning the truth of fundamental beliefs and the justice of fundamental norms from even being raised by the hermeneutically proceeding social scientist.

Ad (1): By "consistency" of communication I mean consistent relationship between verbal expressions, non-verbal expressions, and actions. The discovery that ordinary language as the medium of social interaction is possible only because verbal and non-verbal expressions and actions mutually interpret each other is already implicit in the later works of Dilthey. It has been elaborated in the philosophy of the later Wittgenstein. Both philosophers, however, more or less ignore the actual inconsistencies between these three elements of symbolic interaction which occur in ordinary communication and which, so to speak, indicate gaps in the continuum of meaningful interaction. Where these inconsistencies and contradictions become habitualized, parts of the symbolic field become incomprehensible for the actors and speakers themselves. They no longer recognize themselves and each other in their symbolic objectifications which confront them as an alien text.

Ad (2): This incomprehensibility of parts of a linguistically organized field of interaction (from *within* this field) indicates that communication is inhibited; i.e., it indicates systematic restrictions concerning the convertibility of non-verbal into verbal expressions, of motives into words. There are "meanings" which—as Habermas would put it—are systematically excluded from public discourse and which therefore can come to appear in communicative interactions only as fragments of a mutilated text. Inconsistency and incomprehensibility of communicated meanings indicate a systematic *inhibition* of communication.

Ad (3): This inhibition of communication, in turn, is indicative of a deceptive consensus about beliefs and norms which are considered as valid and adequate in a society. That beliefs are taken for true and norms acknowledged as just seems to imply the idea of a free consent; a consent, however, cannot be free if it is based on a systematic inhibition of communication. We may rather assume that under conditions of systematically "distorted" communication fundamental beliefs and norms, i.e., the basic "rules" of a "language game," in part serve to conceal as well as to legitimate the very distortion of communication which makes a non-enforced, i.e., a "rational" consensus about beliefs and norms impossible.

This rather sketchy explication of what Habermas means by his critique of hermeneutic idealism is of course not a systematic justification of this critique. But let me bypass this problem and assume that the basic argument is correct. It then becomes clear that the linguistic organization of social reality is by no means incompatible with an opposition between this reality and its ideological self-presentations. It is precisely because of the internal relationship which every society has to the idea of truth that social science can question the self-interpretation of groups and individuals and exhibit the delusion as well as the "rational" function of false consciousness: ideology as rationalization (in the Freudian sense). The integration of hermeneutic philosophy into historical materialism consequently does not signify a return to idealism. It rather signifies the elaboration of the conditions of the possibility of historical materialism and of social science as critique. And of course it is not the case that hereby the social phenomena of domination, exploitation, and repression are mysteriously transformed into "merely" linguistic realities. Rather it is the case that as forms of distorted communication they are shown to have their verdict written on their face: they have to be abandoned.

IX

Empiricist materialism and hermeneutic idealism both rest on tacit assumptions concerning the structure of social reality which are equally wrong. While the Empiricist assumes that human history still moves within the closed circle of animal behaviour, the hermeneutic idealist assumes that history already corresponds to the *imago* of humanity which is contained in the first spoken word. Both the empiricist materialist and the hermeneutic idealist cannot come to an adequate conception of history. This is for complementary reasons, namely, that both of them take the human condition as given once and for all and they take it as it could have been realized or could be realized only at the beginning or at the end of history. This, I think, is the reason that empiricist as well as hermeneutic conceptions of the social sciences both contain part of the truth and *only* part of the truth. Hermeneutic analysis is necessary because any historical reality is intrinsically meaningful, and the objectifying methods of causal and functional analysis are necessary because the meaning of history still crystallizes behind the back of the individuals who make it. Historical materialism, correctly understood, is only the elaboration of this truth.

I cannot here discuss the methodological consequences which follow from Habermas' analysis of the epistemological foundations of historical materialism. However, I want to point to one important consequence regarding the relation between social theory and practice. I have already indicated above that the scientific objectification of social (or, for that matter, psychological reality), which treats this reality as "quasi-nature" cannot completely rid itself of the interpretative procedures of a hermeneutic analysis. Since the elemental data of social analysis are constituted as meaningful-in-themselves, they are accessible only as units within the totality of a "language game." If this language game is a foreign one—as is usually the case, e.g., in cultural anthropology—hermeneutic analysis is therefore a necessary first step with regard to the identification of data. This peculiar dependency of the objectifying methods of the social sciences on hermeneutic procedures and the social scientist's pre-understanding respectively does not, however, unambiguously determine the *meaning* of the scientific objectification of social reality. On the one hand, this objectification—i.e., causal, statistical, functionalist, or system-analytic analysis—*can* be understood in analogy to the objectifying methods of the natural sciences. Social science then provides a knowledge which can be used "technologically" for purposes of social engineering. In the latter case the objectification is a final one. The practical application of theoretical and empirical knowledge presupposes a separation between two classes of individuals—social engineers who treat society as quasi-nature and those individuals who are possible objects of their social engineering. This possible meaning of a scientific objectification of social reality obviously corresponds to Engels' vision of social science as an instrument for controlling and steering social processes. On the other hand, the scientific objectification of social reality can also be understood as a tool for, or part of, a hermeneutic analysis which transcends the self-interpretation of the "objectified" individuals to gain access to the concealed meanings, the hidden "depth-grammar" of their interaction. This depth-grammar—exemplified, for example, in the internal relationship between capital and wage labour as analysed by Marx or in the private language of neurotics as analysed by Freud—exerts a quasi-natural force over the life-process of societies or individuals. It reveals a distortion of communication—i.e., an element of violence and repression in the social life-process—which the "surface grammar" conceals. However, in this case the uncovering of quasi-causal mechanisms which operate behind the back of the individuals *does not* serve an interest in social control or social engineering; it rather serves an interest in the *abolition* of such mechanisms, in the "de-naturalization" of history—if "nature" is understood here in the Kantian sense as the being of things insofar as it is governed by general laws—in short, the objectification of social reality here serves an *emancipatory* interest.

This type of objectification, therefore, is essentially *critique*. Social theory penetrates behind the surface grammar of a "language game" to uncover the quasi-natural forces embodied in its depth-grammatical relationships and rules; by spelling them out it wants to break their spell. Its internal *telos* is to enhance the autonomy of individuals and to abolish social domination and repression; it aims at communication free of domination. Such a critical social theory, consequently, can become "practical" in a genuine sense only by initiating processes of self-reflection—a self-reflection which would be the first step on the road toward practical emancipation. The truth claims of a critical social science, however, will ultimately only be substantiated to the degree to which the emancipated individuals can still recognize their own past in the objectifying analyses provided by social scientific theories.

X

The specifically critical task of an objectifying social or psychological analysis does not exhaust the meaning of the theoretical program of historical materialism. I have already indicated above (particularly in sections 6 to 8) that Habermas' reformulation of this program is an attempt to re-integrate the dimension of an epistemological critique and reconstruction into Marx's materialist conception of history. From this point of view the linguistic reformulation of the idea of a social science as *critique* appears as the attempt to interpret the critique of ideologies as the materialist equivalent of the idealist critique of knowledge. Obviously, however, the critique of knowledge in the Kantian as well as in the Hegelian sense means more than a mere destruction of false consciousness; it means also, and primarily, a reflective reconstruction of *genuine* knowledge.[26] To be sure, Marx hoped to surpass the "problematic" of the idealist critique of knowledge once and for all by transforming it into that of a materialist critique of ideologies. However, his articulation of the categories of historical materialism fails precisely at that point where he abandons the dimension of a reflective reconstruction of knowledge together with the idealist presuppositions of the critique of knowledge. This in fact is *not* true for his actual practice of historical materialism in the critique of political economy. It is rather true of the basic categorial framework which Marx used to *explain* his actual practice of historical materialism. This categorial framework only spells out that history is not the history of Mind (i.e., of ideas). It does not spell out, however, that Mind (i.e., objective and subjective Mind) would be impossible without having an *internal* history. To elaborate the epistemological foundations of historical materialism consequently implies the demand genuinely to *transform* rather than to abandon the problematic of an idealist critique of knowledge by unfolding it as a dimension of historical materialism itself.

After what has been said before, a materialist theory of knowledge can be negatively defined by the demand to avoid the pitfalls of empiricism as well as of transcendental and absolute idealism, while retaining the respective truths of these different and mutually incompatible epistemological positions. Roughly speaking, this materialist theory of knowledge will therefore have to assimilate Kant's critique of empiricism and Hegel's critique of transcendentalism as well as the empiricist critique of absolute idealism. Reformulated in this way, Marx's programmatic demand for a naturalism which "is distinguished from both idealism and materialism, and at the same time constitutes their unifying truth" now appears as the fantastic demand for a materialist version of the *Phenomenology of Mind*. Reflection on the epistemological *foundations* of historical materialism thus leads to a new conception of the programmatic *meaning* of historical materialism. If the critique of knowledge is to be incorporated into a materialist theory of history, historical materialism has to be developed as a materialist phenomenology of mind.

Such a materialist "phenomenology of mind" would be neither a scientific theory in the empiricist sense, nor would it be a philosophical theory in the sense of the idealist critique of knowledge. It would also not coincide with a "critical" theory in the sense of Marx's critique of political economy—and yet it would comprise aspects of all these different types of theories. It would be a *materialist* theory in that it reckons with the irreducible empirical contingencies which define the starting point and the boundary conditions of the evolution of the human species; and it would be a *phenomenology* of mind in that it reckons with the fact that the reproduction of the human species is mediated by language, i.e., by the idea of truth, and therefore its evolution is tied to an *internal* progress in the "consciousness of freedom."

Such a theory does not exist today. However, there exist theories which are empirical *and* reconstructive in the sense here indicated— theories which have been developed for the domain of the cognitive, moral, linguistic, and motivational development of *individuals.* These theories attempt empirically to reconstruct the internal logic of developmental processes which take place under the contingent boundary conditions given by the hereditary outfit of human organisms, on the one hand, and specific social relations, on the other. As genetic *explanations* of the formation of various "competences" of the adult individual these theories demand a prior explication of the implicit knowledge which is embodied in these competences (cognitive, moral, linguistic) of a "normal" adult. It is precisely in this sense that Chomsky, e.g., has defined the relationship between the theory of transformational grammar, on the one hand, and theories of linguistic learning on the other. And in extrapolation of Chomsky's ideas, Habermas has developed the idea of a "universal pragmatics" which would provide the meta-theoretical base for the reconstruction of individual as well as social processes of development. However, as far as the genetic explanations *also* have the meaning of a rational reconstruction of the implicit knowledge of the adult, they themselves assume an epistemological meaning: they become fragments of an empirical phenomenology of mind. If this is true, however, the theoretical explication and the genetic reconstruction of the implicit knowledge of the adult can no longer be considered as being in the relationship of meta-theory and theory with each other. Strictly speaking, neither can be developed independently of the other. While this may not create a major problem for the above-mentioned theories of individual development, it does, I believe, create a problem for the materialist reconstruction of cultural evolution.

With my last remark I have indicated one of the reasons which made me hesitate to discuss explicitly Habermas' theory of "pragmatic universals" in this essay. While I consider this theory, as it has been developed so far, an ingenious attempt to provide a theoretical basis for a "linguistically" reformulated conception of historical materialism, I also think that it is still the most controversial part of his theoretical work. This theory of pragmatic universals is an attempt to explicate the universally valid pragmatic rules which every "competent" speaker-actor has learnt to master. Not least, it is an attempt to provide a linguistic explication of the traditional ideas of truth, freedom, and justice, an explication which tries to show that these ideas are operative—and *how* they are operative—in any symbolic interaction. Correspondingly, the theory of pragmatic universals also provides an explication of the idea of "systematically distorted communication," an idea which is of fundamental importance for Habermas' re-interpretation of historical materialism. While it seems to me that such a theory *must* be possible if a systematic reconstruction of cultural evolution as a materialist phenomenology of mind is to be possible at all, I am not clear *how far* it can be developed as a "transcendental pragmatics" of communication prior to and independent of the work of historical reconstruction itself. To deal with these problems, however, and even to make them sufficiently clear *as* problems, would require further work.

XI

In this essay I have tried to reconstruct some of the motives which went into Habermas' reformulation of the conception of historical materialism. Given this reformulation, historical materialism still largely remains a *project,* a theoretical as well as a political one. If Habermas is right, however, this project is deeply rooted in the historical evolution of the human species as an interest in emancipation which, like an invisible and yet explosive force, is operative in the very reproduction process of human societies. This interest in emancipation, according to Habermas, is given with the first spoken word. To say that it is an *interest* in emancipation indicates that with the linguistic organization of social relations reason assumes the force of a material interest. To say that it is an interest in *emancipation* indicates that material needs and interests, once they have become symbolically interpreted needs and interests, are necessarily brought into an internal relationship with the ideas of truth, freedom, and justice. Historical materialism is guided by this interest in emancipation. As a theory, therefore, it is intrinsically tied to the practical project of emancipation from all forms of social repression and political domination. Or, to put it in Habermas' terms, historical materialism is directed to the practical project of making "undistorted communication" a form of social organization.

NOTES

1. T. B. Bottomore (ed.), *Karl Marx's Early Writings* (New York: McGraw-Hill, 1964) p. 202.

2. Ibid p. 206.

3. L. S. Feuer (ed.), *Marx's and Engels' Basic Writings on Politics and Philosophy* (London: Fontana, 1969) p. 283.

4. Ibid.

5. See J. Habermas, "Labor and Interaction: Remarks on Hegel's Jena Philosophy of Mind," in J. Habermas, *Theory and Practice* (Boston: Beacon Press, 1971).

6. Habermas has elaborated this critical point of view in chapters 3 and 6 of *Knowledge and Human Interests* (Boston: Beacon Press, 1971).

7. See Habermas, op. cit., Ch. 3, and A. Wellmer, *Critical Theory of Society* (New York: Herder & Herder, 1971) Ch. 2.

8. Cf. H. Bollnow, "Engels' Auffassung von Revolution und Entwicklung" in *Marxismusstudien*, vol. 1, pp. 77 ff.

9. See A. Schmidt, *The Concept of Nature in Marx* (London: New Left Review Editions, 1971) Chapter 1, section B.

10. F. Engels, "Anti-Dühring," in *Karl Marx/Frederich Engels Werke*, vol. 20, (Berlin: Dietz Verlag, 1968) pp. 131–132.

11. J. Habermas, "Literaturbericht zur philosophischen Diskussion um Marx und den Marxismus," in J. Habermas, *Theorie und Praxis* (Frankfurt: Suhrkamp, 1971) p. 396 (first published in *Philosophische Rundschau*, vols. 3/4, 1957).

12. Cf. Habermas, op. cit.

13. Cf. Habermas, *Knowledge and Human Interests*, Ch. 3, and Wellmer, *Critical Theory of Society*, Ch. 2.

14. G. Lukács, "Reification and the Consciousness of the Proletariat," in *History and Class Consciousness, Studies in Marxist Dialectics*, trans. R. Livingstone, (Cambridge, Mass.: The M.I.T. Press, 1971), p. 91.

15. J. Habermas, *Toward a Rational Society* (Boston: Beacon Press, 1970) p. 112.

16. Ibid.

17. Ibid., p. 113.

18. T. W. Adorno and M. Horkheimer, *Dialectic of Enlightenment* (London: Allen Lane, 1973).

19. Cf. Wellmer, op. cit., Ch. 3.

20. Habermas, *Knowledge and Human Interests*, p. 53.

21. In recent years Habermas has developed in outline a "communication theory" of society. See *Toward a Communication Theory of Society*, Gauss Lectures given at Princeton, Spring, 1971 (unpublished manuscript); see also J. Habermas, "Toward a Theory of Communicative Competence," in H. P. Dreitzel (ed.), *Recent Sociology No. 2.* (New York: Macmillan, 1970), first published in *Inquiry*, vol. 13, nos. 3 and 4; J. Habermas and N. Luhmann, *Theorie der Gessellschaft oder Sozialtechnologie—Was leistet die Systenforschung?* (Frankfurt: Suhrkamp, 1971); J. Habermas, "Der Universalitätsanspruch der Hermeneutik," in *Hermeneutik und Ideologiekritik* (Frankfurt: Suhrkamp, 1971); and J. Habermas, "Wahrheitstheorien," in *Festschrift für Walter Schulz* (Pfullingen: Neske, 1973). See also sections 7–11 below.

22. See e.g. *Knowledge and Human Interests*, Ch. 3. Actually this book as a whole is an elaboration of the thesis presented here. See also *Toward a Communication Theory of Society*.

23. Cf. Ibid.; also see Habermas, "Der Universalitätsanspruch der Hermeneutik," and Habermas, *Zur Logik der Sozialwissenschaften* (Frankfurt: Suhrkamp, 1970), first published as Beiheft 5 of the *Philosophische Rundschau* (Tübingen: Mohr & Siebeck, 1967).

24. P. Winch, *The Idea of a Social Science and its Relation to Philosophy* (London: Routledge and Kegan Paul, 1958); see also Ch. Taylor, "Interpretation and the Sciences of Man," in *Review of Metaphysics*, vol. 25, no. 1, Sept. 1971. Among the numerous works which, in the context of analytic philosophy, have been written on the problems of "Explanation" and "Understanding" in recent years, G. H. von Wright's *Explanation and Understanding* (Ithaca, N.Y.: Cornell University Press, 1971) is of particular importance.

25. See footnote 22 above.

26. Habermas emphasizes the distinction between self-reflection qua *critique* and self-reflection qua *re-construction* in his new Postcript to *Knowledge and Human Interests* (1973).

CONTRIBUTORS

JOHN O'NEILL is director of the Center for Advanced Studies in Social Phenomenology, at York University, Toronto. He is widely known for his studies of Marxism, phenomenology, and contemporary sociological theory. His recent works include *Sociology as a Skin Trade: Essays Towards a Reflexive Sociology* and *Making Sense Together: An Introduction to Wild Sociology.*

BEN AGGER holds a Ph.D. in political economy from the University of Toronto. He is Assistant Professor of Sociology at Bishop's University, Lennoxville, in Quebec.

CHRISTIAN LENHARDT is Associate Professor of Political Science at York University, Toronto. He has a doctorate in political science from the University of California, Berkeley.

IOAN DAVIES is Associate Professor of Sociology and Master of Bethune College, York University. He is the author of *African Trade Unions* and *Social Mobility and Political Change.*

SHIERRY M. WEBER is a marriage and family counselor in private practice in Los Angeles. She holds a doctorate in comparative literature from Columbia, and studied philosophy and sociology in Frankfurt. She has taught the humanities and social sciences at the California Institute of the Arts, Los Angeles, and at the University of California, Irvine.

KEN O'BRIEN worked with the late Dr. Ernest Becker, with whom he developed an interest in critical theory and psychoanalysis. He now teaches social science at the College of Cape Breton, Nova Scotia, and holds a Ph.D. from Simon Fraser University, Vancouver.

PAUL PICCONE is editor of the journal *Telos*. He teaches sociology at Washington University, St. Louis. His recent books include: *History, Philosophy and Culture in Young Gramsci* and *Towards a New Marxism*.

JEREMY J. SHAPIRO is presently coordinator of the Emancipatory Knowledge Network, lecturer in social sciences at the University of California at Irvine, and author of *Zen Socialism* (to be published in 1977). He is currently preparing for publication *Marx and the Self-Reflection of History*.

DIETER MISGELD holds a Ph.D. from University of Heidelburg, where he studied with Hans-Georg Gadamer. He is Assistant Professor in the Department of History and Philosophy of Education, Ontario Institute for Studies in Education, Toronto. He is presently working on a larger study of hermeneutics and critical theory.

FRIEDRICH W. SIXEL (Ph.D. in Anthropology, University of Bonn) is Associate Professor of Sociology at Queen's University, Kingston. His research interest is in social science theory and problems of development.

H. T. WILSON (Ph.D. in political science, Rutgers University) is Professor of Law and Administration at York University, Toronto. He is author of *The American Ideology*.

ALBRECHT WELLMER holds a doctorate in philosophy from the University of Frankfurt, where he worked with Jürgen Habermas. He is Professor of Philosophy at the University of Konstanz, West Germany, and author of *Critical Theory of Society*.